CONTENTS

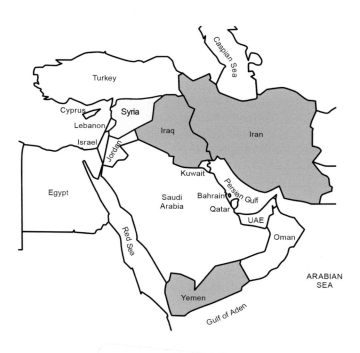

Helion & Company Limited
Unit 8 Amherst Business Centre, Budbrooke Road, Warwick CV34 5WE, England
Tel. 01926 499 619
Email: info@helion.co.uk   Website: www.helion.co.uk   Twitter: @helionbooks   Visit our blog http://blog.helion.co.uk/

Published by Helion & Company 2023
Designed and typeset by Farr out Publications, Wokingham, Berkshire
Cover designed by Paul Hewitt, Battlefield Design (www.battlefield-design.co.uk)

Text © Martin Smisek 2023
Photographs © as individually credited
Colour artwork © David Bocquelet and Tom Cooper 2023
Maps © Tom Cooper 2023

ISBN 978-1-804512-24-1

British Library Cataloguing-in-Publication Data.
A catalogue record for this book is available from the British Library.

For details of other military history titles published by Helion & Company Limited contact the above address, or visit our
website: http://www.helion.co.uk. We always welcome receiving book proposals from prospective authors.

ABBREVIATIONS

AB	Air Base
AOI	Arab Organization for Industrialization
FLOSY	Front for the Liberation of Occupied South Yemen
HTS	*Hlavní technická správa* (Main Technical Administration)
KDP	Kurdistan Democratic Party
KSČ	*Komunistická strana Československa* (Communist Party of Czechoslovakia)
ÚV KSČ	*Ústřední výbor Komunistické strany Československa* (Central Committee of the Communist Party of Czechoslovakia)
MTC	Military Technical College
NATO	North Atlantic Treaty Organization
NLF	National Liberation Front
PDRY	People's Democratic Republic of Yemen
PDRYAF	People's Democratic Republic of Yemen Air Force
SOTI	State Organization for Technical Industries
VAAZ	*Vojenská akademie Antonína Zápotockého* (Antonín Zápotocký Military Academy)
YAR	Yemen Arab Republic
YSP	Yemeni Socialist Party
ZF VAAZ	*Zahraniční fakulta Vojenské akademie Antonína Zápotockého* (Foreign Faculty of the Antonín Zápotocký Military Academy)

INTRODUCTION

Before the Second World War, the Czechoslovak arms industry exported large quantities of weapons to a number of countries in different territories that included Europe (mainly the Baltics and the Balkans), Latin America, the Middle East and Asia. Following the occupation of Czechoslovakia by the German *Wehrmacht* in March 1939, the arms production capacities in the Czech and Slovak territories were fully used for the Nazi war machine. When the conflict finally ended in 1945, Czechoslovak arms factories wanted to reestablish their former positions on the world market. However, because of the emerging Cold War, they had to face a number of insurmountable problems.

Czechoslovakia was considered by the United States to be a country in the Soviet sphere of influence, and so Washington spoiled planned shipments of Czechoslovak military hardware to Latin America. The influence of the Soviet Union in the countries of Central and Eastern Europe after the end of the Second World War meant that there was not as much interest in Czechoslovak arms, as this need could be met by supplies of Soviet military materiel. Therefore, among the last remaining possibilities where it was possible to look for interest in the supply of Czechoslovak arms was the area of the Middle East.

The deteriorating security situation in this territory in the late 1940s and the growing tensions between the Arab and Jewish communities played into the hands of these Czechoslovak efforts. Both Arab and Jewish representatives sought to purchase weapons for the upcoming conflict, and thus both sides expressed interest in military hardware from Czechoslovakia. At the same time, Czechoslovakia was fully integrated into the Soviet Bloc, which was made possible by the communist coup d'état in February 1948. The communist government in Prague, under the patronage of Moscow, decided to deliver armament only to Israel although this meant breaching the UN arms embargo. These arms – mostly infantry weapons and fighter aircraft – played a crucial role in the subsequent 1948 Arab-Israeli War and enabled the Israeli Defense Forces to succeed in the conflict (as described in Volume 1 of this mini-series).

The Israelis were interested in buying more Czechoslovak weapons after the end of the war. However, no further large arms contracts were concluded with Czechoslovakia. When, to the displeasure of both Czechoslovak and the Soviet communist leadership, it became clear that Israel would not become a communist state, Prague severely limited its relations with Jerusalem. The question of the export of Czechoslovak arms to Israel was finally resolved by a decision of the Czechoslovak Ministry of National Defence in July 1950, which banned the supply of all Czechoslovak arms to the Jewish state.

As wished by Moscow, Prague invested huge sums of money in the early 1950s in the development of its own arms industry, primarily for the licenced production of Soviet military aircraft and heavy weapons. Together with the building up of large armed forces, this brought the Czechoslovak economy to the brink of collapse within a few years. Soviet weapons produced in large numbers in Czechoslovak factories were intended not only for the Czechoslovak army, but also for export to other Soviet Bloc countries. However, the extensive armaments production also caused serious economic problems for the remaining communist countries in Central and Eastern Europe, which no longer had the financial means to purchase more weapons from Czechoslovak factories.

Meanwhile, demand for arms from communist Czechoslovakia began to increase in developing countries, including some Arab states in the Middle East. This made it possible to use spare capacities in Czechoslovak arms factories and at the same time to obtain much-needed foreign exchange (British pounds sterling or the United States dollar) for the purchase of goods or raw materials from the West that could not be obtained in the Soviet Bloc countries.

The first Arab country to acquire military hardware from any communist country was Syria in 1955, which bought decommissioned StuG III assault guns from Czechoslovakia. Most subsequent deliveries of Czechoslovak weapons to the Syrian Arab Armed Forces, however, came from new production. The next in line was Egypt that during 1955 ordered massive quantities of Czechoslovak arms which caused great shock and a wave of rage in the West. Several large Czechoslovak-Egyptian arms contracts also involved secret supplies of military hardware from the Soviet Union. The deliveries of armament were followed by the training of Egyptian military personnel in both Czechoslovakia and Egypt (details of Czechoslovak arms deliveries and military assistance to the benefit of Syria and Egypt can be found in Volume 2 and Volume 3 of this mini-series). Against the backdrop of these events, the Mutawakkilite Kingdom of Yemen also became interested in Czechoslovak weapons. Subsequent developments in the 1960s and 1970s created the conditions for Prague to also supply armament and military assistance to Iraq, Iran and South Yemen.

1

IRAN (OPERATION 125, COUNTRY 608)

Before the Second World War, the Empire of Iran (Persia until 1935) was the most important business partner of Czechoslovakia in the Middle East. After 1933, Czechoslovak companies built there, among others, six sugar mills, the power plant at Tehran, a tobacco factory, and more than 100 railway bridges on different sections of the Trans-Iranian Railway. Abundant deliveries of weapons from Czechoslovak production were no exception in this timeframe and the first infantry weapons were contracted in 1929. The most important Czechoslovak arms factories supplying the Imperial Iranian Army were Škodovy závody, ČKD, and Zbrojovka Brno. Deliveries of Czechoslovak weapons to Iran are listed in Table 1

A Czechoslovak-designed and manufactured AH-IV-P tankette in Iranian service in the late 1930s. (Author's collection)

(related contracts were fulfilled even after the German occupation of Czechoslovakia in March 1939). From 1930 to 1938 Czechoslovakia supplied to Iran armament worth 405 million CSK which constituted 55 percent of the overall value of the Czechoslovak export to Iran in that period.[1]

NEW BEGINNINGS

Although diplomatic and business contacts between Czechoslovakia and Iran were reestablished in 1942 and 1945 respectively, their duration in the post-war period was very short-lived. Following the communist coup d'état in Czechoslovakia in February 1948, relations between the two countries deteriorated rapidly and then froze completely. Only the years 1952 and 1953 saw slight improvement when Mohammad Mosaddegh served as the Prime Minister of the Iranian government. Distinct changes in the relationship between Prague and Tehran were apparent only after the normalisation of Iranian-Soviet relations after 1962 when the Shah Mohammad Reza Pahlavi engaged in the tactics of flexible manoeuvring between the West and the East. The important turning point from Prague's point of view was the Shah's official visit to Czechoslovakia in May 1967. During his stay in Prague, Pahlavi visited a nearby Aero Vodochody manufacturing plant and saw a demonstration of L-29 Delfin training aircraft that were produced there.[3]

Improving relations during the 1960s led to the first, but limited, deliveries of Czechoslovak military materiel. During 1964, Czechoslovakia supplied 3.5 million č. 8 A 1 detonators, 1 million metres of safety fuse, and 1,000 electrical fuses. The deliveries continued in the following year when Prague exported to Iran 3 million č. 8 te detonators, 3 million metres of safety fuse, and 122,000 rounds of sports ammunition. Further deliveries were composed primarily of 'nonspecial' items like sports and hunting weapons together with pyrotechnics. A limited amount of 'special material' was supplied to Iran during 1967, apparently for testing purposes only. Three vz. 61 sub machine guns were delivered to Iranian authorities in 1968, probably for local evaluations or as a gift for top-level officials from military or security apparatus.[4]

However, the Main Technical Administration (*Hlavní technická správa*, HTS) of the Ministry of Foreign Trade (*Ministerstvo zahraničního obchodu*) was eager to sell major weapons systems to Iran. The situation looked promising because Moscow concluded the first arms deal with Tehran in January 1967 and further contracts for deliveries of artillery, armoured personnel carriers, and support equipment followed during the subsequent years. Unfortunately for the HTS, dark clouds began to gather over Prague's optimistic outlook. In 1969, General Hassan Toufanian, who was responsible for arms purchases and management of the Iranian military industry, visited Czechoslovakia and during

Table 1: Deliveries of the Czechoslovak arms to Iran, 1929–1940[2]

Type	Number of examples	Note
vz. 98/29, 8mm rifle	240,000	80,000 each ordered in 1929, 1934, and 1939
vz. 24, 7.92mm rifle	30,000	10,000 each ordered in 1929, 1934, and 1939
vz. 98/29, 8mm carbine	30,000	10,000 each ordered in 1929, 1934, and 1939
vz. 26, 7.92mm machine gun	4,954	deliveries in 1929 (100), 1931 (550), 1932 (200), and 1934 (4,104)
Vickers, 0.303 machine gun	99+	28 for Marmon-Herrington armoured cars, 62 for aircraft, and nine for armoured vehicles
vz. 30, 7.92mm aircraft machine gun	80	deliveries in 1939 and 1940
vz. 37, 7.92mm machine gun	1,000	deliveries in 1940
ZB60, 15mm anti-aircraft machine gun	25	deliveries during 1937 and 1939
3,7 KPÚV Beta, 3.7 cm anti-tank gun	50	
H1, 10.5cm light howitzer	248	ordered in 1934 and 1935
K1, 15cm howitzer	20	ordered in 1939
NOa, 15cm heavy cannon	6	deliveries in 1940
4.7cm naval gun (d/44)	3	deliveries in 1935
AH-IV-P, tankette	50	deliveries in 1936 and 1937
TNH, light tank	50	deliveries in 1936 and 1937

The Praga TNH tank manufactured for the Imperial Army of Iran, seen before delivery. (Author's collection)

negotiations at the Federal Ministry of Foreign Trade[5] informed respective officials that the Shah decided not to widen the number of weapon types procured from foreign countries.[6]

In the light of this reserved attitude, it was only gradually that the Iranians changed their opinion: during his second official visit to Czechoslovakia in August 1977, Shah Pahlavi attended a presentation of the latest armament produced by Czechoslovak companies, and new multiple rocket launchers and infantry fighting vehicle sparked his interest. On 13 March 1978, General Toufanian with his two aides (Colonel Generals Massoumi and Moghadam) discussed possible deliveries of the Czechoslovak arms with Ambassador Vladimír Poláček and the HTS business representative Michal Lehocký at the Czechoslovak embassy in Tehran. General Toufanian was interested mainly in the acquisition of 200 to 400 BVP-1 infantry fighting vehicles (Czechoslovak designation for the BMP-1). However, his wishes could not be satisfied swiftly because

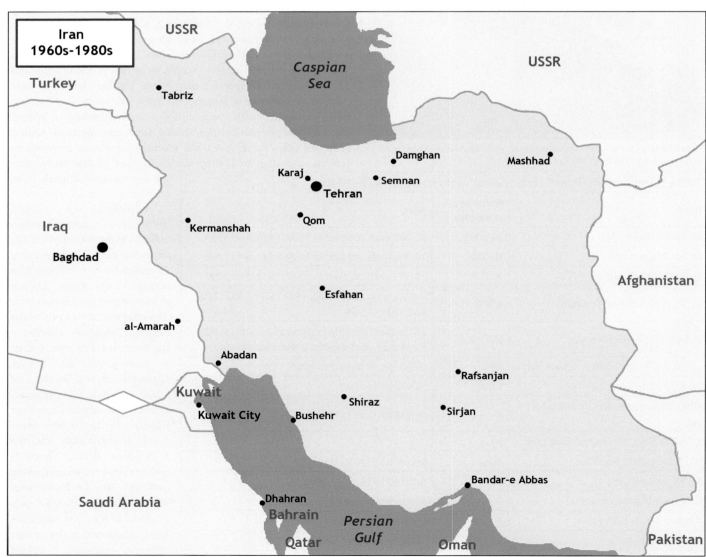

(Map by Tom Cooper)

their production was already sold out for the time coming. Thus, the first deal for the purchase of Czechoslovak armament was signed in May 1978 and included the supply of 160 vz. 70 multiple rocket launchers with ammunition and 320 Tatra 813 tractor trucks to the overall value of 160 million USD.

However, bright times for the HTS concerning Iran were not to last very long as the Iranian Revolution (lasting between 7 January 1978 and 11 February 1979) brought a new theocratic leadership that cancelled the deal completely. Up to this time, the Iranians provided advance payment worth 15.9 million USD and Czechoslovakia delivered just 20 Tatra 813 trucks to the value of 1.4 million USD.[7]

BUILDING IRAN'S ARMS INDUSTRY

Although limited deliveries of various sports and hunting weapons continued unabated, prospects of large-scale shipments of Czechoslovak heavy armament for the Imperial Iranian Army looked bleak in the early 1970s. However, Prague was ready to assist in the development of the Iranian domestic arms industry. Its nucleus was established at Saltanatabad near Tehran (now the Pasdaran district of northern Tehran) during the 1930s. In the beginning, the facility served as a repair and maintenance workshop for weapons used by the Imperial Iranian Army. Its capabilities were later widened with the establishment of works for the production of ammunition for infantry arms and artillery that was further expanded with the manufacture of rifles and machine guns. Czechoslovakia played an active role in these developments. During the 1930s, Zbrojovka Brno established plants for the production of rifles, machine guns, and ammunition at Saltanatabad (licence production of vz. 24 rifles started there in 1940). Simultaneously, Škodovy závody and Konstruktiva delivered and installed machinery for a brass foundry and rolling mill in the same area during 1939 and 1940. The facility, with an annual production rate of 4,200 tonnes (4,134 tons) of semi-finished products from copper and brass, started the production in 1942.

The development of the Iranian arms industry with foreign assistance continued after the Second World War. The construction of new production facilities during the 1950s was assisted by companies from West Germany (Fritz Werner, Lindemann) and Switzerland (Oerlikon). The different Iranian military plants were centralised in 1963 and placed under the Military Industries Organization (MIO) which was headed by General Hassan Toufanian. In 1967, the construction of a rolling mill and drawing plant at Saltanatabad to the value of 52 million DM was completed by Rheinstahl from West Germany. In the early 1970s, the Saltanatabad facility produced small arms ammunition, 81mm and 120mm mortar ammunition, 105mm artillery shells, 20mm cannon ammunition, grenades, signal flares, and anti-tank and anti-personnel mines.[8]

Thanks to the legacy of interwar Czechoslovakia, its communist successor was able to secure the first important contract with Iran related to the arms industry. The deal on reconstruction and modernisation of the brass rolling mill at Saltanatabad worth 40 million CSK (1.6 million USD) was signed in 1971. The Czechoslovak main contractor was foreign trade company OMNIPOL and Škoda was its most important subcontractor and supplier of the machinery. According to the original plan, the facility with an annual production capacity of roughly 12,000 tonnes (11,810 tons) was to be completed in 1974. However, due to several delays, the date of completion had to be postponed to March 1977. In October 1976, Czechoslovak workers finished the installation of almost all machinery except the boiler room and the neutralisation station because the Iranian authorities did not finish the construction of

respective buildings in time. Thus, the Czechoslovak personnel were able to complete the assembly during the spring of 1977. During this year, 10 Czechoslovak experts worked at Saltanatabad. However, the crash of one cylindrical roller during the testing phase postponed the completion date further. The brass rolling mill at Saltanatabad was completed apparently by the end of 1978, in a time of intensifying discontent with the Shah's rule leading to strikes and demonstrations that paralysed the country and resulted in his overthrow.[9]

A-23: FROM A LUCRATIVE PROJECT ...

During the 1973 oil crisis, the price of oil had risen from 3 USD per barrel to nearly 12 USD globally. The massive influx of petrodollars enabled the Shah to spend billions of dollars on purchases of foreign weaponry. At the same time, Mohammad Reza Pahlavi tried to develop a large domestic arms industry to reduce Iran's dependence on overseas suppliers. On grounds of strategic reasons and simple lack of space for further extension of the Saltanatabad installation, the second arms production facility – the so-called Esfahan Complex – started to be built some 60 kilometres (38 miles) southwest of Esfahan in the mid-1970s. The first two newly established plants were to produce anti-aircraft ammunition and Rapier surface-to-air missiles respectively. While the first factory was built with Czechoslovak assistance, the second one was to be established with the help of Great Britain.[10]

In the frame of contracts with the Soviet Union from January 1967, October 1970, and August 1971, Iran ordered 1,000 ZU-23-2 anti-aircraft guns and a further 30 ZSU-23-4 Shilka self-propelled radar-guided anti-aircraft weapon systems. Under its military diversification program, Tehran was anxious to expand the local manufacturing of arms and ammunition. It was against this background that the Union of Soviet Socialist Republics (USSR) approved in 1970 the production of 23mm anti-aircraft rounds for the ordered guns under licence in Iran. This time, Moscow did not forget its satellite country in Central Europe, and as a contemporary CIA intelligence memorandum stated: 'The USSR suggested, however, that the necessary production machinery be obtained from Czechoslovakia.'[11]

The respective contract to the value of some 1 billion CSK was signed in 1973 and OMNIPOL became the main contractor for the delivery of production machinery and technological equipment for the plant that bore the Czechoslovak cover name A-23. The construction of the first structures of this facility started in 1975. Although the Cold War was raging around the globe, lucrative contracts were able to connect the interests of companies from both sides of the Iron Curtain. Although OMNIPOL was based in communist Czechoslovakia, some of its important partners cooperating on the A-23 project were from Western Europe such as West German Blasberg (technology of surface treatment) or Swiss Mikron Hassler (machine tools). The supplier of the boiler room was Yugoslav company Đuro Đaković that used a control system made by West German Siemens. The main supplier of the technology for the A-23 was Czechoslovak company ZVS Dubnica nad Váhom and the remaining foreign partners came from Austria and the Netherlands.

Deliveries of machinery for the plant from Czechoslovakia started in June 1975. As of early 1977, the Czechoslovak main contractor delivered around 75 percent of contracted items. Because of the inability of Iranian authorities to secure proper means of transportation, almost 25 percent of the deliveries waited at the border city of Jolfa in Iran. This led to large delays because the transport of some shipments from there to Esfahan took up to 17

A 23mm twin-barrel ZU-23-2 automatic anti-aircraft gun seen in use by the Islamic Revolutionary Guards Corps during the fighting against Iraq in the Howeizeh Marshes in 1984. (Author's collection)

Another view of an Iranian-operated ZU-23-2, this time from the northern portion of frontlines of the Iran-Iraq War of the early 1980s. (Author's collection)

leadership under the Grand Ayatollah Ruhollah Khomeini started purges of top-level officers of the former Iranian Imperial Armed Forces. One of the victims became General Nowuzi, director of the Esfahan Complex, who was imprisoned and replaced by Dr. Karimi, some 30-year-old returnee from France with no technical education. In April 1979, when the situation calmed down sufficiently, the HTS business representative of the Czechoslovak embassy visited A-23 to assess the situation at the site. He could witness that some 375 workers of the National Defence Industries Organization and contractor companies Chakosh and Iran Thermo were present but did no meaningful work. Upon asking one of the local engineers, the Czechoslovak representative received the answer that this is a 'normal state'.[13]

months. In February 1977, about 70 percent of the main building of the A-23 was ready, while the construction of some objects was nine months behind schedule. In total, 42 Czechoslovak experts worked the A-23 construction site in 1977. Except for the delays, the building of the facility went almost flawlessly until the Iranian Revolution. General turmoil led practically to the suspension of all works related to the construction of the ammunition plant. Following the worsening security situation in Iran, five women and six children, all relatives of the Czechoslovak experts working in the A-23, were evacuated from the country in January 1979. The experts returned to Czechoslovakia apparently only slightly later.[12]

... TO THE NIGHTMARE

After the revolution, a pro-Western authoritarian monarchy was replaced with an anti-Western totalitarian theocracy. New Iranian

Following the Revolution, the new Iranian establishment requested the halting of all assembly works although the facility was completed up to 90 percent. Further work on A-23 was lost in the post-revolutionary turmoil, a de-facto civil war, and then the chaos created by the outbreak of the Iran-Iraq War in September 1980. It was only in 1982 when Tehran asked OMNIPOL for the completion of the installation. The inspection of the construction site showed that a part of the delivered documentation, equipment, machinery, and spare parts was either lost or damaged. However, the reaction from the Czechoslovak side in 1982 and early 1983 was not very fast and this led to a delay of several months. In the second half of 1983,

A young Iranian commando seen in the 1980s during training armed with the Kootah carbine: the Iranian version of the Czechoslovak-designed vz. 98/29. (Author's collection)

dissatisfied Iranians started to vehemently pressure OMNIPOL on the finishing of the facility by the end of the same year.

Despite the presence of some 50 Czechoslovak and further 15 foreign experts at Esfahan, OMNIPOL was not able to complete the project successfully. Deficiencies in West German and Swiss technology, late replacement deliveries from Yugoslavia, and Iranian problems with construction works led to the change of the completion date to February 1984. Contrary to the terms of the contract, the Iranians stopped further payments in early 1984 which caused problems for OMNIPOL, and they were not able to pay for the remaining deliveries from Blasberg. Tensions between OMNIPOL and Iranian officials rose to such proportions that negotiations related to the project were interrupted in March 1984. During the same month, Oplt, the Czechoslovak Ambassador in Tehran, met his West German counterpart to discuss the deliveries from the company Blasberg. West German Ambassador Peterson calmed him down with the words that Blasberg was doing everything that OMNIPOL asked for because, as he added, 'the company successfully cooperates with the Czechoslovak side in other countries as well'.

In the meantime, the A-23 project became the topic for discussion during almost every meeting between high-level Czechoslovak and Iranian representatives. Iranians pressured Czechoslovak officials and threatened that the rapid commissioning of the A-23 was a criterion for further economic and commercial cooperation with Prague. The new timetable for the finishing of the plant was renegotiated during May 1984. Despite the Czechoslovak best efforts, the solution to the problems was not in sight; this time because of Iraqi combat operations that worsened the security situation around Esfahan to such a degree that Czechoslovak and foreign experts working on the factory had to be evacuated back home during early spring 1985. Thus, the construction of the ammunition plant at Esfahan appeared on the agenda in June 1986 again when Iranian Minister of Foreign Affairs Ali Akbar Velayati visited Prague and discussed this matter with Czechoslovak Prime Minister Lubomír Štrougal with the conclusion that 'the matter is going to be straightened out in near future.'[14]

The exact period of completion of the A-23 project remains unknown. According to the state plan for 1989, drawn up in July 1988, deliveries of machinery for the A-23 from Czechoslovakia were to be definitively completed in 1990.[15]

SYRIAN CONNECTION

After the Revolution of 1979, relations between Iran and Syria improved markedly. During the subsequent Iran-Iraq War, Damascus sided with non-Arab Iran against Iraq and became one of Tehran's few Arab allies during the conflict. This attitude showed in practical terms in April 1982 when Syria shut down its section of the Kirkuk-Baniyas pipeline, thus depriving Baghdad of important revenues from oil exports. Returning the Syrian favour, Iran provided Damascus with millions of free or discounted barrels of oil throughout the 1980s. Syrian friendship with Tehran had different practical forms: one of them was the re-export of the Czechoslovak arms to Iran – apparently without the Czechoslovak approval.

In June 1984 the Czechoslovak merchant ship *Sitno* delivered a fresh batch of military materiel to the Syrian port of Latakia. The skipper of the vessel was not very much interested in the fate of the cargo and thus Syrians started to unload the delivery from the Czechoslovak ship onto the nearby-anchored Iranian vessel *Farawan* with no interference. This was done without prior agreement and knowledge of the respective Czechoslovak authorities. However, the Iraqis had good intelligence sources and became very swiftly aware of the developments in Latakia. They complained immediately and Czechoslovak officials had no choice than to intervene to stop the reloading process in the Syrian harbour. Under pressure, the Syrians ended related activities in Latakia and assured the Czechoslovak side that something like that 'will never be repeated'. On 3 July 1984, Prague's official explanation of this incident was provided to the Iraqi ambassador in Czechoslovakia, Tariq Ahmad al-Maroof, who accepted it with satisfaction.

However, this was not the end of the problems with Syrian re-exports as Jan Straka, Czechoslovak Ambassador in Baghdad, was dealing with another complaint in September of the same year. Despite Iraqi claims, the subsequent Czechoslovak investigation did not show misconduct on the Syrian side. At the same time, Bulgarian and Romanian diplomats were challenged by the Iraqis because of alleged arms deliveries to Iran as well. Iraqi officials notified Czechoslovak representatives of their suspicion that Czechoslovak arms were re-exported through Syria to Iran several times later. All of them were categorically rejected on the grounds that all contracts included a clause that prohibited further re-export and that military cooperation with Iran was 'interrupted already before the outbreak of the conflict, immediately after the Shah's fall'.

To the Czechoslovak officials' great astonishment and shock, the Iraqis learned about Prague's involvement in the construction of the A-23 project at Esfahan. On 23 January 1985, Iraqi Minister of Foreign Affairs Tariq Aziz complained directly to Czechoslovak Ambassador Jan Straka and stressed that 'Iraq is exceptionally shocked and irritated that the Czechoslovak side is finishing the ammunition plant at Esfahan'. Already prepared for such eventuality, Straka downplayed the issue and questioned the credibility of Iraqi sources that 'try to disrupt friendly relations between the

Even without direct deliveries, significant amounts of Czechoslovak arms reached Iran – for example in 1982, when a successful Iranian offensive liberated the port of Khorramshahr, mauling four divisions of the Iraqi Army in the process. Amongst the loot collected from the battlefields was this Czechoslovak-manufactured OT-62/R2 TOPAS armoured personnel carrier. (Author's collection)

A column of Iranian commandos seen advancing during the liberation of Khorramshar: visible in the background are two Czechoslovak-manufactured OT-64 SKOT armoured personnel carriers of the Iraqi Army, both of them apparently knocked out by anti-tank weapons. (Author's collection)

Czechoslovak Socialist Republic and Iraq with untrue information'. However, the Iraqis pressed the issue further and several days later Iraqi Ambassador al-Maroof visited František Langer, First Deputy Minister of Foreign Trade and the boss of the HTS responsible for all Czechoslovak arms trading. While Langer rejected the new Iraqi accusation of Iranian arms deliveries through Syria, he was left with no option but to admit the Czechoslovak participation in the establishment of the ammunition production facility at Esfahan. He explained that its construction had started during the Shah's era and Czechoslovakia had to finish the installation otherwise it would face financial penalties.[16]

DOUBLE GAME

While some Czechoslovak officials pretended to be Iraq's best friends, the others tried to sell 'politically acceptable' military materiel to Iran. The issue of the cancelled contract from 1978 for delivery of vz. 70 multiple rocket launchers with ammunition and Tatra 813 tractor trucks remained alive in the relations between Prague and Tehran as Iran had sent higher advance payments than the actual value of trucks delivered before the demise of the Shah's rule. The Czechoslovak economy needed US dollars and the officials at the HTS preferred to keep the money and deliver other goods instead. They did not need to wait long because the bloody conflict with Iraq erupted only shortly later.

In 1981, the Iranian delegation led by General Chegini discussed the possibility of arms deliveries with representatives of the HTS. While the Iranians demanded tanks, infantry fighting vehicles, and artillery, Czechoslovak officials were willing to provide only some types of aircraft and infantry weapons. Simultaneously, OMNIPOL offered new projects for the establishment of arms production facilities with Czechoslovak assistance. However, subsequent negotiations did not materialise because the Iranian delegation conditioned further discussions with the requirement that Czechoslovakia supplied large-calibre artillery ammunition. However, this item was not available and, moreover, Prague was not interested in the export of heavy weapons to Iran because this matter could have 'grave political aspects' – the preservation of good relations with Baghdad remained the top priority of Czechoslovak diplomacy during the times of the Iran-Iraq War. The next round of talks took place in Tehran only in December 1983, in times when the Iranians urgently demanded the return of the retained money for undelivered rocket launchers and trucks. The HTS representatives offered L-410 light transport aircraft, infantry weapons, and related ammunition instead. Apparently, this attempt ended in a failure.[17]

It remains unknown if Czechoslovakia really delivered any weapons to Iran during the times of the conflict with Iraq. Whatever was the case, from the HTS point of view, the Iran-Iraq War ended

CZECHOSLOVAK MERCHANT NAVY

Although a landlocked country, communist Czechoslovakia had its ocean-going shipping company – Československá námořní plavba (Czechoslovak Naval Navigation) – which was established in April 1959.

The embargo imposed on the People's Republic of China, whose ships sailed under the Czechoslovak flag, had the greatest impact on the further development of Czechoslovak shipping. Hence, China participated in the birth of the Czechoslovak company and financially in the construction of a number of ships bearing the Czechoslovak flag. After China's admission to the UN, some of the ships were handed back to China in 1967 and a financial settlement was made.

In terms of trade, the operation of the ships was very profitable. Czechoslovak ships provided exchange of goods with China and Cuba, among others, i.e. with countries that were partly blockaded at that time for political reasons. They made it possible to get the products of Czechoslovak industry all over the world and to import scarce raw materials without much demand for foreign exchange.

The ships operated by the Československá námořní plavba also participated in the deliveries of Czechoslovak arms to various developing countries. For example, in June 1984, the Czechoslovak merchant ship *Sitno* delivered a load of military materiel to the Syrian port of Latakia which was later immediately re-exported to Iran without the knowledge of Czechoslovak authorities.

Mír (*Peace*), a merchantman of the little-known Czechoslovak merchant navy, repeatedly involved in various arms deals of the 1970s and 1980s. (Author's collection)

Czechoslovak merchant Sitno, seen in the mid-1980s. (Author's collection)

A DOK-M universal loader, seen in Iran around 1986. (CIA Photo)

at the least suitable moment. At that time, preparations for arms production for the next five-year plan (1991–1995) were in full swing. The already awarded contracts showed that the approaching decade would be very challenging for the oversized production capacity of the Czechoslovak arms industry. The Warsaw Pact countries were economically in dire straits and their orders dropped dramatically. While Prague's devoted and important clients from Syria, Iraq, and Libya were permanently interested in further wide-scale deliveries of arms, their economies were overburdened with debts and in massive problems. Therefore, the export of goods to these destinations would be possible only thanks to the generous crediting from Czechoslovakia. However, this option was out of the question because each of the mentioned countries already owed hundreds of millions of US dollars to Prague that had its own financial difficulties. Under these conditions, Iran became one of the very limited numbers of the proverbial 'lights at the end of the tunnel'. With the war over, previous suspicions and complaints from Baghdad could be ignored and serious negotiations between the HTS and its Iranian counterparts were well underway in 1989. Tehran had the potential to become a prospective customer of the T-72M1 main battle tank including derived recovery and bridge-laying variants.[18]

However, it was the time when the continued existence of the communist regime in Prague could be counted in months only. After the Velvet Revolution in November 1989, the new Czechoslovak political establishment embarked on a fresh foreign policy oriented towards the improvement of relations with NATO countries and promoting human rights: deliveries of arms to Iran were not a part of this agenda. Thus, no large-scale deliveries of the Czechoslovak weapons ever materialised.

2

IRAQ (OPERATION 118, COUNTRY 607 AND OPERATION 619)

Czechoslovakia maintained diplomatic and trade relations with Iraq before the Second World War. The Czechoslovak Honorary Consulate in Mandatory Iraq (or the Kingdom of Iraq under British Administration) was established in 1930 and functioned there until 1939. The country gained independence from the United Kingdom in 1932 as the Hashemite Kingdom of Iraq, though the British retained military bases, local militia in the form of the Assyrian Levies, and transit rights for their forces. In November of the following year, diplomatic relations were established between the Czechoslovak Republic and the Hashemite Kingdom of Iraq.[1]

The period of the 1930s brought the establishment of Czechoslovak-Iraqi relations into the field of arms deliveries. In 1935, Zbrojovka Brno delivered 20,000 older Lee Enfield rifles, originally from Lithuania, to the Iraqi Army. In June 1936, Zbrojovka Brno concluded a contract for the supply of 200 BREN machine guns by the end of the same year. However, due to delays, the weapons were shipped from the Brno factory only in January 1937. In the meantime, the original order was extended by another 650 BREN machine guns, which were delivered to Iraq in August and September 1937.[2]

POST-WAR PROBINGS

After the Second World War, the Czechoslovak ambassador from Tehran was accredited in Baghdad. However, there were virtually no direct diplomatic relations with Iraq and trading was conducted only indirectly through third countries. Nevertheless, in September 1948, the Iraqi ambassador to Iran visited his Czechoslovak counterpart to express his government's protest that Czechoslovakia was supplying arms to the State of Israel during the ongoing 1948 Arab-Israeli War. The Czechoslovak ambassador wrote in his dispatch to the Ministry of Foreign Affairs (*Ministerstvo zahraničních věcí*) that the Iraqi official simultaneously 'semi-officially stated that his government is interested in buying lighter weapons (machine guns) from us. In both cases, I maintained an extremely reserved position. Please give directives.' The instruction for the ambassador followed shortly thereafter:

1) Our government is anxious to ensure that United Nations resolutions are complied with. [...]

One of the greatest 'prizes of war' for the Iranians during the Iran-Iraq War was the capture of Iraqi main battle tanks, like this Czechoslovakia-manufactured T-72M1, photographed in 1988. (Author's collection)

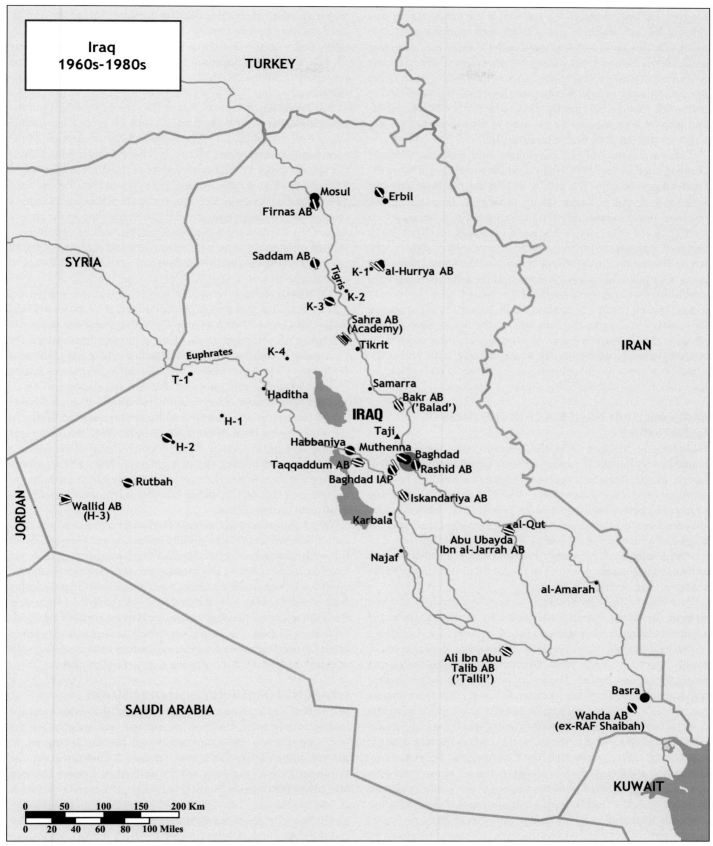

(Map by Tom Cooper)

2) There is no objection to Iraqi officials entering into purchase negotiations with our companies.

Thus, Prague denied its active involvement in the arms shipments for Israel and, at the same time, expressed its readiness to deliver weapons to Israel's enemies.[3]

Surprisingly enough, nothing happened for the next few years, until January 1955, when the Czechoslovak embassy in Den Haag received an Iraqi demand for the supply of 10,000 pistols and rifles, 2,000 sub machine guns, 1,200 light machine guns, 700 heavy machine guns, 310 field guns, and 135 howitzers, including ammunition. However, the outcome of this request was indirectly decided by the Soviet diplomatic steps in the Middle East: 'Given the development of international relations after the severance of diplomatic relations between the Union of Soviet Socialist Republics and Iraq on 8 January 1955, the issue of arms exports from the Czechoslovak Republic to Iraq is unrealistic.'[4]

Lukewarm relations between Prague and Baghdad suddenly changed after 14 July 1958 when a military coup swept away the Hashemite monarchy. The putsch established the Iraqi Republic with Colonel Abd al-Karim Qasim serving in the role of prime minister. While various military factions competed for power on the Iraqi scene with political leaders of the Kurds, the Ba'ath Party, and the Communists, in foreign policy, Iraq abandoned its current strong orientation towards Great Britain and the United States and opted for a policy of non-participation. At the same time, Baghdad established diplomatic relations with the Soviet Union and some of its satellites, especially Czechoslovakia. In August 1959, Iraq opened its embassy in Prague, the only one in the Soviet Bloc outside Moscow. From Prague's point of view, maintaining good trade relations with Iraq was motivated by the fact that in the area of the Middle East it was a relatively rich country thanks to oil revenues, so it was able to pay in cash for Czechoslovak products.[5]

EARLY MILITARY ASSISTANCE IN THE TIMES OF QASIM'S RULE

However, the military relations between both countries still remained very limited. In September 1960, the study of Kamil Petros Hanna at the Antonín Zápotocký Military Academy (*Vojenská akademie Antonína Zápotockého*, VAAZ) in the specialisation of aircraft engines was approved by President of Czechoslovakia Antonín Novotný. Hanna was disabled with an amputated leg at the thigh and a member of the Iraqi Communist Party. He arrived in Czechoslovakia on 30 November 1959 and at first attended a course in the Czech language. His study at the VAAZ in Brno began in the academic year 1960/1961.[6]

In 1960, the Iraqi government, through the Ministry of Land Reform, issued an international tender to develop an offer for aerial surveying, aerial imaging, topographic survey, and mapping of the Iraq Republic. Approximately 20 countries showed interest, mainly the Netherlands, West Germany, the United States, the Soviet Union, and Poland. The tender was also met with a positive response at the HTS of the Ministry of Foreign Trade in Prague, not only in view of the multimillion-dollar scope of the potential contract but also in terms of efforts to strengthen trade and political relations with Iraq. Due to the immense scope of the task at hand, it was originally planned that the Czechoslovak People's Army (*Československá lidová armáda*) would be ordered to carry out such an undertaking. The first estimates showed that it would be needed 225 men, three Il-14 airplanes, one liaison aircraft, and 132 vehicles. Later, the requirement for the participation of military personnel and equipment was reduced and the main role was to be played by the Central Administration of Geodesy and Cartography (*Ústřední správa geodézie a kartografie*). However, Czechoslovakia did not succeed in the tender.[7]

The tenure of Abd al-Karim Qasim ended prematurely in February 1963 due to a military coup perpetrated by the Ba'ath Party's Iraqi wing. Qasim's former deputy, Abdul Salam Arif, became the new president, a function with largely ceremonial

authority, while prominent Ba'athist General Ahmed Hassan al-Bakr was named prime minister. However, the most powerful figure of the new regime was General Secretary of the Iraqi Ba'ath Party Ali Salih al-Sa'di who organised a massacre of thousands of true and suspected Communists, their sympathisers, and other dissidents following the coup.

The Presidium (*Předsednictvo*) of the Central Committee of the Communist Party of Czechoslovakia (*Ústřední výbor Komunistické strany Československa*, ÚV KSČ) approved the recognition of the new Iraqi government on 12 February. However, information about the brutal purges of Iraqi communists enraged the leadership in Prague that adopted radical changes in relations with the new Iraqi government in July 1963. Henceforth, the official agenda included a propaganda campaign against the Ba'ath Party, support for actions against the Ba'athist regime, support for the Ba'athist opposition – including the Kurds – no new agreements and contracts with the current government, and no increase of scientific and technical assistance to Iraq.

The bloody political turmoil in Iraq prompted two young Iraqi officers trained at that time in the Soviet Union to ask for political asylum in Czechoslovakia in June 1963. They made the request to the Soviet military authorities which subsequently contacted the Czechoslovak embassy in Moscow. The first officer was Lieutenant Haddi Awni Jawad who studied at the Soviet flight academy during March 1960 and April 1963 and obtained qualification as an Il-14 pilot. The second officer was the technician of ground-based radars Lieutenant Nasim Mohrin El Idani who attended studies in the Soviet Union from March 1962 to April 1963. The matter was discussed by the Presidium ÚV KSČ which approved the granting of asylum to both officers. This decision was in line with the practice to grant Czechoslovak asylum (or residence permit) to exponents of the former Qasim regime such as Minister of Education Faisal Samir or General Hashim Jabbar.[8]

On 18 November 1963, another coup d'état culminated when the radical Ba'athist faction was ousted from power and the positions of the moderates and soldiers led by Arif were strengthened. Thus, the first Ba'ath establishment was overthrown, and a new, pro-Nasserist government was established with Abdul Salam Arif remaining the Iraqi president. As a result, the Czechoslovak communist leadership reconsidered its relationship with Iraq and eased previous measures. Positive news about the Iraqi government's actions was to begin to appear in the Czechoslovak media, and trade relations together with scientific and technical cooperation were to be expanded.[9]

WEAPONS FOR THE KURDISH OPPOSITION

The radical anti-communist policy of the Ba'athist regime caused Prague to pay more attention to contacts and support for the Iraqi opposition – the Communists and the Kurds. Indeed, at the beginning of July 1963, Jalal Talabani, a spokesman for the Kurdistan Democratic Party (KDP), arrived in Prague. Talabani briefed officials from the Ministry of Foreign Affairs on the situation in Iraq and relations between the Kurds and the Iraqi government, and on the attitudes of some Western countries, communist states, and some African and Asian countries towards the Kurdish issue in Iraq. Finally, he expressed interest in obtaining Czechoslovak moral, political, and military support, which was to consist primarily of the supply of anti-tank weapons.[10]

While Talabani's pleas met no reaction, the situation changed when the personal envoy of KDP leader Mustafa Barzani, Dara Tufik Salihi, visited Prague between 9 and 12 September 1964. Again, he informed Czechoslovak representatives extensively about the current situation in Iraq, Iraqi Kurdistan, in the KDP, and the relation of the Iraqi government towards the Kurdish demands. He asked Czechoslovak officials to maintain contact only with Barzani's faction and not with the group around Ibrahim Ahmad and Jalal Talabani. At the end of his speech, Salihi asked for a donation of a radio station, duplicating machine and typewriters, medicine, and the supply of weapons (especially anti-tank armament) with ammunition to Kurdish units loyal to Barzani. The Presidium ÚV KSČ discussed this matter and on 15 September 1964 approved to donate one Roomayor duplicating machine, four typewriters, and medicaments. At the same time, Czechoslovak diplomats were tasked with exerting pressure on a peaceful solution to the Kurdish issue in international organisations and some countries in the Middle East. Minister of National Defence Army General Bohumír Lomský was to examine the possibility of providing a smaller number of weapons and a radio station.[11]

In the end, the Ministry of National Defence (*Ministerstvo národní obrany*) provided surplus infantry weapons for 2,000 men to the overall value of 4,900,000 CSK (see Table 2) – the radio station could not be delivered. The ministry considered providing an R-102 (from Hungarian licence production) or an R-118 (from Polish licence production), both of which were of Soviet design. However, not only were both types used by the Warsaw Pact armies but they were classified as secret. Subsequently, Prague thought about the provision of the commercial KUV-3/5 radio transmitter. But this type was difficult to maintain and had a high failure rate due to improper handling. Therefore, the Presidium ÚV KSČ approved only the delivery of the weapons for the KDP in the resolution from 13 October 1964.[12]

Although the Czechoslovak People's Army prepared the weapons for shipment on 30 November 1964, their safe transport to Iraqi Kurdistan proved to be an unsolvable problem. Despite numerous attempts, the HTS was unable to deliver the arms into the hands of KDP representatives. For this reason, the Presidium ÚV KSČ agreed with the request of the Ministry of Foreign Trade and cancelled the task on 13 April 1966. Thus, the weapons were never delivered.[13]

This decision did not please the top KDP officials very much, which led Mustafa Barzani to write a letter to President Antonín Novotný on 25 April 1966:

You know for sure that the peaceful Kurdish people in Iraq have been exposed to the cruel consequences of the devastating war imposed on them by the reactionary military regime in Iraq for almost five years. The aim of this war is to exterminate the Kurdish people, simply because it demands autonomy for Iraqi Kurdistan within a democratic Iraq.

[…]

The Kurdish people today urgently need material and moral support, and we firmly believe that Your socialist republic with the other countries of the socialist camp has an understanding of our just cause.

That is why we ask you to continue Your help and continue to support the just struggle of the enslaved Kurdish people, who, alongside all the honourable sons of the Iraqi people, are fighting to establish democracy in Iraq and to gain autonomy for Iraqi Kurdistan.

At that time, however, the Czechoslovak communist leadership no longer had much 'understanding of the just struggle' of the Kurdish people. On the contrary: Prague had a much greater

Table 2: Czechoslovak arms to be delivered to the Kurdistan Democratic Party (unrealised)[14]

Type	Number of examples	Note
vz. 52, 7.62mm rifle	1,600	from the stocks of the Czechoslovak People's Army
vz. 52, 7.62mm machine gun	300	from the stocks of the Czechoslovak People's Army
vz. 26, 7.92mm machine gun	100	from the stocks of the Czechoslovak People's Army
vz. 52, 7.62mm round	3,720,000	from the stocks of the Czechoslovak People's Army
vz. 47, 7.92mm round	600,000	from the stocks of the Czechoslovak People's Army
P-27, light anti-tank weapon	100	from the stocks of the Czechoslovak People's Army
round for P-27	6,000	from the stocks of the Czechoslovak People's Army

understanding of the foreign exchange it could gain by selling arms to the official Iraqi government.[15]

SPOILED DELIVERIES OF JET FIGHTERS AND TANKS

The situation had changed since the second quarter of 1964 when the communist leadership in Prague decided to give permission for supplies of Czechoslovak weapons to the Iraqi government. This change was fully used by the HTS that signed (in the name of foreign trade company OMNIPOL) a contract with Iraq for 5,000 obsolete vz. 24 rifles which were delivered during 1964.[16] During the next year, Czechoslovakia supplied spare parts for Iraqi MiG-15UTI fighter trainers (for 368,000 CSK) and their RD-45FA powerplants (for 127,000 CSK).[17]

In 1964, Iraq expressed interest in the acquisition of 50 T-54AK command tanks and 20 MiG-21F-13 fighters (both from Czechoslovak licence production, the former were to be delivered from the stocks of the Czechoslovak People's Army), including spare parts, worth 160 million CSK in total. After preliminary negotiations, which were conducted by the HTS disguised as OMNIPOL, and after approving consultation with the Soviet officials, the Ministry of Foreign Trade submitted to the Presidium ÚV KSČ a proposal to conclude an agreement with the Iraqi Republic on the supply of this 'special material'. The Presidium ÚV KSČ approved the document on 30 March 1965 under the condition that 'no political damage' may occur to Czechoslovakia due to the Kurdish issue.

If necessary, a 'secret commission' (bribe) should be paid up to 1 percent of the total price of the contract. The Iraqis claimed that the requested military hardware was intended for replenishment of the inventory that Iraq had purchased in the Soviet Union in the past, but which it could no longer obtain because the Soviet military industry had introduced into the production newer types of weapons in the meantime. Prague was afraid of the political repercussions but the economic motives prevailed:

The supply of military hardware, on the other hand, could have a certain negative response in the leadership of the Kurdish movement, to which we have expressed support. Nevertheless, a positive decision is recommended in view of the economic advantageousness of supplies and the fact that it is useful to support the anti-imperialist course of the Iraqi government and to prevent possible supplies of armament from France or Great Britain or other imperialist countries.[18]

Contrary to Czechoslovak wishes, the Kurdish problem escalated into an armed conflict during the spring of the same year. The Czechoslovak embassy in Baghdad reported to Prague at 8:25 a.m. on 22 April 1965 about the recent situation in Iraqi Kurdistan:

In recent days, all soldiers of units concentrated in the north have been equipped with gas masks. News of this spread among the Kurdish population, raising panic and fears of using gas not only against Kurdish troops but also against the population. In some areas, this results in the mass evacuation of villages. On 18 April, the air force carried out the heavy bombing of Barzani's headquarters just near the Iranian and Turkish borders. The bombing is to continue systematically. During a recent visit to the United Arab Republic, Prime Minister Yahya discussed with Nasser, in particular, the possibility of further sending the United Arab Republic units to Iraq. He justified the request by a weakening of security in the interior of Iraq due to the concentration of the army in the north. The situation is especially critical in the south, where only a small number of guard units remained in the garrisons, and moreover, it is precisely in this area that an attempted coup by the pro-British elements cannot be ruled out. Nasser categorically rejected these demands, and as a result of the controversy, Yahya immediately returned to Baghdad.

At 11.00 a.m. during the same day, the Czechoslovak embassy sent another telegram from Bagdad:

The clashes in Kurdistan have already reached the scale of war operations. Heavy weapons and air force are used almost all over the north. The first onslaught by the Iraqi army, which was aimed to break the resistance of the Kurds in strategic sections by lightning actions, was unsuccessful. So far occupied only Ranya and Koisenjaq. The Kurds have chosen a tactic that the Egyptians consider right – not to waste armament and not to resist in the places where tanks can pass – to defend mountain sections of significant importance at all circumstances. According to the Egyptians, the Kurds will hold on until the winter. Now fighting in the mountains of Sephin – Dag south of Shaqlawa, then in the Khanaqin area, where a brigade is deployed with the support of 25 tanks and 500 Salahuddins, in the Darbandikhan and Meidan area, where the army division, two tank regiments and a squadron of MiGs are deployed and in the Shawan and Nakhshina area with artillery and tanks. Attacks in these areas successfully repelled. There are growing cases of desertion in the army and police. In the Khaladja area alone, a company of 46 men deserted. The government forcibly evicted 20 villages from the Dokhuq area to prevent support for the guerrilla movement. Kurds use Iranian territory to heal the wounded. In the revolutionary command, which decided on a violent solution to the Kurdish problem, a crisis occurs at the first failures. The minister of the interior and information and some members of the General Staff against the fighting. Arif, Yahya, commanders of five divisions, and some other military officials for continuation. The Egyptians condemn the start of the fighting, which has led to a further cooling of relations. Government changes are expected, depending on which of the two groups in the government will gain dominance in the military.[19]

On 22 April 1965, General Sergeychik (Chief of the Main Engineering Administration of the State Committee of the Council of Ministers of the Union of Soviet Socialist Republics for Foreign Economic Relations) informed his counterpart at the HTS in Prague that in view of the developments in Iraq, the Soviet government suspended negotiations with the Iraqis on all requests for the supply of additional military hardware and temporarily suspended supplies for all previously concluded contracts. Among other things, the departure of a ship fully loaded with weapons, which was to leave the Soviet port on 23 April, was stopped. In the light of this situation, the HTS hastily recalled home its business team that held negotiations in Baghdad with the Iraqis about the supply of the T-54AKs and MiG-21F-13s.

However, the discussions related to this arms deal continued in May. The Ministry of Foreign Affairs recommended:

… that the actual negotiations on supplies take place as discreetly as possible, preferably in Prague, and that any supplies be made as inconspicuously as possible.

It recommends this discretion in order to avoid the case of Yugoslavia, which, following a report by Iraqi military authorities that Yugoslavia offered to supply arms to the Iraqi army, was called on by the General Secretary of the Committee for the Defence of the Kurdish People's Rights in Paris to refrain from supplying arms to the Iraqi government.

In the course of the negotiations, the Iraqis increased the demand for the supply of MiG-21F-13 fighters by 20 examples. This brought considerable problems to the Czechoslovak aviation industry, because Středočeské strojírny would not be able to ensure the production of an increased number of MiGs for Iraq and at the same time fulfil contracted supplies for the Czechoslovak Air Force (maximum Czechoslovak annual production capacity was 40 MiG-21F-13s).

However, the Ministry of Foreign Trade strongly pushed for the whole deal due to the very advantageous payment conditions. Therefore, on 21 September 1965, the Presidium ÚV KSČ agreed to deliver 40 MiG-21F-13s to Iraq despite the slowdown of the rearmament of the Czechoslovak Air Force. Due to this decision, the MiG-21F-13s manufactured by Středočeské strojírny for the Czechoslovak Air Force would be delivered later than planned since the original proposal to increase the quota for the import of more modern MiG-21PFM fighters from the Soviet Union by 20 aircraft was not approved.[20]

However, at a time when the issue of the possibility of supplying an increased number of MiGs was being resolved in Czechoslovakia, the Soviet Union resumed its negotiations with Iraq. Moscow showed its willingness to supply the required armament under the same conditions as in the past – interest-free on a 10-year credit. Because the terms provided by the Soviet Union were significantly more favourable than the conditions offered by Prague, Baghdad decided to buy tanks, fighter aircraft, and other military hardware in the USSR. During 1965 and 1966, OMNIPOL (alias the HTS) held talks with Iraqi officials on further deliveries of armament. The result of these discussions was only the supply of Czechoslovak infantry weapons in 1965 (worth 5.4 million CSK) and 1966 (to the value of 9.6 million CSK) for Iraqi police forces: 35,000 rifles, 1,655 assault rifles, 150 pistols, 1,500 light machine guns, and 22.5 million rounds of associated ammunition.[21]

SEARCH FOR CONTRACTS

Despite the very limited success, the HTS did not allow itself to be discouraged from trying to sell more Czechoslovak weapons to Iraq. In an effort to secure the supply of heavy weaponry and achieve a higher turnover, it invited a total of three Iraqi military delegations to visit the Czechoslovak Socialist Republic during 1966, which were shown the various types of military hardware manufactured at that time, including the L-29 Delfin training aircraft. The first one led by Chief of the General Staff Abdar Rahman Arif came in April, the next delegation followed in November and was led by the new Chief of the General Staff, General Hamoudi Mehdi. The third delegation was headed by the commander of the Iraqi Air Force, Brigadier Jassam Mohammed as-Saher, who requested delivery of L-29 training aircraft. Also, the possible sale of surplus MiG-15UTI fighter trainers from the inventory of the Czechoslovak Air Force was discussed.

Following these talks, in January 1967 Iraqi officials invited a delegation led by the director of the HTS to pay an official visit to Iraq that took place between 4 and 6 March 1967 with the aim to 'deepen friendly relations.' During their stay, Czechoslovak officials met with the Iraqi president, prime minister, minister of defence, chief of general staff, and commander of the Iraqi Air Force. Despite the Czechoslovak effort, the negotiations ended without a concrete conclusion in terms of awarded contracts. During these talks, Iraqi representatives had repeatedly stated that winning more contracts depended on the credit terms that Prague would provide to Iraq. Thus, Czechoslovak officials at least found out that their existing practice was condemned to failure. Besides, in the face of strong competition mainly in the form of the Soviet Union, from the HTS officials' point of view, it became apparent that paying bribes would be inevitable:

During the talks, the possibilities of cooperation between the Czechoslovak Socialist Republic and Iraq in the field of special materials were discussed. It turned out that the Soviet Union and some other countries continue to provide very favourable payment and credit terms to the Iraqi side so that the sale of Czechoslovak special materials under the conditions we still provide cannot be successfully expanded. In addition, it will be necessary to deepen contacts at key places in the Iraqi Ministry of Defence and to ensure, in an appropriate form, the personal material interest of the relevant Iraqi personalities in supplies from the Czechoslovak Socialist Republic.

For the HTS, Iraq was a country of priority interest at that time because, unlike traditional clients of Czechoslovak military hardware such as Egypt and Syria, the Iraqi economy was in much better shape and thus

Baghdad was able to buy Czechoslovak weapons under financial conditions much more advantageous for Prague. For this reason, the HTS proposed paying bribes of up to 3 percent of the total contract price to the relevant Iraqi military officials.[22]

In the end, however, the outcome for the Czechoslovak armament business was influenced foremost by the courtesy of the Israelis and their stunning military victory during the June 1967 Arab-Israeli War.

DELFINS AND ZLINS FOR THE IRAQI AIR FORCE

Arguably, opportunities for the Czechoslovak 'special material' had arisen before this conflict. One of the main tasks of the new Commander of the Iraqi Air Force Brigadier Jassam Mohammed as-Saher was streamlining the training of new personnel. The training of Iraqi Air Force cadets was undertaken at Shaibah air base on a miscellany of types including de Havilland Canada DHC-1 Chipmunk, Percival Provost, Yakovlev Yak-18, BAC Jet Provost, and Mikoyan-Gurevich MiG-15UTI. The training of aircraft technicians was carried out at the Technical Training Centre at Habbaniya, while the training of technicians for ground-based communication and radar equipment took place at the Technical Training Centre at Taji. The untenability of this situation became even more obvious with the mass introduction of a new generation of Soviet combat airplanes into the inventory of the Iraqi Air Force.

Thus, the first priority became to obtain new suitable training airplanes. The second priority was to unify all air force schools into one training establishment in the newly constructed facility. While the former was realised through the purchase of Aero L-29 Delfin and Zlin Z-526 trainers from Czechoslovakia, the latter requirement led to the establishment of the Air Force Academy at as-Sahra air base near Tikrit.[23]

The Contract 117-0012 between OMNIPOL and the Ministry of Defence – Iraqi Air Force Headquarters, for the acquisition of the first 20 L-29s to the overall value of 48 million CSK (3.3 million USD) was awarded on 18 July 1967. The aircraft, originally intended for the Soviet Air Force, were completed in the Aero Vodochody

A trio of Zlin Z-526F training aircraft manufactured for Iraq, seen prior to their delivery. (Author's collection)

An L-29 Delfin training jet in the markings of the Iraqi Air Force Academy, seen in the early 1970s. Notable are drop tanks, the upper half of which was painted in matt black. (Author's collection)

An overhead view of an L-29 manufactured for Iraq during pre-delivery testing at the Aero Vodochody airfield revealing details of the national markings applied on upper wing surfaces. (Aero Vodochody)

Correspondingly, all Iraqi Delfins were subsequently transferred to as-Sahra where they equipped two squadrons of the Air Force Academy during the 1970s. At the request of the customer, the L-29s for the Iraqi Air Force were equipped with an additional SEMCA air conditioning unit for the cooling of the cockpit while standing on the ramp and before take-off. Until the end of the 1970s, one section (three plus one L-29s) was regularly dispatched for patrolling in Iraqi Kurdistan. Delfins fulfilling these duties were equipped with ASP-3MN gunsights and two RB-57/4M rocket pods (each for four Soviet S-5M unguided rockets). Their crews were composed of instructor pilots from the Air Force Academy. Such operations were staged from Kirkuk or Mosul air bases.[24]

In addition to L-29 Delfins, the Air Force Academy also operated Czechoslovak-made Zlin Z-526 airplanes for elementary pilot training. The Iraqi Air Force ordered 25 Z-526F aircraft and 15 Z-526AF airplanes. Unlike the Z-526AFs operated by the Czechoslovak aerobatic representation team, the Iraqi variant was basically a single-seat version of the Z-526F. For this reason, the Z-526AF operated by the Iraqi

plant at Odolena Voda in early 1968. In an effort to accelerate the development of the Iraqi Air Force, Moscow had agreed to transfer these Delfins to Iraq. Under the code name Course 696, six Czechoslovak instructor pilots from the Higher Aviation Training School (*Vyšší letecké učiliště*) at Košice flew the aircraft to Iraq. Each pilot made two flights. The remaining airplanes were in a partially dismantled state and transported in wooden crates to Baghdad where factory technicians assembled them. The next contract for a further 20 L-29s for 3.3 million USD was signed in 1968. Aero Vodochody managed to deliver all 40 Delfins (Iraqi serial numbers 735 to 794) in three batches by the end of the same year. An additional 38 L-29 trainers for the Iraqi Air Force were delivered between December 1973 and April 1974 (Iraqi serial numbers 1123 to 1160). Thus, the total number of L-29 Delfin aircraft delivered to Iraq reached 78 examples, along with them the Iraqi Air Force also acquired four TL-29 simulators.

The first L-29s delivered in January and February 1968 were initially deployed at Habbaniyah Air Base. Following the construction of as-Sahra air base, the facility became the home of the Air Force Academy which was commissioned there in 1970.

Air Force carried the manufacturer's designation Z-526FI. The first Iraqi Z-526F was test flown at the factory airfield at Otrokovice during February 1970. The shipment of Z-526Fs (Iraqi serial numbers 916 to 940) from the factory took place from August of the same year and lasted until 1971. The Z-526AFs (Iraqi serial numbers 941 to 955) were delivered from June to August 1972. The planes were originally supposed to fly from Otrokovice to Iraq, but Syria did not allow them to overfly its territory. Therefore, the aircraft had to be dismantled and transported to Iraq aboard An-12 transport airplanes. In addition to as-Sahra air base, the Zlins were also operated from the nearby K2 airfield.[25]

In addition, Baghdad bought surplus MiG-15 fighters retired from the inventory of the Czechoslovak Air Force. In February 1969, the Deputy Commander of Iraqi Air Force, Brigadier Mohamed Nasser al-Kasser visited Czechoslovakia to check the flow of the training of Iraqi jet pilots (Course 264, see below) and discuss additional training of Iraqi fliers in Czechoslovakia. During the negotiations with the military and HTS (disguised as OMNIPOL) representatives in Prague, Brigadier al-Kasser expressed his interest in the purchase of 20 MiG-15bis and MiG-17 fighters, including spare parts. In the end, the Iraqi Air Force obtained 10 MiG-15UTI conversion trainers and 39 MiG-15bis fighters (the first order was for 16 airplanes) between 1969 and 1972. All aircraft underwent the overhaul before delivery including new coating with Iraqi insignia and serials (16 MiG-15bis fighters received Iraqi serial numbers 1019 to 1034). According to the Iraqi requirement, the last five MiG-15UTIs were to be transferred to Iraq by Czechoslovak instructor pilots from the Higher Aviation Training School.[26]

COURSE 262: CONVERSION TRAINING ON THE DELFIN

In the frame of the contract for the delivery of the first batch of L-29 Delfins, the Iraqi Air Force ordered conversion training on this aircraft type for the initial cadre of selected pilots and technicians. The Iraqi group was composed of 24 members, future Iraqi Air Force instructors on the L-29 Delfin: three pilots, two technicians – crew chiefs, five technicians for the airframe, five technicians for the engine, three technicians for electrical equipment, two technicians for instrument equipment, three technicians for communication equipment, and one technician for armament. The price of the training reached a value of 13,398 GBP.

Training of the Iraqi personnel received the Czechoslovak cover designation Course 262 and was undertaken between 1 September and 11 November 1967. The actual flight training was provided by the instructors of the 4th Aviation Training Regiment (4. letecký školní pluk) operating from Sliač air base. Training of Iraqi pilots was relatively short – they were trained mostly under the visual flight rules (VFR) conditions during the daylight. The pilots mastered

flying from the back seat during the day and flying according to the instruments in a covered cabin. They were familiarised with flying at night, with the group flying in pairs, with unguided rocket firing at a ground target, and with the bombing. All Iraqi pilots tried to achieve the best possible results during the training.[27]

Additional conversion training of a new group of three Iraqi pilots and 21 technicians on the L-29 Delfin under the Czechoslovak cover name Course 268 took place again at Sliač air base between 29 May and 9 August 1968.[28]

AIRFIELD DESIGNERS IN IRAQ

Prague was more than interested in playing the leading role in the reshaping of the Iraqi Air Force training structure. Czechoslovakia did not only want to supply new training aircraft but was also interested in designing and building a new integrated training facility for training air and ground crews – the future Air Force Academy at as-Sahra air base.

For this reason, under the code designation Course 698, two designers of the Military Design Institute (Vojenský projektový ústav) were sent to Baghdad in March 1968 to discuss the construction of an aviation academy and military airfields. During their one month stay, they found that the Iraqi Air Force was asking to build three complete military air bases with concrete runways and an air academy with two concrete runways worth a total of about 12 million GBP.

On 12 May 1968, the Ministry of National Defence sent to Iraq a new group consisting of three designers of the Military Design Institute (Mužík, Havlena, Malenský) and one officer from the Higher Aviation Training School (Colonel Filouš). The Czechoslovak team aimed to prepare documents for the submission of a bid for the construction of a new air academy – a single centre for the training of future pilots and ground specialists of the Iraqi Air Force. According to Iraqi requirements, Colonel Filouš's task was to prepare a proposal for the organisational structure of the academy and a rough table of numbers and thus give the designers from the Military Design Institute the basis for determining quarters, operating facilities, classrooms, workshops, and other buildings.

The initial Iraqi requirements were enormous – about 5,500 men (including students) were to serve with the academy, whose flying department was to operate 180 aircraft, which were to fly about 30,000 flight hours a year. The Czechoslovak team, therefore, expressed doubts about the enormously high numbers of

Table 3: Course 262 – Iraqi instructor pilots trained on the L-29 Delfin, 1967[29]				
Name	**Number of Flights**	**Number of Flight Hours**	**Period of Training**	**Final Assessment**
Captain Usmet Showket Khaffaf	with instructor: 36 solo: 5 total: 41	with instructor: 13.22 hours solo: 1.52 hours total: 15.14 hours	1 September 1967 – 21 October 1967	Excellent
Major Sabah Saleh	with instructor: 37 solo: 5 total: 42	with instructor: 13.03 hours solo: 2.02 hours total: 15.05 hours	1 September 1967 – 21 October 1967	Excellent
Captain Wathiq Abdullah	with instructor: 35 solo: 6 total: 41	with instructor: 12.55 hours solo: 2.03 hours total: 14.58 hours	1 September 1967 – 21 October 1967	Excellent

Instructors of the Iraqi Air Force Academy seen with one of their L-29s. (Author's collection)

trained students: the Iraqis wanted to graduate 105 pilots and 510 technicians/non-commissioned officers per year. However, the Iraqi Air Force commander initially insisted on these numbers.

During the talks, the Iraqis demanded that an Administrative College for about 60 cadets be included in the academy, which would be intended for the training of administrative forces in the air force. On the night of 20 May, another designer from the Military Design Institute (Malenovský) arrived in Iraq. All four then drew a general layout of the air base and associated air academy for 5,490 persons. The Czechoslovak experts held several consultations with officials of the Iraqi Air Force related to the final form of this facility. After about a month's stay in Iraq, members of the Czechoslovak expert team returned to Czechoslovakia, where they completed their study for the establishment and construction of the air academy.

At this time, an international tender was held for the construction of runways for the Kut and Tallil air bases, in which the Czechoslovak construction company Konstruktiva, represented by the Czechoslovak foreign trade company Strojexport, also took part.[30]

Moreover, in the period from 12 to 25 March 1968, Lieutenant Colonel Miroslav Bílek, an experienced instructor of the Research and Testing Centre 031 (*Výzkumné zkušební středisko 031*), took part in business negotiations in Baghdad (under the code name Course 697), where he demonstrated the Czechoslovak parachutes and gave a short instruction on their use. Although the Soviet Union delivered 1,000 parachutes to Iraq, which no one ordered, the Iraqis were very interested in the Czechoslovak parachutes.[31]

BUSINESS NEGOTIATIONS IN BAGHDAD
The group of four representatives from the HTS and Ministry of National Defence visited Iraq between 22 October and 13 November 1967 in order to discuss future military cooperation between Czechoslovakia and Iraq with Minister of Defence Shakir Mahmud Shukri and other high ranking military officers. One of the outcomes of the negotiations was Contract 5279 (and its Supplements No. 1 and No. 2 – Contract 5279/1 and Contract 5279/2) which was signed in Baghdad on 11 November 1967.

Contract 5279 stipulated basic training of 50 Iraqi cadets on L-29 Delfin aircraft in Czechoslovakia for a total price of 1,170,000 GBP (i.e. 23,400 GBP per pilot). 'Given that the payment will be made in cash and in freely convertible currency and all costs are in CSK, the conclusion of these contracts is very advantageous for the [Czechoslovak] national economy in terms of foreign exchange.'

The reason why the Iraqi Ministry of Defence decided to train its pilots in Czechoslovakia was the insufficient capacity of Iraqi Air Force training establishments. While their capabilities included the training of a maximum of 40 pilots, the Iraqi Air Force leadership required the training of about 120 pilots. Therefore, it was decided to train the remaining pilot cadets abroad – in Czechoslovakia and the Soviet Union. Although Moscow offered training of up to 150 new pilots, Baghdad was interested in the training of the maximum number of its pilots in the Czechoslovak Socialist Republic.

Major General Jassam Mohammed as-Saher put extreme emphasis on the high difficulty of the training. He declared that only cadets able to outstandingly fulfil the duties of fighter pilots could finish the training. All others should be dismissed at the earliest opportunity. Within frame of Contract 5279/1, the Iraqi Air Force ordered an advanced course of the MiG-15 combat employment for pilots previously trained on the L-29 (this agreement was later replaced by Contract 5279/6, see below).[32]

Contract 5279/2 dealt with the training of two communication equipment technicians on the Delfin. The actual training took place under the Czechoslovak code name Course 265 at Zvolen within the Tactical-Technical Courses (*Takticko-technické kursy*) section of the Higher Aviation Training School between 10 January and 10 March 1968.[33]

In May 1969, the Iraqi Air Force requested a reduction of flight hours per pilot on the L-29 Delfin training course and additional training of Iraqi pilots on combat airplanes. Thus, from 22 June 1969 to 4 July 1969, new contracting negotiations were held in Baghdad. Eventually, the cut of flight time on the L-29 and new supplements of Contract 5279 were signed on 3 July. The training on the L-29s was to be completed with a maximum of 130 flight hours for a pilot (the original requirement was 180 flight hours). The follow-on advanced training of 34 Iraqi pilots (graduates of the previous L-29 course) on the MiG-15 with a maximum of 70 flight hours per pilot was awarded as Contract 5279/6 (the original extent according to Contract 5279/1 was 35 flight hours). Besides this, the Iraqis ordered

A MiG-21F-13 of the Czechoslovak Air Force armed with a Soviet-made R-3S ('AA-2 Atoll') air-to-air missile. The type was used for training of Iraqi pilots in Czechoslovakia. (Author's collection)

conversion training of these pilots in Czechoslovakia: 14 Iraqi pilots on the MiG-21 fighter with 32 flying hours per pilot (Contract 5279/7) and training of two groups (each with 10 pilots) on the Su-7 fighter bomber with 30 flight hours per pilot (Contract 5279/8). The total price of these deals was approximately 84 million CSK.[34]

During the meetings in Baghdad, the Iraqis put heavy emphasis on the Su-7 training and threatened that further negotiations could follow only on the condition that Iraqi requests concerning the training on the Su-7s were fulfilled. However, the Iraqi 'training budget' was limited, thus the Iraqis requested the highest possible reduction of prices. If the Czechoslovak Air Force failed to satisfy Iraqi demands, the Iraqis claimed that they would finish the training of their pilots in Iraq and future basic pilot training would be secured by Poland. Therefore, Czechoslovak officials had to make two price reductions. They had basically no other possible choice since the practice of paying bribes had failed – this activity became known to some Iraqi authorities that started to claim that the deal would be completely cancelled if Czechoslovakia continued in this fashion. Eventually, the Iraqis achieved the price reduction by 12 percent per MiG-21 flight hour and by 24 percent per Su-7 flight hour. Thus, the Iraqi Air Force paid 624 GBP for one flight hour on the MiG-21 fighter and 995 GBP for a flight hour of the Su-7 fighter bomber. Nevertheless, in comparison to the Soviet 'price list', the Czechoslovak price was still higher by 28 percent per MiG-21 flight hour and 22 percent per Su-7 flight hour. Moreover, because of the strained budget, the Iraqis had to reduce the number of flight hours for their pilots from the original 35 for both types to 32 and 30 respectively.

In Baghdad, some other issues were discussed as well. Iraqi Air Force officials were highly interested in the new L-39 Albatros training aircraft that was in the final stages of its development. They indicated the need to decide in two to three years what type of airplane would replace MiG-15s and MiG-17s used in the training of Iraqi fighter pilots.[35]

COURSE 264: TRAINING OF IRAQI COMBAT PILOTS

In order to train Iraqi pilots within the frame of Contract 5279 and its supplements, the Czechoslovak Air Force established Course 264 which was to last from 8 January 1968 to 30 October 1970. In the frame of Course 264, the following 'sub-courses' were established (in accordance with supplements of original Contract 5279):

- Course 264 – basic training of 50 Iraqi pilots on the L-29 and MiG-15bis
- Course 264/b – advanced training of 34 Iraqi pilots on the MiG-15bis
- Course 264/c – conversion training of 14 Iraqi pilots on the MiG-21F-13
- Course 264/d – conversion training of 20 Iraqi pilots on the Su-7BM

However, Course 264 did not run as smoothly as Czechoslovak officials expected. Indeed, it became one of the most disastrous training courses for foreign pilots ever undertaken in Czechoslovakia. The Czechoslovak Air Force lost three aircraft with one Czechoslovak instructor pilot and one Iraqi student pilot killed in the process.

After theoretical training, the actual flight training with the 4th Aviation Training Regiment at Sliač air base began in earnest in early May 1968. Due to indiscipline, health reasons, and incapability for flight training, 10 students were sent back home. In August, the training had to be interrupted due to the invasion of Czechoslovakia by Warsaw Pact troops. Sliač air base was permanently occupied by the Soviet Air Force, so the 4th Aviation Training Regiment had to make an involuntary move to Piešťany, where new complications of all kinds arose (temporary accommodation, inadequate food, insufficiently equipped classrooms and gym). Thanks to the maximum efforts of the Czechoslovak personnel, the training activity was resumed there on 15 October.[36]

On 20 October 1969 at 11.00 a.m., a MiG-15UTI (serial number 2759) crewed by student pilot Hikmat Nori Tawfik and instructor Captain Václav Loukotka took off from Piešťany air base on a navigational training flight. After the take-off run of 700–750 metres (2,297–2,461 feet), the Iraqi student started to climb too steeply and brought the aircraft to the stall above the critical angle of attack (27° to 30°). Captain Loukotka reacted at the moment when the horizontal stabiliser was already situated in the wing slipstream, thus becoming ineffective. The pilot and instructor lowered flaps to the 55° position, but it was too late. MiG-15UTI jinked, turned over to its back, and fell to the ground from an altitude of 20 metres (66 feet). The aircraft crashed 32 metres (105 feet) off the runway, exploded, and started to burn. Both crewmembers were killed.[37]

After finishing Course 264, selected Iraqi pilots continued in conversion training at the Air Force Training Centre (Výcvikové středisko letectva) either on the MiG-21F-13 or the Su-7BM. The best of them were selected for the latter airplane. Both courses were largely intended only for basic conversion on the type (circuits, aircraft handling, and aerobatics), only five (Course 264/c) and three training sorties (Course 264/d) were reserved for air combat training. In the case of the MiG-21F-13 conversion, the Iraqi pilots carried out training interceptions simulating the use of R-3S (ASCC/NATO reporting name 'AA-2 Atoll') air-to-air missiles.

The mission of the Air Force Training Centre deployed at Přerov air base was to conduct combat training for students of the Higher Aviation Training School (Vyšší letecké učiliště) at Košice on the MiG-21F-13 and conversion courses for pilots and technicians on the Su-7BM. However, it practically did not perform the latter task and the centre had no complement of Su-7 fighter-bombers of its own. Instead, the required Su-7BMs and Su-7Us (together with instructors) had to be transferred from combat units of the Czechoslovak Air Force – 20th Fighter Bomber Aviation Regiment (20. stíhací bombardovací letecký pluk) and 28th Fighter Bomber Aviation Regiment (28. stíhací bombardovací letecký pluk). In fact, all Su-7U dual seaters from the inventory of the Czechoslovak Air Force were sent to Přerov so that both regiments had to temporarily replace them with MiG-15UTIs. Several Air Force Training Centre instructors hastily underwent refresher courses on Su-7s in order to train Iraqi student pilots as well.

In the course of this training, the Czechoslovak Air Force lost two 'Fitters' through the actions of Lieutenant Abdul Muniam al-Hassan. On 12 June 1970, he, groundlessly and without knowledge of instructor Major Radomír Sprátek, lowered flaps when a Su-7U (serial number 1014) was flying at high speed. As a result of this mistake, not only the flaps but the whole wing was seriously damaged. The Czechoslovak instructor barely managed to land with the damaged aircraft. The Czechoslovak Air Force tried to repair this airplane, but the damage was so heavy that 1014 had to be written off in 1973.

The second incident took place on 2 September 1970. During training in aerobatics, Lieutenant al-Hassan lost speed, and stalled the aircraft that went into a spin. The Iraqi pilot was not able to recover and barely managed to eject at the last moment. The Su-

7BM (serial number 5331), to the value of almost 10 million CSK, was completely destroyed. Following these two incidents, Abdul Muniam al-Hassan was dismissed from the training. According to the assessment of the Czechoslovak instructor pilots, because of his abilities, he could not safely accomplish accelerated training on the Su-7. Nevertheless, they stated that he was well trained on the L-29 and the MiG-15bis so with a higher level of experience and flying practice (an additional 50–80 flight hours), he could successfully master the supersonic aircraft. Otherwise, the outcome of Course 264 was highly appreciated by the leadership of the Iraqi Air Force. In total, 29 pilots graduated from the course.[38]

HEAVY WEAPONS FOR THE IRAQI ARMY

The most significant impetus for the purchase of the Czechoslovak armament for the Iraqi Army came in June 1967 when the Egyptian, Syrian, and Jordanian armed forces suffered a crushing defeat in the face of a surprise Israeli assault. Some three months later, between 18 and 24 September, the Iraqi military delegation led by Minister of Defence Shukri visited Czechoslovakia and in the course of several negotiations raised demands for the delivery of the following arms and military assistance as soon as possible:

- 300 OT-62 TOPAS armoured personnel carriers
- 200 OT-810 armoured personnel carriers
- 265 vz. 53 twin anti-aircraft cannons with ammunition
- 120 Tatra 141 tractor trucks
- 20 AV-8 recovery vehicles
- a large number of 60mm mortars
- various infantry weapons with ammunition
- military assistance, mainly training of 40 to 50 pilots on the L-29

While the pilot training of Iraqi cadets was ordered in Contract 5279 (see the text above), 60mm mortars could not be delivered since weapons of this calibre were never used within Warsaw Pact armies. Eventually, no OT-810 half-track armoured personnel carriers were ordered either because the Iraqis obviously recognised their complete obsolescence (being essentially a close derivative of the Second World War-era Sd.Kfz.251 half-track).

The HTS officials knew very well from the previous negotiations that 'winning major contracts depends on the credit terms we would provide to the Iraqi side'. For this reason, in the resolution from 24 October 1967, the Presidium ÚV KSČ approved the provision of credit up to the value of 21 million GBP (1.320 billion CSK) repayable in seven annual instalments (for weapons from the Czechoslovak People's Army stocks credit repayable in up to 10 annual instalments). At the same time, the Czechoslovak politburo authorised the provision, if necessary, of 'secret commission' up to a maximum of 2 percent of the total value of supplies. And these measures paid dividends.[39]

Due to the fact that the Iraqi Ministry of Defence had more funds available in 1967 and 1968, most of the sales of Czechoslovak weapons were made on more favourable payment terms for Prague (cash payment, short-term corporate credits). Therefore, the government credit approved on 24 October 1967 was used only to finance the purchase of 375 OT-62 TOPAS armoured personnel carriers worth 23.6 million USD, of which the five-year loan was only 18.9 million USD (approximately 510 million CSK). This contract was concluded in 1968. In the same year, Baghdad also purchased an additional 20 L-29 Delfín training aircraft for 3.3 million USD and 280 vz. 53 twin anti-aircraft cannons for 18.1 million USD from military stocks.

The Iraqis subsequently increased the demand for the anti-aircraft cannons, so Czechoslovakia eventually delivered a total of 334 vz. 53 guns in several consecutive contracts along with ammunition for 27.9 million USD, which was paid for in cash (Contract No. 21-8-65, No. 21-8-65/2, No. 21-8-129, No. 21-8-195).[40] The cannons were obtained primarily for the air defence of air bases and stationary objects.[41]

When Iraqi officials ordered the delivery of the last four vz. 53 in the frame of Contract No. 21-8-129, the demand created some tensions within the top leadership of the Czechoslovak armed forces: 'The provision of another four examples of 30mm twin anti-aircraft cannons would therefore mean further reducing the already critical situation in securing the Czechoslovak People's Army with anti-aircraft cannons.' Despite these objections, Prague delivered all contracted guns from the warehouses of the Czechoslovak People's Army.[42]

Czechoslovakia concluded all arms agreements under the name of the foreign trade company OMNIPOL. The deals reached a value of 6.6 million USD in 1967, 43.4 million USD in 1968, and 24.1 million USD in 1969. Thanks to this, Iraq became the largest customer of Czechoslovak military hardware among non-communist countries in these times.[43]

IRAQI OT-64S

The official visit of the Iraqi military delegation led by Vice President Brigadier Saadoon Ghaidan to the Czechoslovak Socialist Republic took place in February 1969. The stay of leading Iraqi military officials resulted in the change of 36 ordered OT-62 armoured personnel carriers into a command version, and the purchase of infantry weapons with related ammunition to the overall value of approximately 15 million USD.[44]

In the frame of Contract No. 21-9-95, Baghdad ordered 600 vz. 52/57 light machine guns and 10,000 vz. 52/57 self-loading rifles all of which were to be delivered in 1969.[45]

Besides, a new contract for the supply of 150 OT-64 SKOT armoured personnel carriers was awarded in April 1969. The Czechoslovak and Iraqi officials discussed the delivery of a total of up to 478 OT-64 vehicles which were to be delivered during the years 1969 and 1970. Due to this short time frame, the HTS requested the Czechoslovak People's Army to provide 250 to 327 vehicles from its inventory. Naturally, this proposal was flatly turned down by the senior Czechoslovak officers because it would mean serious disarmament of two motor rifle divisions. Hence, only an additional 23 vehicles were ordered. Thus, Contract No. 33-607-91 covered, amongst others, the provision of 13 OT-64/R2 command vehicles that were delivered to Iraq during autumn 1970. However, the supplies of OT-64 armoured personnel carriers were further complicated by the incapacity of Poland to provide primary armament for all vehicles – the KPVT heavy machine guns. For this reason, 18 armoured personnel carriers had to be equipped with NS-23 cannons, originally used as an armament of the MiG-15bis fighter. Around August 1970, a team of five technicians from the Repair Plant 026 (*Opravárenský závod 026*) at Šternberk was dispatched to Iraq to install the aircraft cannons with gun mounts and related accessories into the OT-64s. In total, 173 OT-64 SKOT vehicles were delivered to Iraq during the time frame of 1969 to 1970. Baghdad paid for them approximately 10 million USD.[46]

TRAINING COURSES IN CZECHOSLOVAKIA AND IRAQ

Simultaneously with the deliveries, the instructors of the Czechoslovak People's Army carried out the training of Iraqi

Table 4: Training of Iraqi Army personnel in Czechoslovakia, 1968–1972[49]			
Cover designation	Training course	Number of graduates	Period
Course 274	technician for the OT-62	20	5 July 1968 – 20 August 1968
Course 279	instructor for the vz. 53	6	15 August 1968 – 15 September 1969
	technician for infantry weapons	2	15 August 1968 – 15 September 1969
Course 302	technician for the general overhauls of the mechanical components of the OT-62	2	1 October 1969 – 29 January 1970
	technician for the general overhauls of the electrical equipment of the OT-62	2	1 October 1969 – 28 November 1970
	technician for the general overhauls of the communication equipment of the OT-62	1	30 June 1969 – 25 October 1969
	technician for the vz. 59 machine gun	1	12 May 1969 – 6 June 1969
Course 303	commander of a mechanised unit equipped with the OT-62	1	28 April 1969 – 6 August 1969
Course 304	driving instructor for the OT-64	8	16 June 1969 – 22 August 1969
	mechanic of the OT-64	5	16 June 1969 – 1 October 1969
	specialist for the radio stations of the OT-64	2	16 June 1969 – 1 October 1969
	electrical mechanic for the OT-64	3	16 June 1969 – 3 September 1969
Course 313	technician for the vz. 53 general overhauls	6	1 October 1969 – 1 April 1970

A row of T-54 tanks of the Iraqi Army seen in the north of the country in 1966. (Author's collection)

one internal report of the Czechoslovak Federal Ministry of National Defence[47] stated:

The 30mm twin anti-aircraft cannons are very demanding for operation and maintenance (the mechanical and electrical drive of traverse and elevation, electric firing, complex launching device from the transport to the firing position and back). The Iraqi military urgently needs to train technicians-repairmen for these weapons.

Thus, Czechoslovak soldiers trained 26 technicians for the OT-62, 18 technicians for the OT-64, six instructors for the vz. 53 and six technicians for the general overhauls of the vz. 53.[48]

Between 1968 and 1971, a total of 37 Czechoslovak experts were sent to Iraq to ensure the smooth operation of Czechoslovak military hardware and to deepen the training of Iraqi soldiers. To support the operation of the vz. 53 twin anti-aircraft cannons, a total of three groups were dispatched, comprising a total of 11 specialists for training, maintenance, and routine repairs. The length of stay of each group was two to three months. Also, from 1969 to 1971, the Military Repair Plant Bludovice (*Vojenský opravárenský závod Bludovice*) provided three technicians for servicing works as part of the warranty for delivered vz. 53s. As of December 1969, some 54 guns were deployed around Baghdad, an additional 42 examples were in Basra. Other Iraqi units operating twin vz. 53 cannons operated at that time around Mosul and in Jordan.

Another three teams were sent to secure the operation of the OT-62 armoured personnel carriers, the length of their stay in Iraq was two to four-and-a-half months. A total of 15 instructors and technicians provided training for driving, maintenance, routine repairs, and repairs after passing 1,500 km.

personnel for new military hardware in Czechoslovakia, within the confines of the Foreign Faculty of the Antonín Zápotocký Military Academy (*Zahraniční fakulta Vojenské akademie Antonína Zápotockého, ZF VAAZ*). Foremost the training on the delivered vz. 53 twin anti-aircraft cannons was more than important since

Three teams (a total of 10 Czechoslovak instructors) for the support of the Iraqi OT-64 vehicles were involved in the training of drivers and mechanics. Moreover, they carried out instruction in maintenance and routine repairs. The stay of one team was three to five-and-a-half months.

During the early 1970s, one instructor for the construction of the SMS medium bridge set served in Iraq for one-and-a-half months. In 1972, a six-member group of Czechoslovak military specialists worked in Iraq with the task to train Iraqi technical personnel for the general overhauls of the twin vz. 53 cannons.[50]

These overhauls were undertaken at Taji Camp near Baghdad in the military repair plant which was designed and constructed for some four years by the Soviet Union in the late 1960s. In this time, it was the single facility of its kind in Iraq that carried out repairs of all types of artillery weapons, all types of infantry weapons, and tanks operated by the Iraqi Army. When the plant started its regular operation, some 50 Soviet advisors were working there starting with plant management through foremen to assembly team leaders. The facility had two main repair buildings, each with an area of approximately 2,000 square metres (2,391 square yards) and a workshop for repairs of infantry weapons. The annual repair capacity was 100 T-34 or T-54 tanks, 340 guns (up to 75mm calibre), and 200 infantry weapons.[51]

WARSAW PACT COMPETITION

Meanwhile, on 17 July 1968, another regime change took place in Iraq. While President Abdul Rahman Arif was sleeping, his own assistants along with members of the Ba'ath Party led by General Ahmed Hassan al-Bakr overthrew him in a bloodless coup. In the aftermath of Arif's overthrow, al-Bakr was elected Chairman of the Revolutionary Command Council and President: later he was appointed into the position of the prime minister. His cousin Saddam Hussein became Deputy Chairman of the Revolutionary Command Council and Vice President and was responsible for Iraq's security services. In the Soviet Bloc, this change was met with more than positive response, as it marked a fundamental inclination of Iraq towards Moscow. In April 1969, Iraq became the first non-communist state to recognise the German Democratic Republic, and in July of that year, an Iraqi-Soviet oil cooperation agreements was signed, violating the Iraq Petroleum Company's monopoly. In March 1970, the new regime concluded an armistice with the Kurds and in the second half of 1971 released several hundred Iraqi communists from prisons.

However, the events immediately after the coup did not develop favourably in terms of supplies of Czechoslovak weapons to Iraq, since about mid-1969, Iraqi orders of additional armament from Czechoslovakia had stopped, although the Iraqi Ministry of Defence had had a constant interest in these supplies. One of the reasons was the competition from the Soviet Union and other Warsaw Pact states. At

this time, Moscow concluded another agreement for the supply of military hardware on very favourable terms of payment: 30 percent discount and a credit for 10 years at an interest rate of 2 percent per annum. The Polish People's Republic also supplied armament to Iraq on credit at that time, and similar business conditions were offered by the German Democratic Republic as well.

Therefore, Baghdad demanded from Czechoslovakia the provision of credit too. During negotiations with HTS representatives, Iraqi officials conditioned the purchase of Czechoslovak weapons by concluding a credit agreement. The Iraqis justified this demand by saying that their need for new military hardware was greater than could be covered by regular funds. Other Soviet Bloc countries also provided loans for the purchase of their arms. In addition, the Iraqis knew that Czechoslovakia was supplying arms to other Arab countries on credit. Therefore, they expected Prague to provide them with the same terms of payment.

Hence, the Czechoslovak government wasted no time and on 12 March 1970 approved a resolution that allowed the deliveries of weapons to Iraq to the value of up to 55 million USD (1,485,000,000 CSK). The authorised terms of payment were as follows: 20 percent of the amount should be paid in advance, the rest would be provided with a maximum five-year credit with interest at 3 percent per annum. All payments in hard currency only. According to preliminary negotiations, Iraq could purchase the following military hardware:

- up to 213 OT-64 SKOT armoured personnel carriers
- up to 150 OT-62 TOPAS armoured personnel carriers
- up to 100 T-54M tanks
- up to 8 MT-55 armoured vehicle-launched bridges
- up to 100 Tatra 813 tractor trucks
- up to 200 ROD-200 rocket-projected mine-clearing systems
- spare parts for armoured personnel carriers and tanks

The Iraqi purchasing delegation arrived in Czechoslovakia quite unexpectedly on 13 April 1970. Its task was to prepare an agreement, which would later be signed in Prague by Minister of Defence and Vice President Hardan al-Tikriti. However, there was a development of the situation, which the Czechoslovak

An MT-55 bridge-layer of the Iraqi Army, crossing a combination of two (more likely three) bridges laid just minutes before. (Author's collection)

Soldiers of the Czechoslovak People's Army with a vz. 58 assault rifle (left) and a vz. 59 machine gun. (Author's collection)

representatives were not able to predict. The commodity demands submitted by the Iraqi representatives differed significantly from the lists submitted through the Czechoslovak embassy in Iraq. The new Iraqi requirements meant a significant reduction in the originally expected volume of supplies. However, what was worse for Prague, Iraqi officials demanded more favourable payment terms, delivery conditions, and significantly lower prices for the offered weapons. Negotiations with the Iraqi delegation ended with the Iraqis declaring all items, for which Czechoslovak officials were unwilling to accept Iraqi price proposals, as cancelled.

After the meeting, the Iraqi ambassador came to the HTS director František Langer to try to mediate. It was explained to him the unfoundedness and irrationality of the demands made by the Iraqi working group and was told that, under those circumstances, no agreement could be reached. In this context, the fate of Tikriti's visit was discussed with the ambassador because the ambassador expressed concern that no "diplomatic scandal" and disruption of relations would happen, as the signing of the agreement was the main reason for Tikriti's trip to the Czechoslovak Socialist Republic.

Despite these complications, the Czechoslovak-Iraqi arms agreement was signed without major delays on 24 April 1970. In its frame, Czechoslovakia supplied to Iraq the following military hardware:

- 70 OT-62 TOPAS armoured personnel carriers in the ambulance variant
- 8 MT-55 armoured vehicle-launched bridges
- 80 automobile cranes
- 25,000 vz. 58 assault rifles
- 30 million vz. 43 and vz. 59 7.62mm calibre rounds
- 280,000 rounds for the vz. 53 twin anti-aircraft cannons

The total amount of military equipment provided reached 13,600,000 USD (on 6 August 1970, a supplement in the value of 1.1 million USD was signed). Deliveries were paid for with a 20 percent

down payment, and a five-year loan with a 3 percent interest rate per annum for the remaining 80 percent was provided. In all cases, these were newly produced goods, not deliveries from the warehouses of the Czechoslovak People's Army.[52]

IRAQI COMPLAINTS

On 15 December 1970, Czechoslovak Ambassador in Baghdad Miloslav Hruza and four other Czechoslovak representatives (including two HTS officials) visited Minister of Defence Lieutenant General Hammad Shihab who used the opportunity to openly criticise Prague's pricing policy:

The Iraqi side considers the purchase of military hardware to be the content of mutual relations with friends. He [Shihab] stressed that the Czechoslovak Socialist Republic is the second country in terms of the number of supplies of military hardware to Iraq. The training of Iraqi flight cadets and ground technicians is taking place on a larger scale. He stressed that the Czechoslovak Socialist Republic is a highly developed industrial country and yet the prices of the supplied equipment are disproportionately high. Spare parts are more expensive than the French ones. He believed that the government of the Czechoslovak Socialist Republic had set prices incorrectly and that OMNIPOL also did not take into account friendly relations when setting prices and came out only from commercial interests. The Minister of National Defence of the Republic of Iraq stated: "For example, from the Soviet Union we buy a T-54 engine (12-cylinder) for 2,000 GBP while the Czechoslovak Socialist Republic counts us a TOPAS engine (6-cylinder) for 11,004 USD, which means more than 2x more expensive with half of the power output. Spare parts for the TOPAS armoured personnel carrier are also in the same relation. You charge us a V-belt with a width of 1cm and a length of 1.20 m for 71 US $. We can get it on our market for 0.80 US $, etc. I intend to have all Czechoslovak prices reviewed and if no remedy is agreed upon, I am willing to send everything back. In my opinion, the price of spare parts for one unit must agree with the price of the unit. Also, interest rates on special material are twice as high as in the People's Republic of Bulgaria. I am responsible to the Revolutionary Command Council for the proper functioning of the ministry, and in the event that the Czechoslovak prices are not correct, I must inform the council."

Czechoslovak Ambassador Hruza countered:

Czechoslovakia does not normally trade in weapons, but only provides them to friends [sic]. Although our arms industry is advanced, we cannot compare prices with superpowers such as the Soviet Union or the USA due to a lack of raw material base and smaller production runs. Our mutual cooperation must strengthen both states, and therefore the Iraqi side cannot demand prices below production costs. All units supplied by the Czechoslovak side to the Iraqi army are below the world prices. As for the leather parts for the TOPAS, the incorrect prices were caused by an employee who converted the prices from our currency at the wrong exchange rate. […] I have pointed out before that some products can't be cheaper when they're in production and your orders aren't big enough. That is why we need a long-term forward plan for your purchase. […] Purchases are still made for a maximum of one season. As far as spare parts are concerned, it is well known that their price on the world market is 35–60 percent more expensive than the corresponding value of the units.

However, the Iraqi minister of defence continued in his critique:

Modern warfare must be waged with modern weapons. For Czechoslovak weapons, we find an obsolete mechanism, especially the motion one, not corresponding to the current technical level. When it comes to long-term purchasing plans, we are willing to start negotiations because you provide us with a loan and the purchase can be evenly distributed in our financial budgets. Our party and leadership assess the needs of weapons as required by current technology. They must be thorough, most effective at the level of our needs, as effective as [the weapons] our enemies have, scientific, modern. The TOPAS was a good personnel carrier in its time, but at the moment it is completely unsatisfactory.

According to this concept, I ask the Czechoslovak government to offer us modern military hardware, radar-controlled anti-aircraft guns, personnel carriers equipped with modern firing technology, radios and radar for detecting enemy aircraft, tank transporters, etc. If you can offer us modern equipment, submit bids to the operation department and I am willing to fly to the Czechoslovak Socialist Republic at any time in order to get acquainted with the technology on the place.[53]

THE MOTHER OF ALL ARMS AGREEMENTS

Despite this critique, negotiations between the HTS officials and representatives of the Iraqi Ministry of Defence continued unabated. It was primarily Prague that had an eminent interest in further deliveries of military hardware to Iraq:

There is still a political and extraordinary economic interest in developing further relations with regard to the quality of encashment and the optimal payment conditions achieved (relatively short credits). As the Iraqi party has recently shown a tendency to expand its imports of military hardware to other, possibly even Western countries, where it could achieve more favourable payment terms and acquire more modern equipment, it will be necessary for us, considering the interests mentioned above, to take an initiative to maintain our positions.[54]

Czechoslovak efforts culminated in late 1972. From 4 to 15 December, a 19-member Iraqi military delegation led by Minister of Defence Colonel General Hammad Shihab visited the Czechoslovak Socialist Republic. The main task of the Iraqis was to negotiate and sign an agreement for the supply of Czechoslovak military hardware in accordance with the requirements formulated in August 1972. In response to the beginning of the negotiations, the Czechoslovak government adopted Resolution No. 375 on 6 December 1972, in which it approved the provision of credit for the purchase of weapons up to 65 million USD (1.6 billion CSK). However, during the negotiations, the Iraqi delegation presented additional requests (Tatra 813 tractor trucks, low-loading trailers, spare parts for previously delivered armament), thus the volume of deliveries, which were to be included in the agreement, reached 77 million USD (85.5 million USD after the devaluation, 1.9 billion CSK). This change was officially approved by the Czechoslovak government on 5 April 1973 in Resolution No. 99.

With the prior consent of Prime Minister Lubomír Štrougal, an arms agreement was signed on 9 December 1972 between Minister of Foreign Trade Andrej Barčák and Minister of Defence Hammad Shihab. Payments were to be made between 1973 and 1978 in fixed amounts in hard currency (21 percent) and oil (79 percent), provided credit had an interest rate of 2 percent per annum. At the beginning of the negotiations in Czechoslovakia, the Iraqi delegation categorically demanded 100 percent payment for military hardware in oil. Czechoslovak officials explained the problems associated with the purchase of Iraqi oil, mainly due to the lack of economically acceptable oil transportation in the coming years. The Iraqis argued that full payment in oil for arms supplies was accepted not only by the Soviet Union but also by Poland, Bulgaria, and Hungary. It was not until the very end of the negotiations that the Iraqi delegation agreed to the terms and conditions confirmed in the agreement.

During the visit of the Iraqi delegation in August and December 1972, close cooperation with the Federal Ministry of National

Table 5: Military hardware to be delivered to Iraq according to the Agreement from 9 December 1972[56]

Item	List of deliveries	Number of examples	Planned deliveries
1	L-39, training aircraft	50	1973–1975
2	JVBT-55, armoured crane vehicle	30	1973–1974
3	OT-64, armoured personnel carrier	35	1973
4	vz. 53/70, mobile twin 30mm anti-aircraft cannon	40	1973
5	30mm ammunition for vz. 53/70	80,000	1973
6	mobile air traffic control workplace	6 sets	1974–1975
7	RP-3, precision approach radar	3 sets	1974
8	Tatra 813, tractor truck	70	1973
9	P-80, low-loading trailer	70	1973–1974
10	PMS, mobile pontoon bridge	1 set	1974–1975
11	M1 and M2, magnetic mines	1,000	1973
12	100-JPrSv-TK, 100mm high explosive anti-tank round	22,000	1973
13	7.62mm ammunition for Kalashnikov rifles with brass cartridge case	100 million	1973–1976
14	repair plants for armoured personnel carriers, radio stations, and L-29 aircraft		1975–1977
15	spare parts		1973–1977

Note: In the end, contracts for items 6, 7, 10, and 14 were not awarded and the number of OT-64 SKOTs was later reduced to 17 vehicles.

Defence significantly contributed to the positive outcome of the negotiations and the signing of the agreement. It worked very well the impressive demonstration of special hardware in military facilities, the participation of representatives of the Federal Ministry of National Defence in the negotiations, and the personal attention which was paid by Minister of National Defence, Army General Comrade Ing. M Dzúr and the command of the Czechoslovak army to the visit of the Iraqi military delegation, as well as to its leader.[55]

According to the terms of the agreement (Annex No. 1), Baghdad was obliged to buy in Czechoslovakia the military hardware listed in Table 5.

After the October 1973 Arab-Israeli War, and the active participation of the Iraqi Army in combat operations, Baghdad successively asked for additional supplies of Czechoslovak weapons in order to strengthen Iraq's defences. Iraqi requirements included, in particular, L-29 aircraft, tanks, tractor trucks, anti-aircraft cannons, and related ammunition. During the fighting, on 14 October, the Iraqi officials asked whether Czechoslovakia would be able to deliver weapons by transport aircraft. At the same time, they requested the maximum acceleration of deliveries of the ordered 7.62mm ammunition and Tatra 813 trucks. However, unlike Syria (and Egypt), no emergency deliveries of armament from Czechoslovakia to Iraq took place.[57]

Between 27 March and 3 April 1974, Czechoslovak and Iraqi officials met in Baghdad to review the implementation of the Agreement from 9 December 1972. As the relevant contracts for items 6, 7, 10, and 14 were not signed, these items were excluded from the content of the Agreement on 3 April 1974. At the request of the Iraqis, the number of ordered OT-64 armoured personnel carriers was reduced to 17 vehicles. On the other hand, Iraqi officials requested the supply of additional military hardware in connection with the recent war with Israel. This requirement was accepted by the HTS representatives, which led to the changes in Appendix No. 1 of the Agreement from 9 December 1972. The newly required weapons are listed in Table 6. Despite the changes, the maximum financial scope of the agreement remained unchanged (85,555,554.70 USD after the devaluation).[58]

Table 6: Additional military hardware to be delivered to Iraq according to the Agreement from 9 December 1972 (the Exchange Letter from 3 April 1974)[59]

List of deliveries	Number of examples
L-29, training aircraft	38
vz. 53/70, mobile 30mm twin anti-aircraft cannon	16
Tatra 813, tractor truck	70
P-80, low-loading trailer	70
23mm ammunition for NS-23 cannons	63,000
spare parts	

TECHNICAL ASSISTANCE FOR THE IRAQI ARMY

In the meantime, the activities of Czechoslovak military advisors continued directly in Iraq. In 1972, Contracts 4528 and 4529 were signed. Their purpose was to establish general overhaul capability for OT-62 and OT-64 armoured personnel carriers in Iraq. Two Czechoslovak teams, each composed of six instructors, trained Iraqi

technical personnel between 19 January 1973 and 16 June 1974. Simultaneously, within the frame of both contracts, the Repair Plant 026 delivered corresponding assembly jigs, special tools, testing equipment, and repair documentation. Due to delayed deliveries of electric motors from production plants, the Repair Plant 026 was not able to deliver all contracted goods on time. Hence, the last equipment ordered was completed and sent to Iraq in late 1974.

After that, however, complications also arose on the Iraqi side. The Iraqis could not accept Czechoslovak personnel for the assembly and handover of these devices because the foundations for their installation were not completed in time at the repair plant. Two technicians departed Czechoslovakia for Iraq only on 9 March 1976. At the place, they found out that the delivered equipment had been stored for a long time (6 to 18 months) under temporary shelters or in the open air in a partially unpacked state. As a result, a large part of the components were corroded, which caused a number of defects in the handover, which had to be rectified. This led to the extension of the acceptance process by a week. Therefore, the deliveries were not completed until 14 April 1976.[61]

Iraq obtained from Czechoslovakia, among other weapons, M1 and M2 magnetic mines which were never introduced into the inventory of the Czechoslovak People's Army. They were designed by Dr. Sladký from the Research Institute of Engineering Technology and Economics (*Výzkumný ústav strojírenské technologie a ekonomiky*) in Prague. In October 1974, Dr. Sladký was dispatched by the HTS to Iraq to train Iraqi soldiers in the use of the mines. As his interpreter served local HTS representative Lieutenant Colonel Karel Matějíček who was attached to the Czechoslovak embassy in Baghdad from August 1971. After 10 to 14 days of instruction in the classroom, a practical demonstration in the field took place on 4 November 1974. Allegedly due to the incorrect timing of the mine by an Iraqi soldier (instead of one hour it was set to one minute) there was a premature explosion, which fatally wounded Lieutenant Colonel Matějíček.[62]

Also, the training of Iraqi military personnel in Czechoslovakia continued, albeit on a smaller scale than during the late 1960s. In connection with the delivery of JVBT-55 armoured crane vehicles, basic training of three Iraqi technicians on their operation, maintenance, and routine repairs took place at the ZF VAAZ in Brno. The role of instructors was performed by the employees of the production plant (the JVBT-55 was never introduced into the inventory of the Czechoslovak People's Army). The training itself took place from 23 September to 15 December 1973. Further basic training focused on the proper use of the JVBT-55 was provided by members of the service group of the production plant directly in Iraq.[63]

However, everything did not always run smoothly. Within the frame of Contracts No. 51-2-50 and No. 51-3-76, Czechoslovakia delivered to Iraq 56 examples of the vz. 53/70 mobile twin 30mm anti-aircraft cannon which was based on armoured Praga V3S chassis. In 1974, two Czechoslovak military advisors carried out training of Iraqi crews in live firing directly in Iraq, while the service team of the manufacturer, Škoda Plzeň, performed instruction on regular maintenance. Therefore, in October 1976, Iraqi officials requested training in higher levels of maintenance and repairs up to the stage of a general overhaul.

Although since early 1977 HTS officials in Iraq presented several training proposals, the Iraqis did not comment on any of them. But in September 1977, they were fast to complain that the operation of twin vz. 53/70 cannons got into a critical situation 'due to the fact that the Czechoslovak side had not yet carried out the

Table 7: Known Czechoslovak arms export to Iraq, 1948–1974[60]			
Type	Number of examples	Year of delivery	Note
various pistols	150	1965–1966	
	100	1968	254 vz. 27 pistols from the stocks of the Czechoslovak People's Army delivered by 31 August 1969
Sa 23 and Sa 25, 9mm sub machine guns	10	1970	from the stocks of the Czechoslovak People's Army, 200 Sa 23 delivered during 1969–1970, 346 Sa 23 and Sa 25 sub machine guns from the stocks of the Czechoslovak People's Army delivered by 31 August 1969, 371 Sa 23 and Sa 25 sub machine guns from the stocks of the Czechoslovak People's Army delivered by 22 August 1972
vz. 61, 7.65mm sub machine gun	302	1966	
	26	1967	from the stocks of the Czechoslovak People's Army
	570	1968	741 sub machine guns from the stocks of the Czechoslovak People's Army delivered by 31 August 1969
	11	1970	from the stocks of the Czechoslovak People's Army
	503	1971	from the stocks of the Czechoslovak People's Army
	500	1972	from the stocks of the Czechoslovak People's Army, 2,437 sub machine guns delivered by 22 August 1972
vz. 24 and vz. 98 N, 7.92mm rifles	5,002	1964	included the contract for the supply of 5,000 vz. 24 rifles, from the stocks of the Czechoslovak People's Army
	10,013	1966	
	1	1967	35,046 vz. 24 and vz. 98 N rifles from the stocks of the Czechoslovak People's Army delivered by 31 August 1969, altogether 35,296 vz. 24 and vz. 98 N rifles from the stocks of the Czechoslovak People's Army delivered by 22 August 1972
vz. 52, 7.62mm rifle	1	1966	
vz. 52/57, 7.62mm rifle	?	?	two rifles delivered from the stocks of the Czechoslovak People's Army by 31 August 1969
	10,000	1969	from the stocks of the Czechoslovak People's Army
	2,000	1972	from the stocks of the Czechoslovak People's Army
vz. 54, 7.62mm sniper rifle	3	1972	from the stocks of the Czechoslovak People's Army
vz. 58, 7.62mm assault rifle	1,501	1966	
	4	1967	from the stocks of the Czechoslovak People's Army
	4	1968	
	10,000	1969	11,513 rifles from the stocks of the Czechoslovak People's Army delivered by 31 August 1969
	2,200	1970	from the stocks of the Czechoslovak People's Army
	1,000	1972	from the stocks of the Czechoslovak People's Army, 55,923 rifles delivered by 22 August 1972
vz. 26, 7.92mm machine gun	1	1966	
vz. 37, 7.92mm heavy machine gun	400	1966	
vz. 52, 7.62mm machine gun	450	1966	
vz. 52/57, 7.62mm machine gun	600	1969	2,100 machine guns from the stocks of the Czechoslovak People's Army delivered by 31 August 1969
vz. 59, 7.62mm machine gun	1	1966	two vz. 59 machine guns from the stocks of the Czechoslovak People's Army delivered by 31 August 1969

Table 7: Known Czechoslovak arms export to Iraq, 1948–1974 (*continued*)

vz. 68, 7.62mm machine gun	?	?	vz. 59 machine gun for NATO ammunition, 700 vz. 68 delivered by 22 August 1972 (500 as light machine guns and 200 as heavy machine guns)
7.62mm NATO round	?	?	2,000,000 rounds delivered by 22 August 1972
7.65mm round	8,300	1967	
	606,900	1968	from the stocks of the Czechoslovak People's Army, 614,100 rounds delivered by 31 August 1969, 764,300 rounds delivered by 22 August 1972
7.92mm training round	?	?	150,000 rounds from the stocks of the Czechoslovak People's Army delivered by 31 August 1969
vz. 43, 7.62mm round	500	1966	3,000,500 rounds delivered by 22 August 1972
vz. 47, 7.92mm round	200,000	1966	12,000,620 rounds from the stocks of the Czechoslovak People's Army delivered by 31 August 1969
vz. 48, 9mm round	?	?	4,880 rounds from the stocks of the Czechoslovak People's Army delivered by 22 August 1972
vz. 52, 7.62mm round	105	1966	
vz. 59, 7.62mm round	1,000	1966	
	5,000	1968	6,040 rounds delivered by 22 August 1972, 6,006,040 rounds delivered by 30 August 1974
ammunition for small arms and tank machine guns	9,005,900	1972	from the stocks of the Czechoslovak People's Army
F-1, hand grenade	500	1971	from the stocks of the Czechoslovak People's Army
RG-4, hand grenade	7,000	1971	from the stocks of the Czechoslovak People's Army
RG-5 Cv, training hand grenade	1,500	1971	from the stocks of the Czechoslovak People's Army
P-27, light anti-tank weapon	100	1972	from the stocks of the Czechoslovak People's Army
round for P-27	5,000	1972	from the stocks of the Czechoslovak People's Army
vz. 52, 82mm mortar	100	1972	from the stocks of the Czechoslovak People's Army
82mm fragmentation mortar round	10,000	1972	from the stocks of the Czechoslovak People's Army
	24	1973	from the stocks of the Czechoslovak People's Army
vz. 53, towed 30mm twin anti-aircraft cannon	110	1968	from the stocks of the Czechoslovak People's Army
	174	1969	from the stocks of the Czechoslovak People's Army
	50	1970	from the stocks of the Czechoslovak People's Army
30-JFSv-PLDvK 53, 30mm high explosive with tracer and point-detonating fuse	250,000	1968	for vz. 53 anti-aircraft gun, 725,000 30mm rounds from the stocks of the Czechoslovak People's Army delivered by 31 August 1969
other ammunition for vz. 53 anti-aircraft gun	612,000	1970	newly manufactured
	170,000	1971	newly manufactured
	80,000	1973	newly manufactured
	122,680	1974	newly manufactured
JVBT-55 (JVBT-55KS), armoured crane vehicle	14	1973	newly manufactured
	16	1974	newly manufactured
MT-55 (MT-55KS), armoured vehicle-launched bridge	8	1970	newly manufactured
OT-62 TOPAS, armoured personnel carrier	?	1969	newly manufactured, 240 vehicles delivered by 31 August 1969, 375 OT-62 vehicles delivered by 22 August 1972
	70	1971	ambulance version, newly manufactured
OT-64 SKOT, armoured personnel carrier	86	1969	from the stocks of the Czechoslovak People's Army
	?	1970	including 13 OT-64/R2 command vehicles, altogether 173 OT-64 vehicles delivered to Iraq by 30 August 1974

Table 7: Known Czechoslovak arms export to Iraq, 1948–1974 (continued)

100-JOF-ShK 44, K 53, TK, 100mm high explosive round	10	1972	from the stocks of the Czechoslovak People's Army
100-JPSv-ShK 44, K 53, TK, 100mm armour-piercing round	10	1972	from the stocks of the Czechoslovak People's Army
100-JPrSv-TK, 100mm high explosive anti-tank round	10	1968	
	10	1972	from the stocks of the Czechoslovak People's Army
	22,000	1973	from the stocks of the Czechoslovak People's Army
100-JPCvSV-Tk, 100mm training round	10,000	1973	newly manufactured
MiG-15bis, fighter	7	1970	from the stocks of the Czechoslovak People's Army
	26	1971	from the stocks of the Czechoslovak People's Army
	6	1972	from the stocks of the Czechoslovak People's Army
MiG-15UTI, combat trainer	10	1969	from the stocks of the Czechoslovak People's Army
L-29 Delfin, training aircraft	40	1968	newly manufactured
	6	1973	newly manufactured
	32	1974	newly manufactured
Z-526F, training aircraft	21	1970	newly manufactured
	4	1971	newly manufactured
Z-526AF, training aircraft	15	1972	manufacturer's designation Z-526FI, newly manufactured
M-701, jet engine	15	1973	spare engine for L-29 Delfin, newly manufactured
VK-1, jet engine	5	1970	spare engine for MiG-15bis, from the stocks of the Czechoslovak People's Army
	15	1971	from the stocks of the Czechoslovak People's Army
RD-45FA, jet engine	?	?	spare engine for MiG-15UTI, six engines from the stocks of the Czechoslovak People's Army delivered by 31 August 1969
	3	1970	from the stocks of the Czechoslovak People's Army
NS-23, 23mm aircraft cannon	100	1970	spare cannon for MiG-15bis, from the stocks of the Czechoslovak People's Army
OZT and BZ, 23mm HEI-T and API round	50,000	1970	for NS-23 aircraft cannon, from the stocks of the Czechoslovak People's Army
OVP-65, parachute	10	1966	
Tatra 813, tractor truck	131	1973	newly manufactured
	9	1974	newly manufactured
P-80, low-loading trailer	140	1973-1974	newly manufactured, for Tatra 813 trucks
PTO, mobile tank workshop	?	?	on Praga V3S chassis, four workshops from the stocks of the Czechoslovak People's Army delivered by 31 August 1969
PTDA-M, mobile tank workshop	?	?	on Praga V3S chassis, two workshops from the stocks of the Czechoslovak People's Army delivered by 31 August 1969
automobile crane	80	1970–1971?	newly manufactured, probably AV-8 recovery vehicles using Tatra 138 chassis
PT-Mi Ba II, Bakelite anti-tank mine	?	?	two mines from the stocks of the Czechoslovak People's Army delivered by 31 August 1969
PP-Mi Šr, anti-personnel shrapnel mine	?	?	two mines from the stocks of the Czechoslovak People's Army delivered by 31 August 1969
M1 and M2, magnetic mines	1,000	1973?	newly manufactured
vz. 53, raincoat poncho	100,000	1974	from the stocks of the Czechoslovak People's Army

A Czechoslovak-manufactured Tatra 813 tractor with P-80 trailer carrying a T-55 tank of the Iraqi Army through the streets of Baghdad, in the 1970s. (via Ivan Bouchal)

A column of Czechoslovak-manufactured Tatra 138 VN trucks of the Iraqi Army, seen navigating the streets of the southern outskirts of Damascus, during the Iraqi deployment in Syria, in the course of the October 1973 Arab-Israeli War. (Author's collection)

GENERAL OVERHAULS OF DELFINS AND NAVIGATOR TRAINING

In accordance with Resolution No. 21 of the Czechoslovak government from 1974, the general overhauls of L-29 training aircraft of the Iraqi Air Force were carried out in Czechoslovakia at the Aircraft Repair Plant Trenčín (*Letecké opravny Trenčín*). This facility performed the repairs in the same way as in the case of the Delfins of the Egyptian Air Force. The dismantled airplane was transported to Czechoslovakia on board an An-12 transport aircraft. After the overhaul and a test flight at the Trenčín airfield, the L-29 was dismantled again, loaded into the An-12, and transported back to Iraq. There, a small Czechoslovak team of several technicians and one test pilot assembled the Delfin once more and performed its additional test flight. Following this procedure, the airplane was officially handed over to the Iraqi authorities. The Aircraft Repair Plant Trenčín performed an average of 10 overhauls of the Iraqi L-29s per year.[65]

In late summer 1973, the Iraqi Ministry of Defence requested the training of 15 navigators for transport aircraft in the training facilities of the Czechoslovak Air Force. 'The minister of foreign trade states that its fulfilment is very desirable from the point of view of trade and political reasons'. Minister of National Defence Army General Martin Dzúr approved the undertaking on 27 September 1973. The actual training of 14 Iraqi students began at the Military Aviation University (*Vysoká vojenská letecká škola*, VVLŠ) at Košice in November 1974 (the actual flying was performed from Piešťany air base). This was preceded by the study of the Czech language at the ZF VAAZ in Brno. The graduation ceremony and ceremonial conclusion of the training course, for which the Iraqis paid 580,380 USD (11.7 million CSK), took place on 26 April 1976.[66]

required training of Iraqi specialists in the repair and maintenance of these vehicles'. At that time, four pairs of cannons were in very poor technical condition. In response to Iraqi complaints and HTS insistence, the Czechoslovak People's Army prepared a new training syllabus. This work also came to naught, this time due to the chaotic communication between individual departments in the HTS. Finally, in March 1978, the HTS informed the Federal Ministry of National Defence that the required training would be performed by the manufacturer within the frame of a new contract for an additional 36 twin vz. 53/70 cannons.[64]

REPAIRS OF ARMOURED VEHICLES AND TRUCKS

In summer 1972, Baghdad requested that Prague establish a repair plant for communication equipment. However, this demand had to be turned down due to a lack of capacity to realise such a project. Hence, the Iraqis turned to the Soviet Union with the same request. In 1973, the Iraqis requested that Czechoslovakia help with the establishment of an ammunition maintenance plant. This requirement was approved by the Czechoslovak government on 24 January 1974 in Resolution No. 22. The facility was designed by the design bureau of the Military Design Institute in Bratislava.[67]

Within the frame of the Agreement from 9 December 1972, Czechoslovakia was obliged to establish several military repair plants on behalf of the Iraqi armed forces. The most important was the facility for the repairs of armoured personnel carriers and heavy trucks. The Iraqis demanded a repair plant with an annual capacity of 1,400 general overhauls of vehicles while maintaining about 25 percent reserve for the production of spare parts. Due to the already realised deliveries of military hardware, 45 percent of the capacity was to be set aside for Soviet types, 40 percent for Czechoslovak vehicles, and the remaining 15 percent for other types, mostly of Western origin. According to the Iraqi demands, the annual scope of the overhauls should be as follows: 150 OT-62s and BTR-50PKs, 100 OT-64s, 50 BTR-60PBs, 50 Panhard AMLs and M3s together with 50 M113s, and 1,000 heavy trucks.

The repair plant was to be built in Taji Camp near Baghdad, where a tank repair facility built by the Soviet Union was already operating (at the end of spring 1973, the Soviets began building a motor plant here).

During negotiations in Iraq between 22 May and 6 June 1973, Czechoslovak officials found out that the Iraqis had not requested the delivery of repair documentation for Soviet vehicles in the Soviet Union and approval to carry out repairs of Soviet types in a repair plant which was to be built by Czechoslovakia. Therefore, two meetings were held with Soviet representatives in Iraq:

The talks were aimed at mutual information, unification, and discussion of further progress in terms of common interests and gaining experience of the Soviet side in building industrial works in Iraq. In the negotiations, the Soviet comrades indicated their interest in securing their own repairs of their equipment even within the repair plant being built by the Czechoslovak side.[68]

During the meetings of the working groups in Moscow in September 1973 and in February 1974, the basic technical issues and the scope and forms of mutual cooperation were specified. It was agreed that the Soviet Union would take over the role of general designer of the military repair plant and that Czechoslovakia would provide the necessary technical documentation and relevant consultations. This change came in more than handy because the then design capacities of the Military Design Institute were heavily used. On 23 August 1974, Soviet and Iraqi officials signed a protocol on assistance in the establishment of the military repair plant. At the same time, the Iraqi side informed the Soviets about their demand for the project to be completed as soon as possible.[69]

Despite Iraqi wishes, it took almost another five years before the Soviet-Czechoslovak project of the repair plant was approved and the necessary buildings and structures were built. Between 1979 and 1980, 20 technical advisors from Czechoslovak military repair plants were to be sent to Iraq for the installation of the supplied equipment and the start-up of the repair plant for a period of one year. At the same time, 15 Iraqi technicians were to be trained in Czechoslovakia at the ZF VAAZ and repair facilities of the Czechoslovak People's Army.[70]

THE AIRCRAFT REPAIR PLANT

The Agreement from 9 December 1972 stipulated also the establishment of an aircraft repair plant. According to the first Iraqi plans, Czechoslovakia was to introduce general overhauls of L-29 and later L-39 training aircraft in the existing aircraft repair plant. This facility, with the assistance of Soviet advisors, carried out repairs of Soviet combat aircraft introduced in the inventory of the Iraqi Air Force. However, it was only in January 1975 when a team of representatives from the HTS, INPRO Praha (main supplier), and Czechoslovak Air Force experts on aircraft repairs visited Iraq to assess the actual state of the existing aircraft repair plant.

The task of the Czechoslovak group was to assess the condition of technical and repair equipment and its possible extension for overhauls of L-29 aircraft, specify the required repair capacity with respect to technical equipment in the existing repair plant, specify the need for technical and technological documentation for L-29 repairs, specify necessary qualification of Iraqi technicians for the training in Czechoslovakia, and to propose the necessary Czechoslovak specialists needed for deployment to Iraq for the start of overhauls and training of Iraqi personnel.[71]

The survey of the Iraqi aircraft repair plant, which was established with Soviet assistance, showed that the facility includes about 80 percent of the equipment needed and had enough space for repairs of L-29 aircraft. For this reason, the Czechoslovak side only needed to secure the supply of special equipment, test devices, technical repair documentation, and assist in the training of Iraqi personnel in the Czechoslovak Socialist Republic and Iraq.[72]

A rare 'air-to-air' photograph of an Iraqi L-39C or L-39ZO, seen in the 1980s. The type was operated exclusively by the Iraqi Air Force Academy but also saw some combat against Kurdish insurgents in the north of the country. (Author's collection)

Table 8: Overview of L-39 Albatros training aircraft delivered to Iraq, 1975–1989[75]

Year	Variant	Number of examples	Hand over, overflight
1975	L-39C.2	6	14 – 15 May 1975
1975/1976	L-39ZO.6	16	20 November 1975 – 3 February 1976
1976/1977	L-39ZO.6	28 (27)	28 October 1976 – 15 June 1977, one aircraft crashed on 28 January 1977 during the overflight to Iraq
1977	L-39ZO.6	1	2 November 1977
1981	L-39ZO.7	10	12 August 1981 – 6 October 1981
1984	L-39ZO.7	10	3 October 1984 – 31 October 1984
1985	L-39ZO.7	10	7 November 1985 – 3 December 1985

Another view of an Iraqi L-39, revealing details of national markings applied under the wing. (Author's collection)

Final batches of L-39ZOs manufactured for Iraq wore a standardised camouflage pattern instead of the original 'trainer' livery in white and grey. This is a close-up of the front cockpit of one, together with the crest of the Iraqi Air Force Academy. (Author's collection)

In 1979, the Czechoslovak deliveries for the Iraqi Air Force repair facility reached a value of 10,878,953 CSK.[73]

THE ALBATROS FOR THE IRAQI AIR FORCE

Iraq became the second export user of the L-39 Albatros jet trainer right after the Soviet Air Force. Within the frame of the Agreement from 9 December 1972, Czechoslovakia undertook to supply the Iraqi Air Force with 50 aircraft of this type. Although the Iraqis demanded that deliveries of the airplanes were to begin as early as 1973, this requirement could not be realised because almost the entire production of L-39 aircraft in 1973 and 1974 was intended for the Soviet Union. Therefore, the first six L-39C trainers and 16 L-39ZO training and light combat aircraft were delivered in several batches during 1975 and 1976. These were supplemented by 28 L-39ZOs during the years 1976 and 1977. The deliveries of Albatros airplanes were completed in the period from 1981 to 1985 when the last 30 L-39ZO jets were supplied to the Iraqi Air Force. Together with the aircraft, the TL-39 flight simulators and the NKTL-29/39 ejection simulator were delivered as well.

The airplanes were transferred to Iraq by Czechoslovak pilots. Initially, the first L-39s flying along the route Bratislava – Belgrade – Sofia – Ankara – Diyarbakir to Tikrit or Baghdad. Later, the flights avoided Yugoslavia and the only landings were performed in Turkey. Sometimes they led even through Greece. During one of the overflights, on 28 January 1977, an L-39ZO aircraft was destroyed near Trnava in a crash into the ground during a failed landing attempt in adverse weather conditions. The factory crew Miloslav Šmídt and Vlastimil David died in the accident.

With the introduction of the Albatros into the inventory of the Iraqi Air Force, the L-29 Delfins were relegated to the role of the basic trainer. The L-39s served for the advanced portion of the flight training that prepared new pilots for MiG-21 and MiG-23 fighters (and later Mirage F.1EQs).[74]

The syllabus of Iraqi flight training in the 1980s consisted of elementary training on FFA AS-202 Bravo piston aircraft and Embraer EMB-312 turboprop trainer. After mastering them, training flights followed on the L-29 Delfin and then on the L-39 Albatros with 80 flight hours on each type. Then the pilots switched to MiG-15UTI and MiG-21U combat trainers.

In addition to training duties at the Air Force Academy, the L-39ZOs took over the combat role which was previously performed by the L-29 Delfins. A section of four aircraft (one of them was spare) was regularly deployed to air bases at Mosul and Kirkuk from where they performed patrol flights over Iraqi Kurdistan and undertook an attack mission there against Kurdish rebels using S-5 unguided rockets and FAB-250 bombs. The patrol duties were carried out also during the Iran-Iraq War. During the attack of the Islamic Republic of Iran Air Force on the Kirkuk air base in 1983, two L-39ZOs were destroyed there.[76]

THE PROSPECTIVE EDUCATIONAL ASSISTANCE AND CZECHOSLOVAK ASSESSMENTS

The Iraqi officials began considering Czechoslovak assistance in the development of the Iraqi military education system as early as 1969. Between 1970 and 1972, the Iraqis expressed interest in building a military technical academy with Czechoslovak assistance. At the invitation of the Iraqi military, a Czechoslovak delegation led by the Chief of the VAAZ Lieutenant General Jaroslav Mašek visited Iraq from 18 February to 4 March 1972. The Czechoslovak experts inspected Iraqi military educational institutions and then assessed the needs of the local military school system. Moreover, they had the opportunity to visit several military units and installations of the Iraqi armed forces:

During our visit, basic training of individuals took place in Iraqi Army units. Great emphasis is placed on physical and moral maturity, on external manifestations of discipline, paying tribute, and orderliness. At the 2nd Division, stationed in Kirkuk, we saw a demonstration of special forces training (Commandos). Although they were novices, they showed relatively good training, they were led to overcome fear (shooting with blanks right at the head of creeping soldiers), they were trained in self-defence, overcoming obstacles, etc. Live shooting or training with military hardware was not shown to us.

Each division has its own technical repair shop, in which they make all repairs, including general ones. The repair shop at the 2nd Division, which we visited, was well organised, the workplaces were in order, the tools and machines in rare cases were of a good standard, some operations on combat hardware were done in a primitive way. Conscripts work in repair shops, the repair shop carries out its own technical training. Team leaders are sergeants, graduates of a special training school.

The Iraqi Air Force has its own independent headquarters, as well as its own training centre for flying and technical personnel. From the discussion with the commander of the air base in Mosul, it is clear that there is no special cooperation between the ground forces and the air force during military exercises. At the same time, we were told that their pilots, trained in the states of the Warsaw Pact, are poorly trained in terms of shooting, they only undergo training in shooting at ground stationary targets and cannot conduct air combat. That's why they have to provide further training for all of them at home.

We also visited a base near Baghdad to train paratroopers and parachute instructors. The newcomers leave for Iraqi Army units after six months of training. The training facilities were mostly self-made, some very primitive. The classroom of diversionary means was also quite primitive. Since 1959, they have used exclusively Soviet and Czechoslovak parachutes. The commander of the base showed great interest in the methodology of training of Czechoslovak paratroopers and also in the supply of training aids and devices as well as in the armament and equipment of paratroopers of the Czechoslovak army.

The assessment of the Iraqi Army leadership was as follows:

As for our knowledge of the Iraqi Army and its leadership, our knowledge is less favourable. The overwhelming part of the leadership, especially division commanders and staff officers are typical representatives of the old English school at the level of World War 2 with all the negative phenomena: conservatism, parochiality, external manifestations of superiority, the popularity of the drill of soldiers. Conversations about technical readiness, tactical level, use of combat hardware were avoided. Likewise, in the political sphere, they were reluctant and, if they spoke, they were supporters of taking help (military hardware, training methods) from both sides, without a more fundamental political orientation. They also use outdated English regulations from the years before World War 2. They take delight and enjoy demanding individual training. They refused our request to allow us to visit the technical division school at the 2nd Division.

[…]

Each division has infantry and technical training centres that officers go through. This, too, is a remnant of the old English school: to solve everything with short courses, without any solid and comprehensive training.

We agreed with the Soviet comrades that this leadership could not be re-educated and that therefore the establishment of a new military college was politically desirable to strengthen the positions of socialist states in Iraq, keep Iraq on the side of socialism and establish a new leadership of the Iraqi Army as counterbalances to the current one.

After the return of this delegation back to Czechoslovakia, a draft concept for the establishment of a new military technical academy was prepared. However, no further initiative was taken by the Czechoslovak side during the consulting negotiations due to significant commitments in the development of the Military Technical College in Cairo.[77]

NEW IRAQI MILITARY TECHNICAL ACADEMY

The Iraqis continued in their efforts which culminated on 14 August 1973 when the Military Technical College (MTC) was established in Baghdad. Its main purpose was to prepare new technical officers for the Iraqi military and university-educated technical professionals for the local arms industry. At the same time, the college was to become a centre of domestic military scientific research.

At the end of 1975, Baghdad renewed its interest in cooperating in the development of the newly established MTC. The Iraqi chief of the general staff requested the conclusion of a government technical protocol on cooperation in military education between the Czechoslovak Socialist Republic and Iraq. In May 1976, the Iraqi embassy in Prague requested that 12 Czechoslovak teachers be sent to the MTC and that consultation be held at Czechoslovak military universities for a roughly 10-member Iraqi delegation of MTC professors and students.

The requested consultation took place in October 1976, when six Iraqi officials, including the MTC commander Brigadier Ismail Sultan Jabir, visited the VAAZ in Brno to learn about local teaching methods and scientific work. At the same time, they were shown several classrooms and training workplaces. During the stay in Czechoslovakia, the Iraqi delegation submitted a draft government protocol on cooperation in military university education, including specific requirements. The negotiation with OMNIPOL officials was held too. During the meeting, the Iraqi officers presented requests for the transfer of experience, curricula, and programs for planning the teaching process at the MTC. The direct deployment of 11 Czechoslovak military experts, with the ability to give lectures in English, to teach selected subjects directly in the MTC was also requested.[78]

In accordance with Resolution No. 68 of the Czechoslovak government from 10 March 1977, Minister of National Defence Army General Martin Dzúr was authorised to sign a protocol on Czechoslovak-Iraqi cooperation in the field of military university education. Despite this step, the cooperation did not take place, as the relevant intergovernmental protocol was not negotiated or signed. However, the Iraqis soon changed their minds and the Protocol on Technical and Scientific Cooperation in Military University Technical Education for the Years 1978–1980 was finally signed on 26 June 1978.[79]

OMNIPOL and the Iraqi Ministry of Defence then signed the relevant contracts. The most important was General Contract No. 45610 on the conditions of activities of Czechoslovak university lecturers at the MTC. According to this deal, Prague was to send experts to provide teaching and scientific training at the MTC in Baghdad. The numbers and specialisations of experts were addressed in the relevant supplements which were then concluded separately before each school year and formed an integral part of the contract.

These developments came just in time for Prague. The gradual reduction of the Czechoslovak involvement in the development of the Military Technical College in Cairo came to an abrupt end when the Egyptians unilaterally terminated the whole event in the autumn of 1977. Therefore, it was possible to immediately use the freed capacity for the needs of securing the new undertaking in Iraq. At the moment, it was very advantageous for the Czechoslovak side to accept the submitted Iraqi offer for the assistance in the build-up of the MTC in Baghdad, with regard to Czechoslovak foreign and trade interests and mainly also for reasons of obtaining foreign exchange funds.[80]

Based on signed contracts, 15 Czechoslovak university professors worked at the MTC in Baghdad, and 15 Iraqi students commenced studied at the VAAZ to obtain a Master of Science degree (Contract No. 45613). The MTC officials assumed that upon completion of this stage, these graduates would continue their follow-up studies to achieve a Doctor of Philosophy degree. In 1980, two members of the Iraqi armed forces began postgraduate studies in Brno. A one-year study stay of an Iraqi researcher, head of the department at the MTC, was also made possible at the VAAZ (Contract No. 4596) from autumn 1979. Under contracts signed up to July 1980, the VAAZ provided assistance for the MTC to the value of 620,000 USD (8.7 million CSK) per year.[81]

IRAQI ARMS INDUSTRY

Until 1958, there were only two smaller plants in Iraq for the production of ammunition for pistols and sub machine guns. However, the production capacity of these factories did not even cover the needs of the Iraqi military and police forces.

After the coup d'état in July 1958, the first thoughts on building an independent arms industry began to emerge. However, it remained only in the considerations and the basic concept of possible weapons production was not elaborated. At the end of the 1960s, there was a change and the arms production department at the Ministry of Defence drew up a long-term concept for building a domestic arms industry. After another coup in July 1968, the concept gained the full support of the ruling Ba'ath Party. Following the 8th National Congress of the Ba'ath Party, this concept was further developed and expanded.

After these steps, the first organisational measures were taken to ensure the implementation of plans to build the Iraqi arms industry. The crucial one was the creation of the State Organization for Technical Industries (SOTI) as the supreme planning and management body of the entire Iraqi arms production. SOTI was officially subordinated to the Ministry of Industry but, in fact, the first deputy prime minister was directly in charge of it. The primary tasks of this organisation were the planning and management of the construction of arms factories together with research, development, and production of armament and other military equipment.

The production capacity of the created Iraqi arms industry was to exceed the needs of the Iraqi armed forces. The Iraqi leadership anticipated Iraq not only becoming a politically and economically leading force among Arab countries, but also the largest military force in the Arab world. According to these visions, Iraq was to become a major supplier of military hardware to other Arab countries and, in the long run, to other developing countries as well.

In the first phase of planning the construction of its arms industry, Iraq envisaged cooperation with other Arab countries in connection with their existing or planned arms industry. There were also proposals from Iraq for the unification of armaments and, at the same time, propositions for the construction of joint plants for the production of weapons, ammunition, and other military hardware.

Iraq also sought admission to the Arab Organization for Industrialization (AOI), an Egypt-based Arab organisation established in 1975 by Egypt, the Kingdom of Saudi Arabia, the United Arab Emirates, and Qatar to supervise the collective development of the Arab arms industry. Minimal cooperation in arms production between Iraq and Egypt had persisted since the times of the reign of Gamal Nasser in Egypt. However, Iraq's efforts were in vain, probably due to the fact that the states associated in the AOI feared that Iraq would gain a dominant position in the organisation during a short period of time.

The enormous scale of the planned construction of the Iraqi arms industry had exceeded even the supply capacity of individual foreign states. Thanks to this, a number of countries were able to participate simultaneously in the construction and development of the Iraqi arms industry. In the development of its arms production, Iraq had sought to apply the principle of a balance between the West and the East. Hence, Baghdad was looking for potential suppliers not only among NATO and Warsaw Pact states but also in countries outside these blocs. Until the early 1980s, Yugoslavia had the largest share in the construction and development of the Iraqi arms industry. Czechoslovakia was also involved in these matters, albeit on a relatively smaller scale.

The original intention was to concentrate the Iraqi arms industry in one area around Baghdad and southwest of the Iraqi capital (Iskandariya, Musayib), where facilities were established for nuclear research and the production of infantry and artillery ammunition, infantry weapons, mortars, optical and electronic devices, chemicals, explosives, and incendiary substances. These plans were quickly reconsidered with the start of the Iran-Iraq War in September 1980. Since then, it had been decided to locate newly built arms factories in places such as Falluja, Mosul, Samarra, Tikrit, Taji, and Basra.

During the decade from the early 1970s to the early 1980s, several arms factories were built to produce ammunition (5.56mm, 7.65mm, 7.62mm, 12.7mm, 14.5mm, 122mm, and 130mm), pistols (7.65mm and 9mm), sub machine guns (7.65mm and 9mm), hand grenades, bombs for mortars (60mm and 82mm), RPG-7 anti-tank rocket-propelled grenade launchers including ammunition together with tools, instruments and different jigs for the local arms industry.[82]

CZECHOSLOVAK PARTICIPATION IN THE EXPANSION OF IRAQI ARMS PRODUCTION

Czechoslovak participation in the growth of the Iraqi arms industry began with the deliveries of forging lines for the Huteen State Establishment, which was being built by the Soviet Union in Iskandariya for the production of large-calibre artillery ammunition (57mm to 152mm) in the late 1970s and early 1980s. The value of Czechoslovak supplies was 11.7 million USD. In total, Prague delivered three lines (for 122mm and 130mm ammunition) manufactured by ŽĎAS between 1977 and 1980 which were put into operation in 1981.[83]

At the beginning of 1976, SOTI's management informed HTS representatives about its development plans and proposed the participation of Czechoslovakia in the program of construction of the Iraqi arms industry. After considering the Czechoslovak capabilities and after an agreement with the SOTI, it was decided to participate in the tenders (always simultaneously with several competing bidders) for the construction of:

- a plant for the production of special tools,
- a plant for the production of infantry ammunition,
- a rolling mill for non-ferrous metals – profiles for the arms production,
- a plant for the production of spherical powders.

The tender for the construction of a plant for the production of special tools was completed at the end of 1976. Although the HTS submitted a bid comparable in price and technology to the rival competitors, the contract was concluded with Gildemeister from West Germany. Despite this setback, intensive technical negotiations between Czechoslovak and Iraqi officials took place in 1976 on a plant for the production of vz. 43 and vz. 59 7.62mm ammunition (annual capacity 54 million rounds) and 12.7mm ammunition (annual capacity 5 million rounds). The approval of the Soviet Union had to be sought to introduce the production of 7.62mm ammunition in Iraq. These rounds had been manufactured in Czechoslovakia according to Soviet licence documentation since the 1950s (but since then the production technology had been significantly reworked by the Czechoslovak manufacturer).

After the first meeting with representatives of the SOTI in April 1976, the possibility of securing the supply of production equipment and technology for both calibres only from Czechoslovakia was examined. However, it was found that the production of 12.7mm ammunition had been cancelled 15 years earlier and that the Czechoslovak industry (enterprises associated in the production and economic unit Závody všeobecného strojírenství Brno) was unable to provide not only deliveries of production machines but also to devise the production technology.

Thus, in August 1976, the SOTI was informed that Czechoslovakia could not submit a complete offer. The Iraqis subsequently agreed that Prague would only offer the introduction of 7.62mm ammunition production and that the Iraqi side would secure the introduction of 12.7mm ammunition production itself, under the condition that it provided the Czechoslovak side with the data needed to prepare the project. In September 1976, a technical protocol was signed between both parties containing detailed specifications.

Based on this, a design study was prepared, which was discussed with the SOTI in April 1977. For further design work, it was necessary to obtain the needed data for the production of 12.7mm ammunition. However, the information provided by the Iraqis was completely insufficient. From the HTS point of view, it was clear that an incomplete Czechoslovak offer would be at a competitive disadvantage.[84]

OPERATIONS BETA AND JANTAR

Therefore, the HTS additionally agreed with the Yugoslav organisation Federal Directorate of Circulation and Reserves of Special Purpose Means to submit a joint bid – the complete production of 12.7mm ammunition would be secured by Yugoslavia as a part of the overall offer of the OMNIPOL foreign trade company. Although Yugoslavia's involvement allowed the Czechoslovak representatives to submit a complete offer according to the SOTI requirements, the Yugoslav project had a number of drawbacks, especially the diversity of production machinery from various manufacturers from Western Europe (primarily France and West Germany), resulting in a high price.

At a meeting in Iraq in September 1977, the final specification of the general layout of the ammunition plant and the individual buildings was made. It was also mutually agreed that Czechoslovakia would submit a final bid by 16 November 1977. At that time, OMNIPOL's main competitor was Manurhin of France. The estimated financial scope of the contract was approximately 120 million USD, of which Czechoslovak supplies were some 72 million USD. Deliveries from Yugoslavia amounted to 15 million USD and the price for the construction of buildings was roughly 33 million USD.

In the end, Czechoslovakia managed to win the deal but in a reduced form. In July 1978, a contract was signed for the technological portion of the introduction of 7.62mm ammunition production worth 44.8 million USD (approximately 672 million CSK). The scope of the deal was to expand the Al-Yarmook ammunition plant in Baghdad that produced rounds in 7.62mm, 12.7mm, and 14.5mm calibres. The project received the Czechoslovak cover name Operation BETA, while Iraqis used the term Project SAAD 3. The overall value of Czechoslovak deliveries in the frame of Operation BETA amounted to 47.2 million USD.

The principal Czechoslovak suppliers were Blanické strojírny Vlašim and Průmyslové stavby Gottwaldov. While the former prepared a technological project and was a supplier of technology and production equipment of main and auxiliary facilities, the latter was a construction designer and general contractor of the construction part, including non-production technological assemblage. Other participating Czechoslovak companies were, for example, ČKD Dukla, Janka Radotín, INPRO Praha, Sigma Hranice, Kovofiniš Ledeč nad Sázavou, ZPA, and Synthesia Semtín.

Around the same time, HTS managed to secure the contract to the value of 7.5 million USD for the establishment of the plant for the production of spherical powders. This project received the

Czechoslovak cover name Operation JANTAR and was a part of the Al Bakr Chemical Complex which was built by Yugoslav companies for the manufacturing of explosives.[85]

THE COMPETITION FROM THE WEST

Despite considerable supplies of military hardware under the Agreement from 9 December 1972, Baghdad's interest in weapons from Czechoslovakia persisted. The 1973 oil crisis and subsequent skyrocketing oil prices meant that Iraq no longer needed loans to buy Czechoslovak armament. Thus, since 1974, deliveries had taken place on the basis of contracts covered by a letter of credit. However, the prospects for further significant HTS success did not look very optimistic.[86]

Table 9: Financial value of the Czechoslovak arms deliveries to Iraq and related military assistance, 1975–1981[87]

Year	Value (million USD)
1975	2.8
1976	1.8
1977	16.3
1978	52.9
1979	32.3
1980	42.7
1981	49.7 (as of 30 June)

Iraq's focus on obtaining military hardware almost exclusively from the Soviet Union and its satellites lasted until about the early 1970s. Especially after the accession of Saddam Hussein to the leading positions in the state, Iraq's efforts to balance arms imports to gain independence from both superpowers were beginning to show. At this time, the first major purchases in the West began, and the Iraqi Ministry of Defence was exploring the possibility of purchasing fighter jets, tanks, and missiles in countries other than the Soviet Union.

In the first phase, purchases of radars and communications equipment were made in the United Kingdom, France, and Italy. These were followed by acquisitions of helicopters from France, light ships from Italy, anti-tank guided missiles from West Germany and France, and Panhard armoured vehicles from France. West European arms companies had waged a tough fight to win contracts for the supply of armament to the Iraqi Ministry of Defence. The result of this competitive struggle was, among others, that there was a delay of three to five years in the decision of the Iraqi officials, what types of combat airplanes and tanks should be purchased.

Competition from the West severely undermined the position of HTS, which was further hampered by other factors: the relatively narrow range of military hardware produced in Czechoslovakia, insufficient manufacturing capacity, long delivery times for spare parts, lack of spare parts, or lengthy and expensive repairs of L-39 training aircraft performed in Czechoslovakia. This was reflected in the words of Chief of the General Staff General Abdul Jabbar Khalil Shanshal during the reception of the Czechoslovak embassy representative in May 1977:

Shanshal used the meeting to re-criticise spare parts deliveries and the exorbitant prices of some spare parts. As for the scope of our supplies for the Iraqi military and the construction of industrial works for the military, Shanshal said that our capabilities are

not being used and that there is the possibility of substantial expansion. However, he did not forget to mention the case of Czechoslovak mines used in 1974 by Kurdish rebels against the Iraqi Army. I replied that the matter had long been explained and closed. Shanshal added that this problem is closed from their side.

This remark only confirms our earlier view that Shanshal's relationship to the Czechoslovak Socialist Republic is cold.[88]

MOSCOW'S PRESSURE

The HTS managed to secure several large deals with Baghdad between 1977 and 1980. The most important were contracts for the delivery of 10 L-39ZOs training and light combat airplanes for 12 million USD, 30 JVBT-55 armoured crane vehicles for 7.4 million USD, and 100mm tank ammunition for 18.5 million USD. All of this happened at a time when trends were taking place in Iraq, which the communist leadership in Prague considered negative because since the mid-1970s the Iraqi regime had resumed harsh repression against opposition forces – the Kurds and the Communists. These issues, however, were just minor details for the respective HTS officials. Quite surprisingly, much bigger problems for Czechoslovak arms export to Iraq came after the outbreak of the Iran-Iraq War.

Following a long-running history of border disputes between Baghdad and Tehran, Iraqi military forces invaded Iran on 22 September 1980 intending to annex oil-rich Khuzestan Province and the east bank of the Shatt al-Arab. Hoping to take advantage of Iran's post-revolutionary chaos, the Iraqi advance lasted only until December 1980. While the offensive of the Iraqi Army had stalled, the Iranians began to gain the upper hand and regained almost all lost territory by June 1982. The war subsequently degenerated into the protracted armed struggle which was terminated at the cost of massive economic, material, and human losses for both warring sides in August 1988.

The Soviet Union did not have a clear favourite state in the conflict. As early as 30 September 1980, Soviet leader Leonid Brezhnev said that the two countries were friends of Moscow and called on them to end the fighting. On a practical level, the Soviet Union refused to side with Baghdad, mainly because of fears that Tehran could reestablish its strategic partnership with the United States if Iraq gained a significant advantage over Iran. This was also the reason why the Soviets imposed an arms embargo upon Iraq, after the outbreak of war.[89]

Immediately after the start of the conflict, the Iraqis came forward with demands for the accelerated fulfilment of already signed contracts and also submitted a number of new requests for the supply of military hardware. Therefore, a delegation of Iraqi officials arrived in Czechoslovakia to discuss these matters in closer detail. While Saddam Hussein's special envoy Naim Haddad held talks with the top-ranking Czechoslovak politicians, Colonel Abdul Rahman negotiated at the HTS for acute deliveries from the list that all Soviet Bloc countries were to receive. This list included requirements for infantry ammunition (7.62mm), tank ammunition (100mm), artillery ammunition (30mm, 57mm, 122mm, 152mm, 122mm Grad rockets), Strela surface-to-air missiles, Malyutka anti-tank guided missiles, and spare parts for military vehicles.

However, even before this meeting happened, the Ministry of Defence of the Union of Soviet Socialist Republics 'recommended' to the Federal Ministry of Defence in Prague 'restraint' in this matter. The HTS officials, therefore, decided not to make any improvisations and evasively told Rahman that Czechoslovakia does not produce most of the demanded items and that the required special material produced in Czechoslovakia has a relatively long delivery time, given the long-term commitments already made with the other Warsaw Pact countries. However, Colonel Rahman was prompt and immediately asked the Czechoslovak representatives to supply the required commodities from the stocks of the Czechoslovak People's Army.

The HTS officials informed their counterparts in the Soviet Union about this request who indicated that 'the Soviet side had not yet addressed similar Iraqi demands. Based on this position, the Czechoslovak side took a restrained stance to solve the new Iraqi demands.' At the end of 1980, Soviet special envoy Botvin passed to the Czechoslovak state leadership information on Moscow's stance on the Iran-Iraq War. 'The information recommends suspending arms supplies to Iraq and Iran in line with a decision taken by the Soviet government and expresses its belief that this position will be properly understood by the leadership of the allied countries, some of which continue to deliver arms to Iraq under previously signed agreements.' And this was the case of Czechoslovakia as well.[90]

THE SUSPENSION OF ARMS SHIPMENTS

Prague strictly followed Soviet 'recommendations' and, indeed, had taken a reserved stance not only on Iraq's new arms requirements but also suspended the shipments of already contracted military materiel. In jeopardy were deliveries of L-39ZO Albatros aircraft and their general overhauls in Czechoslovakia, supplies of JVBT-55 armoured crane vehicles, 100mm ammunition, 7.62mm ammunition (compensatory shipment for the settlement of complaints), spare parts, small arms, and provision of technical assistance together with shipments of related machinery for Operations BETA and JANTAR. The financial scope of Czechoslovakia's commitments in the area of military hardware supplies for 1981 was 33,341,199 USD (of which 6,432,086 USD was in the first quarter).[91]

Understandably, this attitude angered the Iraqi leadership. Baghdad repeatedly called for the fulfilment of existing deals and a positive response to newly submitted requests. During talks with the Czechoslovak ambassador, Iraqi officials openly stated that mutual economic relations directly depend on whether Czechoslovakia would deliver military hardware. During his visit to Czechoslovakia in January 1981, Minister of Industry and Minerals Taher Tawfiq al-Ani informed Czechoslovak officials that 'Iraq's relations with other countries will be judged on their behaviour during the war.' 'Czechoslovakia is able to supply weapons, [...] the success of his entire visit to Czechoslovakia depends on it.'

When Czechoslovak representatives were still evasive about the issue of arms supplies, Tawfiq al-Ani requested a personal meeting with Czechoslovak Prime Minister Lubomír Štrougal on 23 January:

If Czechoslovakia's current position on weapons issues remains as it has been so far, then he says straight away that there will not be much cooperation. E.g. there will

be no cooperation with Zetor tractors and they will, e.g., choose a Finnish company that can make even better tractors than Czechoslovakia. They know we sell weapons to Libya and Syria and why not to Iraq. It pays in cash.[92]

The situation for Prague became serious. A situation arose where, due to the non-fulfilment of contracts to the value of dozens of millions of US dollars, Czechoslovakia was exposed to the risk of Iraqi retaliation measures, which would mean that the Czechoslovak Socialist Republic would lose orders worth almost 2 billion USD in the next four to five years. At the same time, Iraq had already begun to apply these sanctions when it contracted projects promised to Czechoslovakia to third countries.[93]

THE GREEN LIGHT FROM MOSCOW

Fortunately for the Czechoslovak politburo, in March 1981, the Soviet Union changed its position and informed Prague about the new attitude, according to which it was possible to supply military hardware to Iraq ordered in the frame of previous deals and at the same time address some of Baghdad's new demands. The suspension of Czechoslovak arms deliveries lasted until April 1981. In spite of these developments, the Aircraft Repair Plant Trenčín did not send its technical team (several technicians and one pilot) to Iraq to assemble and test fly the L-39 Albatros airplanes after the general overhaul in Czechoslovakia even in June 1981, although this was their duty under the terms of the effective contract. The HTS representative in Iraq complained bitterly that 'the air force headquarters has repeatedly urged the deployment of these experts. This seriously jeopardises the position of the FMZO-HTS in the Iraqi Air Force.' On the other hand, the deliveries and technical assistance provided within the frame of Operation BETA and JANTAR continued almost flawlessly and 'the customer appreciates the high working morale and technical expertise of our employees'.[94]

The change in Prague's arms export policy paid its dividends very early on. During the official visit of Iraqi Deputy Prime Minister Taha Yasin Ramadan al-Jizrawi to Czechoslovakia from 22 to 24 April 1981, several business negotiations were held which led to the export of Czechoslovak goods and construction of civilian industrial

A knocked out Iranian M60 main battle tank, captured by the Iraqis during their invasion of 1980. Barely visible in the background is a West German-made Faun HZ 32.25-40 Herkules tank transporter, carrying a Czechoslovak made-JVBT-55, both in service with the Iraqi Army. (Author's collection)

A large portion of armour deployed by the Iraqi Army during the invasion of Iran in September 1980 was of Soviet and Czechoslovak origin. Visible in this photograph taken in the Dezful area in 1982 are, amongst others, a JVTB-55 armoured recovery vehicle (left centre), and a T-55, together with a row of T-62Ms. (Author's collection)

The burned-out hulk of a Czechoslovak-manufactured OT-64 SKOT armoured personnel carrier of the Iraqi Army, seen in the Khorramshahr area in 1982. (Author's collection)

Not only the Western states but also the Union of Soviet Socialist Republics supply the most modern hardware.

A more pressing issue was the lack of available manufacturing capacity of the Czechoslovak arms industry because the production of Czechoslovak arms factories for the 7th five-year plan (1981–1985) was already almost completely exhausted. Therefore, the HTS under cover of foreign trade company OMNIPOL was able to sign contracts with the Iraqi Ministry of Defence to the overall value of 'only' 64.2 million USD between April 1981 to early March 1982. The largest share was again 100mm and 122mm ammunition worth 46.7 million USD.[96]

CZECHOSLOVAK MILITARY TEACHERS DURING THE WAR

While the Iran-Iraq War raged on, the Czechoslovak military advisors continued to perform their duties at the Military Technical College in Baghdad. On 3 July 1980, the Czechoslovak government approved the continuation of military assistance for the MTC. Thus, the protocol on technical assistance for the years 1980 to 1982 was signed in Bagdad on 6 September 1980, just several days before the outbreak of the Iran-Iraq War. The signing of the protocol and related General Contract No. 45014 extended the assistance provided by Czechoslovakia to Iraq in the field of military education until 31 August 1983. The agenda of the Czechoslovak military-business delegation also included issues of ongoing postgraduate studies of Iraqis at the VAAZ in Brno.[97]

During the school year 1980/1981, the ranks of the MTC in Bagdad were augmented by 13 Czechoslovak, six Egyptian, three Indian, and three Pakistani experts. With the start of the conflict, the study period was extended to a full six days a week. Initially, the mood of the Iraqi students was overly optimistic, but it began to decline rapidly due to failures at the frontline. In the meantime, the wives and children of Czechoslovak advisors were evacuated to Czechoslovakia.

The MTC was situated in a military camp that served simultaneously as the staging area for Iraqi armoured vehicles

works in Iraq worth 138.3 million USD while Iraqi imports to Czechoslovakia were to reach a value of only 6.6 million USD. Naturally, the shipments of Czechoslovak weapons were discussed as well.[95]

However, Prague's capability to fulfil all Iraqi wishes was quite constrained. The room for manoeuvre was severely limited by Iraq's demands for state-of-the-art weapons supplies:

The requirements of the Iraqi armed forces are increasing very significantly in terms of the quality and technical level of the special material. The state leadership and the leadership of the Iraqi armed forces are demanding and will require state-of-the-art armament. Iraq has enough funds for this and has enough willing suppliers, as the practice of recent months confirms.

A Czechoslovak-manufactured OT-62 TOPAS armoured personnel carrier of the Iraqi Army, seen on the streets of an Iranian border town in late 1980. (Author's collection)

Long columns of Czechoslovak-manufactured T-72M1 main battle tanks of the Republican Guards Forces Command seen during a parade in Baghdad in 1990. (Author's collection)

before their deployment at the front. The armour was taken to the frontline by tank transporters and constantly supplemented so that the number of combat vehicles in the camp was still maintained at the same number. The chief of Czechoslovak advisors at the MTC estimated the number of T-55 and T-72 tanks in the camp at about 300. There was also a place where Iraqi and Iranian military

hardware disabled in the fighting was brought from the front. As for the damaged Iraqi combat vehicles, the most numerous were the OT-62 TOPAS armoured personnel carriers. The Czechoslovak reports from Iraq stated that the Iraqis complained that the BMP-1 'is not very rigid, that its hull deforms when hit, which leads to blocking the door, so the crew remains trapped in it. They also point to difficult conditions in Soviet tanks, mainly because they do not have air conditioning in the crew compartment, which American tanks [used by Iranians] allegedly have.'[98]

The commander of the MTC, Brigadier Farooq Hussain Salman, was more than satisfied with the work of Czechoslovak advisors. Hence, he planned to extend the contract for the coming years, at least in the same number of experts. Correspondingly, new General Contract No. 82215 was signed on 13 August 1982. Despite Salman's promises, the number of Czechoslovak experts on the MTC was scaled down. The official reason was the arrival of new Iraqi pedagogues trained abroad. The actual cause was the rising financial difficulties of Iraq's economy that was becoming increasingly unable to appropriate foreign exchange for Prague's military assistance. Therefore, the role of Czechoslovak experts was focused on leading postgraduate studies and research work.

THE TERMINATION OF CZECHOSLOVAK ASSISTANCE AT THE MTC

Before the Iran-Iraq War, the engineering studies at the MTC were essentially the same as at Iraqi civilian technical universities. With the outbreak of the conflict, the Iraqi military realised that the MTC was a military university, so the college began to plan and implement activities in which the armed forces had an overriding interest. It was mainly a two-year postgraduate education program to obtain a Master of Science degree in the fields of military engines and operational art. In 1983 and 1984, nine Czechoslovak military advisors were attached to the MTC in Baghdad, six of whom worked in the mechanical department and three in the electronics department.[99]

In the autumn of 1983, the Iraqis asked for the expansion of the Czechoslovak military group. However, they had to soon reduce this demand considerably again due to the lack of foreign exchange. The assessment of the situation from Prague's point of view was as follows:

However, the original interest in 12 of our teachers was gradually reduced to four, mainly for financial reasons. For Czechoslovak teachers, who are the largest group of foreign teachers at the school, Iraqis pay about 2,100 a month in dollars, while for teachers from other countries (Egyptians, Indians, and Pakistanis) they pay 40% in dinars and 60% are transferred in hard currency to the homeland. At the same time, the rate for an Egyptian is about 3/4 and for an Indian even half the rate for Czechoslovak teachers. The current lack of interest in the originally considered number of Czechoslovak teachers has its reason in the fact that Iraqis currently have a surplus of their own teachers – officers trained at home or abroad (England, France, the Union of Soviet Socialist Republics, Czechoslovakia, and Japan). However, most of these Iraqi teachers do not have the theoretical or practical experience in military technical disciplines at the required level.[100]

All Czechoslovak experts working in the electronics and mechanical department of the MTC ended their activities at the MTC and returned to Czechoslovakia in the summer of 1984. During August 1984, Iraqi and Czechoslovak representatives signed Supplement No. 2 to the General Contract No. 82215 which extended Czechoslovak involvement in the development of the MTC for the school year 1984/1985. According to the conditions of this deal, Prague was obliged to send two experts for the electronics department. Since one of them refused to serve in Iraq for family reasons, in the end, only one Czechoslovak associate professor was attached to the college, officially from 11 August 1984 to 11 August 1985. After August 1985, no Czechoslovak pedagogue worked at the MTC in Baghdad.[101]

Meanwhile, Iraqi military students and candidates performed their studies at the VAAZ in Brno. In total, between 1960 and 1994, 328 Iraqis took turns at the VAAZ in various courses in different specialisations.[102]

Table 10: Deliveries of newly manufactured armoured vehicles from Czechoslovakia to Iraq, 1975–1992[103]

Type	Number of examples	Note
JVBT-55 (JVBT-55KS), armoured crane vehicle	44	deliveries 1981–1982
T-72M1, main battle tank	90	deliveries 1986–1987

THE LAST ARMS AGREEMENT

Iraqi Ministry of Defence had an enormous interest in the acquisition of T-72 tanks and BVP-1 infantry fighting vehicles manufactured under licence in Czechoslovakia. In this area as of 1982, deliveries from the Soviet Union did not cover Baghdad's demands even from half. Because Czechoslovak manufacturing capacity of tanks and infantry fighting vehicles was fully used up in the 7th five-year plan (1981–1985), Prague only managed to deliver T-72M1 tanks, the production of which was planned for the 8th five-year plan (1986–1990).[104]

Despite the end of cooperation between Prague and Baghdad, Czechoslovak-made military vehicles continued dominating the Iraqi Army. This photograph shows an OT-62 TOPAS (right), and an IFA W50 truck (left), together with Soviet-manufactured URAL 375 truck (centre) being washed down during a break in the fighting for the Qassr-e Shirin area, in the mid-1980s. (Author's collection)

A Czechoslovakia-manufactured T-72M1 captured by US Army troops in Kuwait during Operation Desert Storm in 1991. (US Department of Defense)

A front view of a captured Iraqi T-72M1, seen next to a captured ZSU-23-4 Shilka self-propelled anti-aircraft gun. (US Department of Defense)

Due to the raging war with Iran which devasted the Iraqi economy and caused severe losses in terms of people and military materiel, Baghdad began to feel not only inadequate numbers of new weapons but most importantly critical financial problems. Hence, the supply of Czechoslovak weapons and their payments were among the main topics of the official visit of Czechoslovak Prime Minister Lubomír Štrougal to Iraq in late November and early December 1985. In confidential talks, Iraqi Deputy Prime Minister Taha Yasin Ramadan al-Jizrawi made complaints about shipments of weapons from communist countries to Syria and Libya which were subsequently re-exported to Iran. He mentioned specifically Poland but because the Iraqis repeatedly complained about Czechoslovak

weapons entering Iran via Syria, Štrougal assured his Iraqi partners that the Czechoslovak Socialist Republic was supplying armament to Syria and Libya solely for their defence and received assurances that the weapons would not be delivered to a third party (for more details, see the chapter on Iran). During the visit, the terms of a 500 million USD loan for further arms deliveries from Czechoslovakia were agreed upon.[105]

The corresponding credit agreement was signed on 16 July 1986. Up to the end of November of the same year, the Iraqi Ministry of Defence used the terms of this agreement and ordered the Czechoslovak armament to the overall value of 186 million USD. During negotiations in Prague between 24 and 30 November

1986, the Iraqis requested delivery of 260 T-55 tanks, 105 VT-55 or VT-72 armoured recovery vehicles, 150 BVP-1 infantry fighting vehicles, 100 AMB-1 ambulance vehicles on the BVP-1 chassis, 140 Tatra 815 8x8 trucks, 160 to 200 tank transporters using Tatra 815 tractor trucks, and AV-15 recovery vehicles on Tatra 815 chassis. Furthermore, requirements were raised for the possibility of supplying large-calibre guns, light infantry weapons, small-calibre and large-calibre ammunition, together with communication equipment. Baghdad demanded deliveries in 1986 or 1987 and considered shipments at a later date to be too distant.

Contrary to Iraqi expectations, Prague's response was largely negative. The production of T-55 and VT-55 vehicles had ceased several years earlier and the Czechoslovak People's Army was unwilling to provide them from its stocks. The VT-72 recovery vehicles could be supplied only after 1990. In the case of Tatra 815 8x8 trucks, some technical issues had to be solved and tank transporters could not be delivered before 1989. The deliveries of AV-15 vehicles could be expected at the earliest from 1988 with the number of around 10 examples per year. From the remaining requests, only offers on 7.62mm ammunition and hand grenades could be submitted.

At the same time, Iraqi officials requested a deferral of payments due for the supply of military hardware in 1987, stating that they were able to pay only 25 percent of the instalments that year. Although they increased this value to 35 percent during the negotiations, the Czechoslovak representatives were only prepared, at worst, to accept a deferral of payments of a maximum of 50 percent by one year.[106]

ON THE WAY TO DEBTS

Although the Iraqi military tested the Czechoslovak heavy wheel loader together with LIAZ 151.154 and Tatra 815 trucks in 1987, the Ministry of Foreign Trade in Prague knew very well that the days when Iraq was a lucrative trading partner supplying Czechoslovakia with hard currency were long over. The outstanding receivables for the supply of civilian goods and weapons to Baghdad grew unstoppably. In 1987, Iraq was unable to pay 34.6 million USD in receivables for the supplied Czechoslovak armament. One year later, Iraq's total debt to Czechoslovakia from arms and civilian contracts reached 0.5 billion USD. In comparison with other socialist states, the situation of Prague was one of the best in this respect.

According to the information of the Czechoslovak Ministry of Foreign Trade, at that time Iraq owed to the Soviet Union 10 billion USD, to Yugoslavia 1.5 billion USD, to East Germany 1 billion USD, to Bulgaria 0.9 billion USD, and to Poland 0.7 billion USD.[107] The analysis from September 1989 commented:

In the mid-1980s, the positive development of mutual cooperation was replaced by a slowdown, resulting mainly from the escalation of the Iran-Iraq conflict, which had a negative impact on the Iraqi economy. Complications in trade and economic relations

have led to Iraq's current high indebtedness to the Czechoslovak Socialist Republic (as of 31 December 1990, Czechoslovak receivables due will amount to 520.4 million USD) and the Iraqi side's demands to defer repayment of previously granted loans.

This all came at a time when the condition of the Czechoslovak economy began to collapse as a result of many years of communist mismanagement. Therefore, during 1989, several diplomatic delegations were sent to Baghdad to persuade Iraqis to pay their debts as soon as possible. The high-profile delegation led by Czechoslovak Prime Minister Ladislav Adamec which visited Iraq between 14 and 17 October 1989 had the same objective:

At the request of the Iraqi president, L Adamec gave a detailed explanation of current developments in the countries of the socialist community and explained the essence of the process of democratisation and reconstruction of the economic mechanism in the Czechoslovak Socialist Republic. He pointed out the difficulties we face in external economic relations, mainly due to high credit exposure in some developing countries, including Iraq. He stressed the interest in continuing mutually beneficial cooperation between the two countries, provided that the Iraqi side settles at least part of its obligations to the Czechoslovak Socialist Republic primarily by supplying oil.

However, Iraqi President Saddam Hussein was not much touched by Czechoslovakia's economic problems. During all negotiations, the Iraqis refused to accept Czechoslovak demands for debt repayment. Finally, it was agreed that further negotiations on this issue would take place in December 1989.[108]

However, while the communist regime in Prague crumbled in November 1989, the Iraqi debts remained even in 1993 when Czechoslovakia split into the Czech and Slovak Republic. The Iraqi amount receivable was divided between successor states with Prague taking over two-thirds of the sum. In 2006, an intergovernmental agreement was signed between the Czech Republic and Iraq on the settlement of Iraqi debt, according to which 60 percent of the Iraqi debt was forgiven. Another portion of Iraq's debt (20 percent) was forgiven at the end of 2008 following the International Monetary Fund assessment. The rest was recorded as a receivable, with an

Worn out hulks of Czechoslovak-manufactured armoured vehicles of the Iraqi Army found by US troops during the invasion of 2003. Visible in the centre is the front hull of a vz. 53/70 self-propelled twin-barrelled 30mm automatic anti-aircraft gun: this is surrounded by several OT-62 TOPAS armoured personnel carriers. (US Department of Defense)

Thanks to the acquisition of a large number of aircraft, and huge volumes of spare parts and support equipment for them, L-29s remained in service with the Iraqi Air Force well into the 1990s. Indeed, several aircraft of this type ended their careers as test-rigs for remotely piloted drones. This row was photographed at Sahra AB in 1997. (Author's collection)

An L-29 of the Iraqi Air Force Academy, as found by US troops at the Sahra AB, in 2003. (US Department of Defense)

concluded on 16 August 1938 and ratified on 12 March 1939. However, the subsequent occupation of Czechoslovakia by the *Wehrmacht* and the events of the Second World War prevented its practical use.[1]

Nevertheless, limited contacts between the two states continued throughout the 1940s. In October 1949, Zbrojovka Brno applied to the Ministry of National Defence and the Ministry of Foreign Affairs for permission to deliver 10,000 Karabiner 98k rifles, 250 vz. 26 light machine guns, and 150 vz. 37 heavy machine guns with ammunition to Yemen. The request was probably rejected.[2]

Imam Yahya Muhammad was assassinated in an unsuccessful coup d'état in 1948 but was eventually succeeded by his son, Ahmad bin Yahya. In 1956, Yemen turned to the Soviet Bloc countries with a request for development assistance. Crown prince Muhammad al-Badr, the Imam Ahmad bin Yahya's oldest son, became the main protagonist of Yemen's rapprochement with Egypt and the communist states. Although the communist leadership in Prague considered Yemen as 'a particularly backward absolutist feudal monarchy with considerable elements of slave relics', upon pressure from Moscow, Czechoslovakia carried out large-scale arms deliveries for the Mutawakkilite Kingdom. However, their ultimate outcome for Prague can only be described as a financial disaster.

interest rate of 5 percent. Subsequently, between the years 2009 and 2018, Iraq repaid approximately 1.24 billion CSK from its principal sum according to the agreed repayment schedule. Nevertheless, as of 31 December 2018, Iraq still owed to Czechoslovakia 3.057 billion CSK (134.7 million USD): over the following year, Baghdad managed to repay only 147 million CSK to Prague. Thus, Iraqi debts from the times of the Iran-Iraq War will haunt the Czech treasury even in the foreseeable future.[109]

3
NORTH YEMEN (OPERATION 110, COUNTRY 611)

The Mutawakkilite Kingdom of Yemen was one of the most isolated and undeveloped countries of the Arab world, but despite the isolation of his country, Yemeni ruler Imam Yahya Muhammad tried to establish diplomatic relations with foreign countries. One of them was the Soviet Union, with which the friendship and trade agreement was signed in 1928. The friendship treaty between the Mutawakkilite Kingdom and the Czechoslovak Republic was

PLAYING THE SOVIET PROXY AGAIN

On 23 February 1956 a Czechoslovak business delegation left Cairo and through Djibouti arrived in Yemen. During the stay in the Mutawakkilite Kingdom from 25 February to 10 March, Czechoslovak representatives were, among other points, asked for possible deliveries of armament for the Yemeni military. In early March, the Yemeni ambassador in Egypt approached his Czechoslovak counterpart and told him that the Yemeni government planned to ask Czechoslovakia for deliveries of weapons for the reorganisation of local armed forces. Additionally, around the same time, Yemeni *chargé d'affaires* in London contacted the local Czechoslovak ambassador and asked him if Czechoslovakia could supply military materiel and heavy weapons. Moreover, on 7 March 1956, the Soviet *chargé d'affaires* in Prague – Sytienko – visited Czechoslovak Prime Minister Viliam Široký and informed him that Yemeni officials had requested delivery of Soviet small arms, technical equipment for artillery, tanks, self-propelled guns, piston

This is a reconstruction of one of 20 Tatra 813 trucks delivered by Czechoslovakia to Iran in the late 1970s. They were originally developed as medium artillery tractors and 11,751 examples were manufactured in military and civilian variants from 1967 until 1982. In addition to Iran, by 1989, Tatra 813s had been exported to Bulgaria, Cambodia, East Germany, India, Iraq, and Romania. (Artwork by David Bocquelet)

This OT-62/R2 TOPAS armoured personnel carrier mobile command post version was originally delivered to Iraq, then captured by the Iranian forces during the war between the two countries of 1980–1988 and pressed into service by its new owners. A total of 140 OT-62/R2s were manufactured by Podpolianske strojárne Detva for the Czechoslovak People's Army for command sections of motor rifle and tank battalions of the Czechoslovak People's Army, and equipped with R-105, R-112, and R-113 radios. In Iran, they served a similar function well into the 1990s. (Artwork by David Bocquelet)

The DOK-M (*Dozer otočný kolový*) engineering vehicle was developed under the acronym UŽAS (*Univerzální ženijní armádní stroj*) for the Czechoslovak People's Army, as a replacement for the earlier Soviet-made D-271 dozer. This original version was followed by the slightly improved DOK-Ms. About 110 were manufactured by Stavostroj in Nové Město nad Metují, from 1967 until around 1977, and exported to the East Germany Army. This is a reconstruction of an example confirmed as operated by Iranian military engineers in 1986–1988, during the Iraq-Iraq War. (Artwork by David Bocquelet)

This is a reconstruction of a vz. 53/70 self-propelled anti-aircraft gun operated by Iraq since the mid-1970s. Manufactured by Závody 9. mája in Trenčín-Kubra between 1959 and 1961, where a total of 950 examples were rolled out, this vehicle originally included twin 30mm vz. 53 guns on an Praga V3S chassis with armoured body. The slightly improved vz. 53/59B – equipped with a radio station and intercom – emerged in 1970 and was manufactured for the Czechoslovak People's Army and for export, at Škoda Plzeň. Iraq eventually acquired 92 vz. 53/70s, but little is known about their service with their army. (Artwork by David Bocquelet)

The OT-62A was a slightly improved variant of the OT-62 TOPAS armoured personnel carrier, based on the Soviet-made BTR-50, and including no armament. Its spacious crew compartment had space for two crew and up to 18 passengers. Alternatively, it could serve as a command post and staff workplace, or for transporting personnel, various cargoes and material around the battlefield, and was also manufactured as the UMU mine layer, in ambulance and recovery vehicle sub-variants. This example was acquired by Iraq in the early 1970s and survived long enough to end its days while operated by the 45th Mechanised Infantry Division in southern Iraq in 1991, where it was destroyed by an AMX-30B2 main battle tank of the 4th Dragoon Regiment of the French Army, during Operation Daguet, the French component of Operation Desert Storm. (Artwork by David Bocquelet)

Only 188 JVBT-55 armoured crane vehicles (known as BTS-3 Medium Armoured Tractor to the Soviets) were manufactured for export, but Iraq acquired over 120 of them. At least one was assigned to the maintenance section of each armoured battalion, and they saw heavy utilisation in the October 1973 Arab-Israeli War, the Second Iraqi-Kurdish War of 1974–1975, and especially the Iran-Iraq War of 1980–1988. This vehicle is shown wearing the typical camouflage pattern of wide vertical stripes of blue-green atop of its original dark yellow sand colour, as widespread in the Iraqi Army of the late 1970s and early 1980s. Eventually, it was found in derelict condition at Diwaniyah in 2003. (Artwork by David Bocquelet)

The MT-55A was a bridge-layer tank based on the chassis of the T-55A main battle tank. A total of 1,278 were constructed by Turčianske Strojárne between 1969 and 1983 for the Czechoslovak People's Army, and allied forces of the Warsaw Pact. An additional 191 were manufactured for export, of which Iraq purchased eight in the version also known as MT-55KS. Each was equipped with a scissors-type bridge capable of spanning 18 metres and supporting a load of 50 tonnes, designed for easy and quick crossing of anti-tank barriers, like trenches, and other large obstacles. This example is shown in service in 1980, when most Iraqi MT-55s saw deployment during the invasion of Iran. (Artwork by David Bocquelet)

The OT-64 SKOT was a wheeled medium armoured personnel carrier with amphibious capability, designed in Czechoslovakia, but also manufactured in Poland. The Iraqi request for nearly 500 could not be meet by the Czechoslovak industry within the required period of time, and the Czechoslovak People's Army refused to sell any from its own stocks: thus, Baghdad eventually acquired a total of only 173 OT-64As and OT-64/R2s (all equipped with the same 14.5mm KPVT-armed turret as the Soviet-made BRDM-2 armoured car) in 1969–1970. In the Iraqi Army, the type served in motorised infantry formations, and saw action during the wars with Israel, the Kurds, and Iran. (Artwork by David Bocquelet)

In the Arab world, Czechoslovak-manufactured T-72M1s had a reputation of being of far better quality than Soviet-made examples and unsurprisingly, there was heavy demand for them. However, huge Libyan orders from the early 1980s, and the requirement to equip the Czechoslovak People's Army with them, kept the local industry busy. Thus, Iraq eventually obtained just 90 T-72M1s in the 1986–1987 period. All were distributed to the armoured and mechanised divisions of the Republican Guards Forces Command and saw intensive action during the closing stages of the war with Iran in 1988, the invasion of Kuwait in 1990, and the Second Persian Gulf War in 1991. The T-72M1s in question retained their overall cardboard colour, and rarely wore any insignia other than the tactical markings of the brigades and divisions to which they were assigned, usually applied on the rear turret storage box. (Artwork by David Bocquelet)

Between 1969 and 1972, Iraq acquired a total of 39 MiG-15bis and MiG-15UTI fighter-bombers and two-seat conversion trainers, respectively. The latter were primarily required for the newly established Air Force Academy, while the former – which wore Iraqi serial numbers 1019 to 1034, and one of which (1021) is illustrated here – were operated as fighter-bombers. Indeed, ex-Czechoslovak MiG-15bis saw intensive action during the early stages of the Second Iraqi-Kurdish War of 1974–1975, when they flew hundreds of strike sorties from air bases in the Erbil and Mosul areas. As far as is known, most were left in bare metal overall – covered by two layers of clear lacquer mixed with 5 percent and 10 percent aluminium powder, respectively – throughout their careers, which ended in the 1990s. (Artwork by Tom Cooper)

Between 1967 and 1974, Iraq acquired no fewer than 78 Aero L-29 Delfin jets from Czechoslovakia. They lacked internal armament and primarily served as basic and advanced trainers at the Air Force Academy outside Tikrit. However, time and again, a squadron-sized sub-unit of the advanced jet training element of this institution was deployed for counterinsurgency purposes against the Kurds, armed with Czechoslovak-made RB-57/M pods for four S-5M 57mm unguided rockets, as illustrated here on an example from the first two batches of this type delivered to Iraq, wearing the serial number 786. Throughout most of their operational service, Iraqi L-29s retained this livery in highly polished bare metal overall, with large surfaces in dark red. (Artwork by Tom Cooper)

Aiming to further expand their Air Force Academy, the Iraqis were highly enthusiastic customers for the Aero L-39 Albatross jet trainer. However, due to huge Soviet orders, they had to wait years for them. Eventually, the Iraqi Air Force acquired no fewer than 81 L-39s: the first of these were L-39C.2 and L-39ZO.6s, delivered in 1975–1977, and usually painted in white on supper surfaces, and light grey on lower undersurfaces. The last three batches delivered beween 1981 and 1985 wore camouflage colours including 6600 *žluť dubová* (dark yellow sand) and 5450 *zeleň khaki* (khaki green) on upper surfaces and sides, and 4265 *modř pastelová* (pastel blue) on undersurfaces. Fin-tips and wing-tip-installed drop tanks were in yellow, but noses were in dark red. Illustrated here is the example with serial number 1375. (Artwork by Tom Cooper)

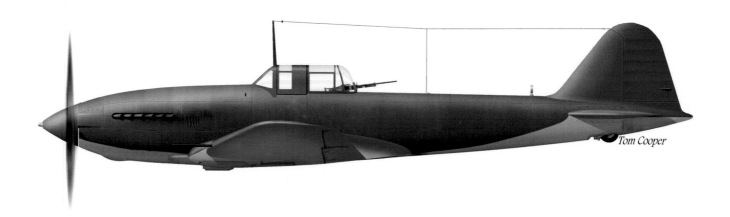

This is a reconstruction of an Avia B-33 piston-engined ground attack aircraft – the licence version of the Soviet-designed Ilyushin Il-10 – as delivered to the Imamate of Yemen (North Yemen) in 1957. Taken from surplus stocks of the Czechoslovak Air Force, the aircraft retained their livery in 5450 *Smalt Avion* 2036 (khaki green) colour on top surfaces and sides, while undersides were painted in *Avion* 2036.65 (light blue). As far is known, no national markings or other insignia were ever applied. (Artwork by Tom Cooper)

In 1956–1957, Czechoslovakia arranged the delivery of 50 SU-100 tank destroyers to the Imamate of Yemen. These were manufactured by the Ural 14.5 Machine Building Works (Sverdlovsk), and the Omsk State Factory No. 174, in the USSR, between 1944 and 1948, or – under licence – by ČKD Sokolovo in Prague and Závody J. V. Stalina in Martin, in Czechoslovakia, from 1953 to 1957. Miraculously, several Yemeni SU-100s remained in service for more than 60 years to participate in the Yemeni Civil War fought from 2014 until 2022. (Artwork by David Bocquelet)

In a little-known deal concluded in 1957, Czechoslovakia delivered 30 T-34/85 medium tanks to the Imamate of Yemen. Additional examples were subsequently delivered directly from the USSR. This example – painted in dark yellow sand, with a disruptive pattern in (very bleached) olive green – then remained in service long enough to be operated in November 2016 by the forces loyal to the ousted President of Yemen, Abdrabbuh Mansur Hadiduring, during the Yemen Civil War of 2014–2022. (Artwork by David Bocquelet)

The vz. 53 towed, twin-barrel 30mm automatic anti-aircraft gun was introduced to service in the Czechoslovak People's Army in 1953, even though full-scale production began only a few years later. Hundreds were acquired by Iraq, and they saw intensive deployment during the Iran-Iraq War of 1980–1988, both in their intended anti-aircraft role, and in ground combat. Dozens were mounted atop BTR-50PK armoured personnel carriers, converting them into self-propelled fire-support vehicles, highly valued at a time when the primary threat the Iraqi army faced was the infiltrating and roaming Iranian infantry. (Artwork by David Bocquelet)

Czechoslovakia delivered a total of 18 vz. 52 anti-tank guns from surplus stocks of its army to the Yemen Arab Republic (North Yemen) in 1964. Developed by Škodovy závody in Pilsen under the designation A22, the gun was manufactured by Závody K. J. Vorošilova at Dubnica nad Váhom. The essence of their construction was the same D-5T gun used on the T-34/85 tank, with a muzzle brake, installed on a mount originally developed for the 105mm H9 field howitzer. In this fashion, a new gun was developed quickly and introduced to service to the Czechoslovak army in 1952, under the designation vz. 52. (Artwork by David Bocquelet)

Czechoslovakia usually delivered only infantry weapons to the People's Democratic Republic of Yemen (South Yemen). One exception was the little-known vz. 59A 82mm recoilless guns. The weapon was manufactured by Závody K. J. Vorošilova at Dubnica nad Váhom in the early 1960s, and 12 were delivered to Aden in July 1981. They saw combat deployment not only during the South Yemen Civil War (also known as the 'Events of '86'), that ravaged the country's armed forces between 13 – 24 January 1986, but especially during the Yemeni Civil War of 1994, pitting the pro-union northern states against the separatist southern Yemeni states. (Artwork by David Bocquelet)

The attempt of the Yemen Arab Republic (North Yemen) to purchase L-39s in 1985 was fruitless. However, in 1998 Sana'a returned to the idea and placed an order for 12 L-39Cs from Prague. All the resulting aircraft, taken from a batch originally manufactured for the Soviet Union but never collected, received a standardised camouflage pattern in the Czechoslovak colours 6700 *okr světlý* (light tan), 5700 *zeleň na vagony* (wagon green) and 5450 *zeleň khaki* (khaki green) on top surfaces and sides, and 1010 *šeď pastelová* (pastel grey) on undersurfaces. (Aero Vodochody)

In the Yemen Air Force (YAF), L-39Cs were assigned to the Flight School and served as basic and advanced jet trainers, and also for weapons training purposes. This example was photographed prior to delivery in 1999, by when YAF introduced the practice of applying its crest on most of its combat aircraft. (Aero Vodochody)

In 2005, the YAF acquired another batch of 14 second-hand but overhauled L-39Cs from Ukraine: these aircraft received an entirely new camouflage pattern in two shades of sand and duck egg blue. Shortly before the collapse of the central government in Sana'a in 2014 the Yemeni Air Force still operated 22 L-39Cs, but very few survived the Saudi-led invasion of the following year. (via Tom Cooper)

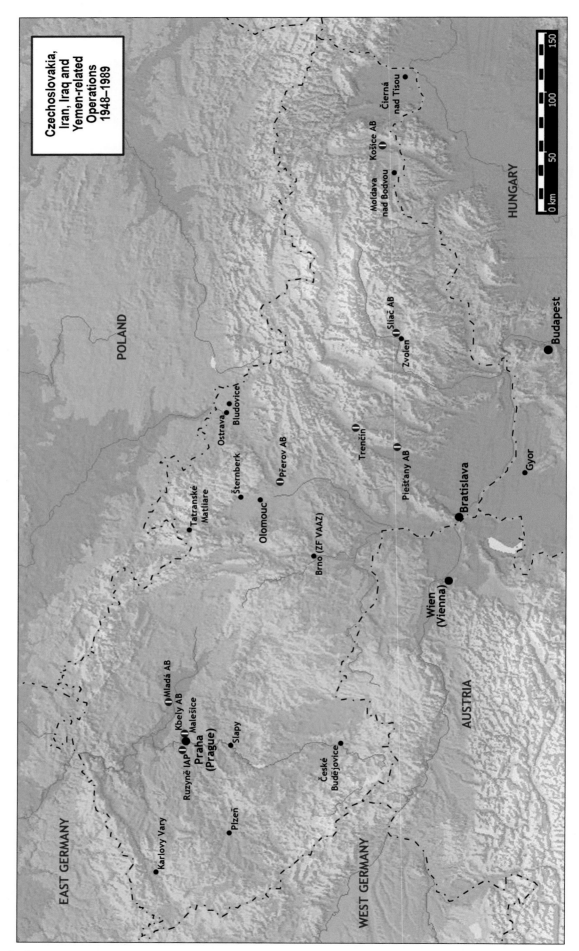

A map of the facilities in Czechoslovakia used in relation to training and stay of military personnel from Iran, Iraq, North Yemen and South Yemen (Map by Tom Cooper)

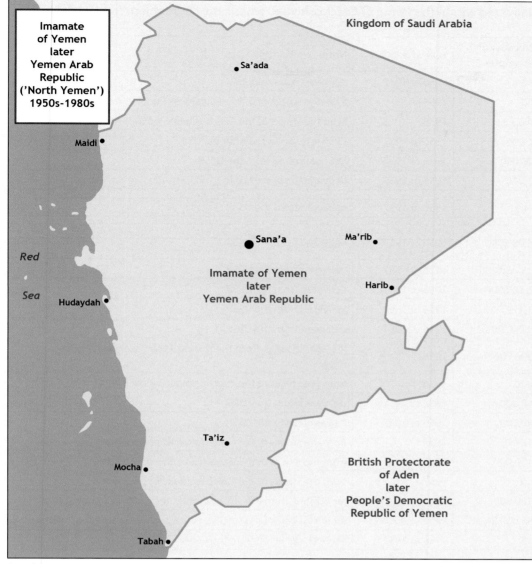

(Map by Tom Cooper)

informed during June that all Yemeni requirements would be fulfilled by Moscow. However, in early July Soviet representatives arrived in Czechoslovakia and notified respective officials that the Soviet Union would secure not all Yemeni demands but only 60 percent of them. Moreover, upon Yemeni pleas, Moscow offered very favourable prices and lucrative terms of payment – 70 percent discount, credit for 10 years, and an interest rate of just 1 percent.

This abrupt change of events caused quite a problem for Prague – the realisation of the rest of the deal under the identical payment conditions was to be carried out by Czechoslovakia. This was a bitter pill even for the most loyal members of the Politburo ÚV KSČ since the final price for the provided weapons was lower than their manufacturing costs. The first secretary of the ÚV KSČ Antonín Novotný bitterly observed, 'politically clear – basically free of charge.' President Antonín Zápotocký was also afraid that the deliveries to Yemen could spoil the lucrative arms deals with Egypt and Syria. It was expected that Cairo and Damascus would get wind of the generous terms of payment and demand the same conditions. The situation was further exacerbated by urgent deadlines for the supply of weapons. The armament, with ammunition, maintenance equipment and spare parts for three years of service, was to be delivered between September and December 1956. Moreover, the Ministry of National Defence warned that a complete lack of proper expertise in the operation of modern weaponry on the part of the Yemeni military would mean intensive involvement of the Czechoslovak People's Army in training and support of Yemeni troops.[4]

Left basically with no other option than to salute smartly, the Politburo ÚV KSČ approved the deliveries of arms for the Mutawakkilite Kingdom according to the Soviet demands on 9 July 1956. The corresponding agreement for the delivery of military materiel to Yemen to the overall value of some 218 million CSK was signed in Prague on 11 July 1956 with the Yemeni delegation led by crown prince al-Badr. The agreement between the Czechoslovak Republic and the Union of Soviet Socialist Republics for the re-export of Soviet arms to Yemen was concluded on 14 August 1956, the Soviet share was circa 165 million CSK. After the negotiated price reduction, Sana'a was supposed to pay just 65.685 million CSK (Soviet share was 49.987 CSK) in 11 instalments by 1966.[5]

aircraft, communication equipment, and other materiel for the year 1956. Simultaneously, he notified Široký that the Soviet government was ready to accept Yemeni demands and that it would be useful to arrange the arms supplies for Yemen in the same way as in the case of recent deliveries to Egypt. Hence, Czechoslovakia would play the role of the middleman camouflaging the actual Soviet involvement again.

Moscow planned to fulfil all Yemeni demands, except those types of weaponry or equipment that were not manufactured in the Soviet Union. Široký readily gave consent to the Soviet proposal. On 27 April 1956, *chargé d'affaires* Sytienko notified Czechoslovak officials that the related dealings in Cairo between the Soviet and Yemeni representatives were in full swing and that the Yemenis would like to finish the negotiations and sign a corresponding agreement with Czechoslovakia. During the next day, Prime Minister Široký informed Sytienko that the Czechoslovak government had authorised direct negotiations with the Yemenis in Prague and the conclusion of an agreement related to the supplies of weapons to the Mutawakkilite Kingdom.[3]

Correspondingly, the Politburo (*Politické byro*) of the ÚV KSČ ordered the Ministry of Foreign Trade in the resolution from 28 May 1956 to make an agreement, with the Soviet assistance, for the deliveries of weaponry to Yemen. Prime Minister Široký was

Type	Number of examples	Year of delivery	Note
Table 11: Military hardware delivered within the frame of Czechoslovak-Yemeni arms agreement from 11 July 1956[7]			
Binoculars, 6x30	360	1956 or 1957	delivered from the USSR
vz. 44, 26.5mm signal pistol	80	1956	from the stocks of the Czechoslovak People's Army
26.5mm signal round	4,000	1956	from the stocks of the Czechoslovak People's Army
7.62mm sub machine gun	2,000	1956 or 1957	PPSh-41?, delivered from the USSR
7.62mm carbine	20,000	1956 or 1957	SKS?, delivered from the USSR
DP, 7.62mm light machine gun	1,000	1956 or 1957	delivered from the USSR
SG-43, 7.62mm heavy machine gun	400	1956 or 1957	delivered from the USSR
7.62mm round for sub machine gun	6,000,000	1956 or 1957	delivered from the USSR
7.62mm light round	25,288,000	1956 or 1957	delivered from the USSR
7.62mm armour-piercing round	3,100,000	1956 or 1957	delivered from the USSR
7.62mm incendiary round	1,112,000	1956 or 1957	delivered from the USSR
7.62mm heavy round	9,000,000	1956 or 1957	delivered from the USSR
7.62mm rimfire round	990,000	1956	for T-34/85 tanks, from the stocks of the Czechoslovak People's Army
RG-4, hand grenade	800	1956	from the stocks of the Czechoslovak People's Army
offensive hand grenade	50,000	1956 or 1957	delivered from the USSR
defensive hand grenade	50,000	1956 or 1957	delivered from the USSR
P-27, light anti-tank weapon	1,000	1957	from the stocks of the Czechoslovak People's Army
round for P-27	100,000	1957	from the stocks of the Czechoslovak People's Army
ROKS-3, flamethrower	50	1957	from the stocks of the Czechoslovak People's Army
propellant cartridge	100,000	1957	for ROKS-3, from the stocks of the Czechoslovak People's Army
flammable fill	35,000 litres	1957	for ROKS-3, from the stocks of the Czechoslovak People's Army
82mm mortar	15	1956 or 1957	M1941?, delivered from the USSR
82mm mortar round	18,000	1956 or 1957	delivered from the USSR
DShK, 12.7mm anti-aircraft machine gun	100	1956 or 1957	delivered from the USSR
M1939 (61-K), 37mm anti-aircraft gun	100	1956 or 1957	delivered from the USSR
M1942 (ZiS-3), 76mm field gun	100	1956 or 1957	delivered from the USSR
M1931/37 (A-19), 122mm gun	24	1956 or 1957	delivered from the USSR
12.7mm incendiary round	800,000	1956 or 1957	delivered from the USSR
12.7mm armour-piercing round	1,200,000	1956 or 1957	delivered from the USSR
37mm time setting round	164,000	1956 or 1957	delivered from the USSR
37mm armour-piercing round	36,000	1956 or 1957	delivered from the USSR
76mm time setting round	120,400	1956 or 1957	delivered from the USSR
76mm armour-piercing round	14,000	1956 or 1957	delivered from the USSR
76mm armour-piercing discarding sabot round	5,600	1956 or 1957	delivered from the USSR
122mm high explosive round	9,120	1956 or 1957	delivered from the USSR
122mm armour-piercing round	480	1956 or 1957	delivered from the USSR
AST, artillery periscopic binocular	90	1956 or 1957	delivered from the USSR
BMT, artillery compass	62	1956 or 1957	delivered from the USSR

Table 11: Military hardware delivered within the frame of Czechoslovak-Yemeni arms agreement from 11 July 1956 (continued)

T-34/85, medium tank	30	1957	from the stocks of the Czechoslovak People's Army, delivered including 8 V-2 spare engines (in 1957) and four spare guns (in 1956)
SU-100, self-propelled gun	50	1956 or 1957	delivered from the USSR
85-JOF-TK 44, K 52, PLK 39, 85mm high explosive round	10,500	1956	for T-34/85 tank, from the stocks of the Czechoslovak People's Army
85-JPSv-TK 44, K 52, PLK 39, 85mm armour-piercing round	4,000	1956	for T-34/85 tank, from the stocks of the Czechoslovak People's Army
85mm armour-piercing discarding sabot round	800	1956 or 1957	for T-34/85 tank, delivered from the USSR
100mm high explosive round	10,500	1956 or 1957	for SU-100 self-propelled gun, delivered from the USSR
100mm armour-piercing round	6,000	1956 or 1957	for SU-100 self-propelled gun, delivered from the USSR
SPK-5, crane tank	2	1956 or 1957	delivered from the USSR
BTR-40, armoured personnel carrier	100	1956 or 1957	delivered from the USSR
B-33, ground attack aircraft	20	1957	the Czechoslovak licence of Il-10, from the stocks of the HTS
CB-33, combat trainer	4	1957	the Czechoslovak licence of UII-10, from the stocks of the Czechoslovak People's Army
C-11, training aircraft	3	1957	the Czechoslovak licence of Yak-11
BZT, 23mm armour-piercing incendiary round with tracer	16,000	1957?	for B-33 aircraft (NS-23KM gun), from the stocks of the Czechoslovak People's Army
OZT, 23mm high explosive incendiary round with tracer	4,800	1957?	for B-33 aircraft (NS-23KM gun), from the stocks of the Czechoslovak People's Army
23mm dummy armour-piercing round	10,000	1957?	for B-33 aircraft (NS-23KM gun), from the stocks of the Czechoslovak People's Army
PZ, 20mm armour-piercing incendiary round	4,200	1957?	for B-33 aircraft (BTN-20E gun), from the stocks of the Czechoslovak People's Army
NChSv, 20mm round	6,000	1957?	for B-33 aircraft (BTN-20E gun), from the stocks of the Czechoslovak People's Army
12.7mm incendiary round	12,600	1956 or 1957	for C-11 aircraft (UBS machine gun), delivered from the USSR
12.7mm armour-piercing round	5,400	1956 or 1957	for C-11 aircraft (UBS machine gun), delivered from the USSR
PTAB-2,5, anti-tank shaped charge bomblet	600	1957?	from the stocks of the Czechoslovak People's Army
ZAB-2,5, incendiary bomblet	600	1957?	from the stocks of the Czechoslovak People's Army
TAD-4, training bomb	200	1956 or 1957	delivered from the USSR
PPU-70, training bomb	500	1957?	from the stocks of the Czechoslovak People's Army
OFAB-100, high explosive bomb	360	1957?	from the stocks of the Czechoslovak People's Army
FAB-250, general purpose bomb	180	1957?	from the stocks of the Czechoslovak People's Army
PLK-45, pilot emergency parachute	36	1957	from the stocks of the Czechoslovak People's Army
Searchlight	10	1956 or 1957	delivered from the USSR
airfield lighting system	2	1957?	from the stocks of the Czechoslovak People's Army
aircraft spare parts and airfield ground support equipment (including POL-1 mobile workshop, gantry cranes, compressors, communication equipment, fire-fighting equipment)		1957	from the stocks of the Czechoslovak People's Army

Table 11: Military hardware delivered within the frame of Czechoslovak-Yemeni arms agreement from 11 July 1956 (continued)

GAZ-63, light truck	100	1956 or 1957	delivered from the USSR
ZiS-150, medium truck	75	1956 or 1957	delivered from the USSR
YaAZ-210, heavy truck	24	1956 or 1957	delivered from the USSR
PAZ-653, ambulance	10	1956 or 1957	delivered from the USSR
mobile crane 5t	3	1956 or 1957	delivered from the USSR
Tatra 111 C, fuel tank truck	2	1957	ground support equipment for delivered aircraft, from the stocks of the Czechoslovak People's Army
communication trailer with RSI-6 radio station, Lambda receiver and Pelikan transmitter	3	1957	ground support equipment for delivered aircraft, from the stocks of the Czechoslovak People's Army
PAR-3B, non-directional radio beacon	2	1957	ground support equipment for delivered aircraft, on ZiS-150 or ZiS-151 chassis, from the stocks of the Czechoslovak People's Army
AKZS-40, mobile oxygen-filling station	2	1957	ground support equipment for delivered aircraft, on ZiS-150 chassis, from the stocks of the Czechoslovak People's Army
PTDA, mobile tank workshop	8	1957	on Praga V3S chassis, from the stocks of the Czechoslovak People's Army
PTDB, mobile tank workshop	5	1957	on Praga V3S chassis, from the stocks of the Czechoslovak People's Army
PM-2, mobile regimental artillery workshop	1	1956 or 1957	delivered from the USSR
Zetor 25, tractor	2	1957	ground support equipment for delivered aircraft, from the stocks of the Czechoslovak People's Army
RM-31T, radio station	8	1956	from the stocks of the Czechoslovak People's Army
R-106, radio station	20	1956 or 1957	delivered from the USSR
RBM1, radio station	20	1956 or 1957	delivered from the USSR
EC 15 kVA, power generating set (trailer)	12	1957	from the stocks of the Czechoslovak People's Army
NS-1250, charger set 1.25 kW	5	1956	from the stocks of the Czechoslovak People's Army
PK-12, compressor	1	1956 or 1957	delivered from the USSR
mine	2,000	1956 or 1957	delivered from the USSR
steel helmet	10,000	1956 or 1957	delivered from the USSR
leather ammunition pouch	30,000	1956 or 1957	delivered from the USSR

The overview of arms supplied from Czechoslovakia and the Soviet Union for the Mutawakkilite Kingdom is shown in Table 11. Prague provided the arms and ammunition mostly from the stocks of the Ministry of National Defence. A large part of the deliveries from Czechoslovakia was taking place during the first half of 1957.[6]

An Avia B-33 ground attack aircraft of the 2nd Squadron, 32nd Ground Attack Regiment, Czechoslovak Air Force. (VÚA-VHA Praha)

FOLLOW-UP DEALS

Despite the obvious economic disadvantageousness for Prague of the Czechoslovak-Yemeni arms agreement from 11 July 1956, negotiations related to additional armament deliveries were underway and culminated in March 1957 with the signing of three

contracts for spare parts, artillery weapons, and fuel (listed in Table 12). However, unlike the first agreement, these shipments were to be paid for by the Yemenis in British pounds through Switzerland.[8]

In June 1957 the Yemeni minister of defence requested new shipments of 100 M-72 motorcycles, eight PTDA and four PTDB

A T-34/85 medium tank seen on the streets of Sana'a in 1962. (Author's collection)

Table 12: Additional Czechoslovak-Yemeni arms contracts, 1957–1958[11]

Contract	Date	Value	Note
Contract No. 121/1	25 March 1957	7,500 GBP	spare parts for B-33 aircraft for 3 to 5 years of service (discount provided, original value 80,000 GBP)
Contract No. 121/2	25 March 1957	457,000 CSK	artillery armament and spare parts for T-34/85 tanks, see Table 13 (discount provided, original value 464,500 GBP)
Contract No. 121/4	25 March 1957	39,048 GBP	fuel and lubricants for delivered armament
Contract No. 220342	3 August 1957	54,967 GBP	Z-126 Trenér training aircraft
Contract No. 220723	24 July 1958	8,919 GBP	two DK-2 compressors and engineer equipment (explosives, safety fuses, etc.)
Contract No. 220413	1958	41,444 GBP	military assistance (training) in Yemen 1956–1959

mobile workshops, 104 military tents, and armoured vehicles from Czechoslovakia's military stocks including 30 StuG III assault guns, 30 T-34/85 tanks, and 30 SD-100 self-propelled guns. However, the commander of the Czechoslovak tank and mechanised troops, Lieutenant General Vladimír Janko, declined additional provision of T-34/85s and SD-100s from the inventory of the Czechoslovak People's Army. Instead, the oldest vehicles from army warehouses were offered and these were composed of Cromwell and Challenger tanks together with ISU-152 self-propelled guns. While the HTS of the Ministry of Foreign Trade refused to accept the supply of tanks of British origin as they were thought inappropriate, StuG III and ISU-152 guns could only be supplied without spare parts which was considered as unsuitable too. In the end, no deliveries materialised.[9]

During summer 1957, crown prince Muhammad al-Badr personally contacted the representative of the HTS in Yemen, Colonel Foršt, with a request for help. The political situation in Yemen had worsened after the serious illness of his father, the Imam Ahmad bin Yahya. In the case of his death, his son and Muhammad al-Badr's younger brother Hasan, at that time Yemeni representative in the United Nations, was poised to become the new ruler of the Mutawakkilite Kingdom. According to al-Badr's claims, this move was reportedly supported by the United States. Simultaneously, a propaganda campaign intended to remove Muhammad al-Badr

from his position started in earnest with the radio broadcast accusing him of acquisitions of arms in 'communist states' and calling him 'the dog' buying weapons instead of building schools. Crown prince al-Badr warned Colonel Foršt that this was an apparent effort by the Americans and British to change the orientation of Yemeni foreign policy. In such a case, Yemeni financial obligations vis-à-vis Prague could be in jeopardy. In order to strengthen his position, al-Badr asked for further deliveries of Czechoslovak materiel worth 20 million CSK together with the deployment of Czechoslovak and Soviet military experts. Among the requested items were four Il-14 aircraft, 100 trucks, 40 off-road passenger cars, 10 buses, two coastal patrol boats, a radio transmitter, and support equipment for three airfields. At the same time, the activities of Czechoslovak advisors in Yemen were to be prolonged. Moreover, a Czechoslovak doctor with the sole task of treating Imam Ahmad bin Yahya was to be dispatched as well.[10]

Czechoslovakia promptly informed Moscow about these developments through the Soviet embassy in Cairo. Prague was generally ready to fulfil all Muhammad al-Badr's wishes except the sending of the Czechoslovak doctor on grounds that the 'Imam is very seriously ill and the possibility of his early decease is expected. Imam's death, in the case of his treatment by a Czechoslovak doctor, could be misused against al-Badr both inside the country and on the international political forum'. The Politburo ÚV KSČ approved further steps in this matter in the resolution from 20 August 1957.

At the same time, the Czechoslovak communist leadership began to fully appreciate the effects of massive arms deliveries on the Yemeni internal situation. The large number of supplied weapons impelled the Yemenis to establish large, conventional, and relatively modern armed forces that could exceed the limited resources of the Mutawakkilite Kingdom to finance them. This could, in turn, elicit economic problems with subsequent unfavourable implications on domestic political stability. Moreover, before the deliveries, nobody had paid attention to the actual condition of the Yemeni military. The armed forces, in the concept as understood in Czechoslovakia, were basically non-existent in Yemen at that time, and the existing military had too limited personnel resources to absorb all the weapons and military assistance properly. The low level of general education together with completely missing technical skills meant that the operation and maintenance of newly delivered weapons were met with immense difficulties because of the lack of appropriately educated and trained soldiers.[12]

Despite the politburo's decision to help the Yemeni crown prince's case, Czechoslovakia provided no material that was requested by

Muhammad al-Badr. Additional deliveries of Czechoslovak arms to Yemen during the years 1957 and 1959 are listed in Table 13.

Table 13: Czechoslovak arms export to Yemen, 1957–1959[13]			
Type	Number of examples	Year of delivery	Note
vz. 44, 26.5mm signal pistol	116	1958	
26.5mm signal round	4,000	1958	
vz. 24, 9mm pistol	603	1958	
vz. 52, 7.62mm rifle	2	1957	from the stocks of the Czechoslovak People's Army
	3	1958	
	1	1959	
vz. 98 N and vz. 24, 7.92mm rifle	540	1959	Czechoslovak designation of German Karabiner 98k (vz. 98 N) and Czechoslovak variant of Gewehr 98 (vz. 24), from the stocks of the Czechoslovak People's Army
9mm round	600	1958	for vz. 24 pistol
vz. 52, 7.62mm round	1,200	1957	for vz. 52 rifle, from the stocks of the Czechoslovak People's Army
	1,200	1958	
	300	1959	
T-21, bazooka	20	1957	Contract No. 121/2, from the stocks of the Czechoslovak People's Army
round for T-21	2,000	1957	Contract No. 121/2, from the stocks of the Czechoslovak People's Army
round for T-21 with reduced charge	1,000	1957	Contract No. 121/2, from the stocks of the Czechoslovak People's Army
drill round for T-21	5	1957	Contract No. 121/2, from the stocks of the Czechoslovak People's Army
drill round for P-27	20	1958	
training round for P-27	200	1958	
Bakelite cartridge for P-27	2,000	1958	
vz. 43, 57mm anti-tank gun	50	1957	Contract No. 121/2, the Czechoslovak licence of M1943 (ZiS-2), from the stocks of the Czechoslovak People's Army
57-JO-PTK 43, 57mm fragmentation round	6,000	1957	Contract No. 121/2, for vz. 43 anti-tank gun, from the stocks of the Czechoslovak People's Army
57-JPSv-PTK 43, 57mm armour-piercing round	24,000	1957	Contract No. 121/2, from the stocks of the Czechoslovak People's Army
Z-126, training aircraft	10	1957	Contract No. 220342
extension pole antenna (9 metre)	3	1958	
Náložka 200g, explosive block	500	1958	Contract No. 220723
Náložka 100g, explosive block	5,000	1958	Contract No. 220723
Rozbuška Ž, detonator	900	1958	Contract No. 220723
detonating cord	600 metres	1958	Contract No. 220723
safety fuse	240	1958	Contract No. 220723
detonator crimping pliers	2	1958	Contract No. 220723
DK-2, compressor	2	1958	Contract No. 220723
Souprava pneumatických nástrojů 11, pneumatic tools set	2	1958	Contract No. 220723
SMS, medium bridge set	1/3	1957	Contract No. 121/2, from the stocks of the Czechoslovak People's Army

A vz. 52 anti-tank gun of the Czechoslovak People's Army towed by a Tatra 111 truck. (Československý voják)

several aircraft technicians, and two interpreters responsible for bringing the delivered airplanes to working order.

The last instructor group under the leadership of Major Tambor was responsible for advising the Yemenis in terrain reconnaissance and road treatment. The last assignment of this team – made up of the commander, one additional officer, and a civilian interpreter – was training in the use of delivered engineer equipment.[16]

CZECHOSLOVAK ADVISORS

A couple of months after the signing of the Czechoslovak-Yemeni arms agreement from 11 July 1956, a Czechoslovak military preparatory team (including one Soviet tank officer) was sent to Yemen in September 1956 in order to check local conditions for the disembarkation of the weapons, their assembly, and follow-up training of Yemeni soldiers under the guidance of Czechoslovak and Soviet instructors. The deliveries of armament from the Soviet Union started during the second half of 1956. Therefore, as of 31 December 1956, three Soviet advisors were dispatched in the Mutawakkilite Kingdom.[14]

The Czechoslovak-Yemeni arms agreement had a provision that obliged Czechoslovakia to provide technical assistance in the assembly of newly delivered arms and proper training of their crews for the subsequent service within the Yemeni military. This provision resulted in two supplements that were signed at Sana'a in March 1957 and that defined the conditions for activities of Czechoslovak instructors in Yemen (Supplement No. 1) and training of Yemeni troops in Czechoslovakia (Supplement No. 2).[15]

In total, 28 Czechoslovak advisors (including five civilian interpreters, one doctor, and one cook) and 12 Soviet military instructors were sent to Yemen during the first half of 1957. The Czechoslovak and Soviet military materiel was transported to the bay north of the port of Salif and unshipped there using a pontoon. One team of Czechoslovak soldiers, five conscripts from the Training Tank Regiment (Školní tankový pluk), was tasked to unload 30 tanks together with 50 self-propelled guns and drive them initially to Hudaydah (also known as Hodeida) and from there to Sana'a. However, because of the impassable Hudaydah – Sana'a mountain road, all T-34/85s and SU-100s were moved to Taiz, Hudaydah, and Bajil instead.

Experiencing the first of many instances of Yemeni incompetence, the activity of the Czechoslovak tank instruction team led by 1st Lieutenant Mleziva, and composed of a further eight members (six officers and two interpreters), proved to be a complete failure. Despite numerous urgings to crown prince Muhammad al-Badr, the Yemenis were not able to select candidates for the training. The same issue repeated itself in the case of the aviation training team with the task to train Yemeni pilots on B-33 ground attack aircraft. Only the commander of the group – Major Jiří Sedlář – was sent to Yemen before it became known that no training would materialise. Another Czechoslovak advisory team was composed of a factory pilot,

YEMENI 'KOMBAJN'

The hopelessly obsolete Avia B-33 ground attack aircraft, nicknamed 'Kombajn' (combine harvester) in the Czechoslovak Air Force, was to become the mainstay of the fledgling Yemeni military air service. However, such optimistic plans never became reality. In fact, their supply to Yemen was surrounded by controversies basically from the moment when the idea reached the leadership of the Czechoslovak Air Force. The chief technical officer Colonel Žďárský repeatedly warned the HTS officials that the B-33 was completely unsuitable for Yemeni conditions. The aircraft were not only demanding of maintenance and repairs but sensitive to the local subtropical hot climate as well. Their engines were prone to overheating even in Czechoslovakia during the summer months. However, the die was cast, and 20 B-33 and 4 CB-33 were sent to Yemen despite the complications that could potentially arise later. All B-33 and CB-33 were dispatched to Yemen in transports 9644, 9645, and 9646 on 18 May 1957. At the same time, 25 M-42 engines were ready for shipment.

And this was just the beginning of the problems. Before the delivery, the aircraft and their power plants underwent technical inspection. On 16 and 20 April 1957, a team of experts from the Aircraft Repair Plant Malešice (Letecké opravny Malešice) checked out two M-42 engines ready for shipment to Yemen. They detected heavy rust on different sections of the power plants with some of their parts jammed. It was assumed that the remaining M-42s were in similar condition. On 8 May, the technicians of the Aircraft Repair Plant Kbely (Letecké opravny Kbely) noted heavy corrosion and mould on the airframes. The airplanes were duly classified as not airworthy. Although the HTS officials were informed about the poor technical condition of the aircraft in time, they did nothing to remedy the situation (probably because of financial reasons of the whole Yemeni deal). This prompted Colonel General Václav Kratochvíl, Chief of the General Staff of the Czechoslovak People's Army, to warn Minister of National Defence Colonel General Bohumír Lomský that without the corrective action, the lives of Czechoslovak instructor pilots in Yemen would be in jeopardy.[17]

In May and June 1957, Major Jiří Sedlář (pilot of the 45th Artillery Reconnaissance Aviation Regiment [45. dělostřelecký průzkumný letecký pluk]), Václav Bohata (the factory pilot of the Aircraft Repair Plant Kbely), Warrant Officer Bohumír Rektořík (the operator of ground support equipment from the 25th Airfield Battalion [25. letištní prapor]) and five technicians (four from the Aircraft Repair Plant Kbely and one from Let Kunovice company) left for Yemen in order to assemble and test fly recently delivered B-33, CB-33, and

An 'almost legendary' photograph of the row of assembled Yemeni B-33s, covered by tarpaulins to protect their engines, cockpits, and fins from the sun. (Author's collection)

A 'factory fresh' Avia C-11 (Czechoslovak version of the Yak-11 training aircraft), as exported to Yemen. (VÚA-VHA Praha)

C-11 aircraft. The dismantled airplanes were unloaded from the ship near Salif harbour and transported to the nearby airfield some five kilometres (three miles) away, using a road built recently by a French company. The mission of the aviation team met only partial success due to the problems in the dispatching harbour and poor working morale of some of the team members during the first half of their stay in Yemen. The outcome was that only nine B-33s, two CB-33s, and three C-11s were assembled, test flown, and flown to Sana'a airfield (the local runway was extended by 200 metres (656 feet) during this timeframe).

At the moment the flying training was to begin in earnest, the Yemenis found out that they had no suitable pilots that could undergo conversion training. Therefore, new pilots had to be trained from scratch. Without any aircraft for the basic flying training, 10 Z-126 Trenér airplanes were hastily ordered in Czechoslovakia. The first four of them were sent to Yemen on 19 July 1957 and subsequently assembled and flown to Sana'a as well.[18]

FINISHING THE AIRCRAFT ASSEMBLY

The Czechoslovak aircraft assembling team returned back home in December 1957 without accomplishing the job. Therefore, under the code name Course 514, a new group of Czechoslovak aircraft specialists had to be dispatched in Yemen to finish the task of the original team. The six-member group with Czechoslovak Air Force technicians led by Osvald Šťourač (employee of the Aircraft Repair Plant Kbely and the member of the previous assembly group), factory pilot Václav Bohata, and Warrant Officer. Bohumír Rektořík arrived in Salif on 12 February 1958. One Z-126 was flown from

Sana'a during the next day and it subsequently served for liaison and courier duties of the Czechoslovak group.

Meanwhile, the technicians went immediately to work and began to assemble the aircraft remaining at Salif (11 B-33s, two CB-33s, and six Z-126s). On 7 March, the whole team moved to Sana'a where it carried out engine conservation and maintenance of Czechoslovak airplanes already stationed there. The complete group returned to Salif eight days later and continued the assembly of ground attack aircraft which was followed by the completion of the rest of the Trenérs. After the test flight of the recently assembled airplane, Václav Bohata flew it to Sana'a. Osvald Šťourač, using the group's sole Z-126, picked him up and both returned to Salif for the flight of the next aircraft. Simultaneously, technical equipment such as power generating sets, tractors, or spare parts were readied for transport to Bajil. All work at Salif was completed on 25 April 1958 (all aircraft were transferred by 21 April) and the group moved to Sana'a.

The local airfield had absolutely no ground support equipment, except one smaller old building which was adapted by the Czechoslovak technicians to a small warehouse and workroom. They had to even provisionally manufacture the basic furniture. The Czechoslovak team performed maintenance of aircraft and related support equipment that was partially stored in a nearby farm under completely insufficient conditions. The buildings had to be cleared of up to half a metre of manure and repaired in order to serve as a warehouse for spare parts for the delivered aircraft. Again, the Czechoslovak technicians had to manufacture the required racks, although Yemeni authorities provided locals for this work. However, they proved to be completely unsuitable for the task at hand. Two Yemeni workers produced one rack after 45 days while the same piece of equipment was manufactured by the Czechoslovaks in just two days.

All Z-126 aircraft were parked at Sana'a airfield in the open air and thus exposed to the strong sun and dust. Therefore, and because the start of flying training of Yemeni pilots was nowhere in sight, Osvald Šťourač decided to dismantle eight Trenérs and store them in two rooms at the farm. In early May one Tatra 111 C fuel truck towing a communication trailer was driven from Bajil to Sana'a airfield (the remaining two communication trailers were at Bajil airfield and Hudaydah barracks). This was the first time that such heavy and large-sized transport drove through the local mountain roads. Using the same pattern, the remaining Tatra 111 C and one Tatra 128 (POL-1 aircraft workshop) were transferred to Sana'a. Meanwhile, the Czechoslovak technical team prepared the airfield at Sana'a for regular flying with all necessary equipment ready for operation: even the lighting system was set up for trial purposes. In this condition, the airfield was presented to crown prince Muhammad al-Badr on 4 June 1958. Moreover, Czechoslovak pilots undertook several night flights using one Z-126. During the same month, several trial take-offs with B-33s were carried out in order to find out their actual performance in the hot and high conditions of the local airfield: primarily the length of runway needed for a successful take-off.

Two members of the group (Václav Bohata and Bohumír Rektořík) returned to Czechoslovakia on 26 August 1958. The rest of the group continued the maintenance and conservation of the delivered airplanes and ground support equipment. Around the same time, the construction of the flying school began in earnest. However, the work of Yemeni workers proceeded at a very slow pace. Thus, Czechoslovak technicians had to complete some parts of the building themselves before they were able to install delivered teaching aids into the schoolroom. Harsh weather prompted Osvald Šťourač to produce tarpaulins for covering rudders and their hinges on the B-33 airplanes. Later, covers for complete aircraft were manufactured. On 21 November, after the maintenance and new conservation of aircraft at Sana'a was carried out, three technicians arrived back in Czechoslovakia (1st Lieutenant Václav Hořejší from the 28th Ground Attack Aviation Regiment [*28. bitevní letecký pluk*], 1st Lieutenant Miroslav Krpata from the 32nd Ground Attack Aviation Regiment [*32. bitevní letecký pluk*], and 2nd Lieutenant Josef Jurečka from the Aviation Training School [*Letecké učiliště*]). Thus, only Osvald Šťourač (with an interpreter Josef Muzikář) remained in Yemen and performed the basic maintenance of Czechoslovak aircraft and ground support equipment at Sana'a airfield until his return to Czechoslovakia on 8 March 1959.[19]

Simultaneously, tank technician Zdeněk Jára from the 25th Tank Repair Plant (*25. tankový opravárenský závod*) carried out the maintenance and conservation of some T-34/85 tanks and SU-100 self-propelled guns during his stay in Yemen between 9 February to 26 August 1958. Like all other Czechoslovak military advisors deployed to the Mutawakkilite Kingdom, he had to live in very austere conditions.[20]

PRINCE'S PRIVATE PILOT

While the team operating under the cover name Course 514 was busy assembling aircraft at Salif, the Czechoslovak Ministry of National Defence provided additional military assistance for Yemen in the form of a personal pilot for Muhammad al-Badr. Captain Karel Bahenský from the 1st Transport Airdrop Aviation Regiment (*1. dopravní výsadkový letecký pluk*) was selected for this task. He was informed about his forthcoming mission with five months' notice. When he asked his superiors what he could expect and which personal equipment would be needed in Yemen, he was told, 'Comrade, you learn everything in time'. He was left in uncertainty until the time for his departure was approaching. He was hurriedly

summoned to the HTS headquarters on Friday and informed that he would be on the way to Yemen on Sunday!

Bahenský arrived in Yemen on 30 March 1958, his mission receiving cover name Course 517. His task was to fly with a couple of Aero Commander 500 series of utility aircraft of the Yemen Airlines, which operated as a private air fleet of the Imam rather than as a normal commercial enterprise. Some two weeks after his arrival, Captain Karel Bahenský was received by the crown prince who promised to provide him with an aircraft so he could perform his duty soon. At that time Yemen Airlines had only three pilots – one Swede and two Yugoslavs. Around May 1958, three Yemeni pilots returned from the training in Italy. This, in turn, meant that Bahenský was left without an available airplane and thus with nothing to do. Therefore, he was attached to the assembly team at Salif and performed transfer flights of Czechoslovak aircraft to Sana'a. After additional questions, Yemeni authorities informed the HTS representative Colonel Foršt that they would provide no aircraft for Bahenský. It was planned that he could serve as an instructor pilot training Yemeni pilots instead. However, Yemeni officials were not able to organise a group of cadets again, thus no flying training took place and Karel Bahenský returned home on 26 August 1958.

During his stay in Yemen, he had the opportunity to learn some specifics of the local military firsthand. Czechoslovak aircraft technicians were assisted by Yemeni citizens who did the auxiliary works. Not only were their numbers too low, but Yemeni authorities also failed to pay their wages regularly and in an adequate amount. Thus, when one relatively competent Yemeni driver did not receive his pay, no one saw him on the Sana'a airfield again.[21]

SOVIETS STEP IN

Despite the continuous breaching of all training contracts due to the Yemeni incompetence in finding proper trainees, after the high-level meeting in Prague on 30 October 1958, Czechoslovak officials decided to prolong the military assistance provided to the Mutawakkilite Kingdom, but only on the minimal possible scale. Hence, a new technical group, with cover name Course 536 and under the command of Lieutenant Colonel Jan Maďarka, was dispatched to Yemen with the task of maintaining aircraft, tanks, and self-propelled guns in working order. Their additional task was 'to try to persuade' the Yemenis to finally provide some men for the contracted military training in order to become self-sufficient at least in attending the delivered armament. The team was composed of three aircraft technicians, a tank technician, and one interpreter who arrived in Yemen successively on 17 February and 7 April 1959. While Lieutenant Colonel Maďarka was in the first echelon, the interpreter arrived later which meant that cooperation with Yemenis was completely minimal until 13 April. In the meantime, at least the repeated conservation of C-11s, Z-126s, and B-33s was carried out during March and April.[22]

Meanwhile, Moscow deployed its first military advisors to Yemen. A team of Soviet tank instructors arrived in Yemen in November 1958. At first, they checked the mountain roads in order to move the T-34/85 tanks and SU-100 self-propelled guns from Hudaydah to Sana'a to begin the training of Yemeni crews in the latter city. The Soviets requested some 60 students and informed Yemeni officials they had one month to find suitable candidates. Otherwise, the Soviet military team would return home. The initial movement of three self-propelled guns commenced on 18 January 1959 and took around 12 days. Another road march from Hudaydah arrived in Sana'a on 22 February 1959 and comprised three tanks and two mobile workshops on Praga V3S chassis with hooked up

One of 100 BTR-40 armoured cars delivered to the Imamate of Yemen by the Soviets in 1956 or 1957. This example is seen after its capture by Royalist insurgents, in the Sa'ada area in November 1962. (Author's collection)

EC 15 kVA power generating sets, all with Yemeni drivers behind the steering wheels. Around the same time, the Soviets trained one radio operator and a small group of engineers in the use of delivered land mines. Taking Soviet threats seriously, the Yemenis made ready the required number of trainees within a given period of time.[23]

However, when the Soviet advisors found out the circumstances under which the actual training was to take place, they declined to instruct Yemenis on the ground of lack of technicians and interpreters. Upon urgent pleas from the commander of the Royal Guard, Colonel Abdullah al-Sallal, recently arriving Czechoslovak tank technician Major Oldřich Císař started the training on T-34/85 for 12 officers of the Crown Prince's Regiment at Sana'a on 18 April 1959. Their instruction was taking place extremely slowly and with great difficulty due to the lack of proper education of the prospective Yemeni tank officers and the language barrier because Czechoslovak interpreter Fiedler was not fluent in technical terminology. At that time, except for five tanks at Sana'a and Taiz, all other T-34/85s were stored at Hudaydah and Bajil. According to the report of Soviet advisors, most of them were in very poor technical condition.[24]

On 25 May, the whole Czechoslovak military group was flown to Hudaydah in order to conserve armoured vehicles stored at this place. After finishing the work, the Czechoslovaks left the area in one Praga V3S mobile workshop with the communication trailer in tow. Upon request from Yemeni officials, they travelled to Salif to check the technical condition of one unserviceable vehicle and repair it. As soon as they appeared there, it was found out that the vehicle in question was a Soviet PAR-3B truck-mounted non-directional radio beacon. However, without spare parts, Czechoslovak technicians could do nothing to bring the truck into working order. Thus, they moved to Bajil and they took the second Praga V3S mobile workshop with the communication trailer there. With two trucks and two trailers, the Czechoslovak team returned to Sana'a between 8 and 9 June 1959.[25]

EGYPTIAN MILITARY INSTRUCTORS

When the Czechoslovaks came back to Sana'a airfield, they found the Egyptian aviation advisory team of three pilots and some 10 technicians there. The Egyptians acted here as though at home and behaved arrogantly towards the Czechoslovak technicians who were requested to do menial works at the airfield. During May and early June 1959, a larger number of Egyptian military instructors, upon the invitation from Muhammad al-Badr, was dispatched to Yemen with the orders to train Yemeni infantry and artillery troops (the Soviets were to provide instruction for the remaining branches of Yemeni land forces while Czechoslovak advisors would train air force personnel). However, the last Egyptian advisory group was composed of aviation and tank instructors. While the latter took over the training of tank specialisation from Major Císař promptly, the former were preparing themselves to teach Yemeni pilots at Sana'a airfield.

The Egyptian technicians readied C-11 training aircraft and Egyptian pilots then underwent a couple of familiarisation flights with them. After a couple of sorties, the pilots complained about the airfield's high altitude above sea level and the low performance of the powerplants. Thus, the flying with C-11s was ceased. Instead, the Egyptians asked the Czechoslovak technicians to prepare several Z-126 Trenérs for flying operations. With the assistance of the Egyptian technicians, the Czechoslovaks duly did what they were asked for. Although Lieutenant Colonel Mad'arka suggested to the commander of the Egyptian aviation advisory team that they complete technical training on the Z-126, the proposal was ignored, and the Egyptian pilots continued flying with Czechoslovak airplanes around the airfield.

Some 10 days later, an Egyptian lieutenant colonel showed up at Sana'a and sent his adjutant to Lieutenant Colonel Mad'arka with the question of whether Egyptian technicians had passed exams for operating the Z-126 and warned that it would be Czechoslovak responsibility if anything bad were to happen. The Czechoslovak commander answered tersely, 'we did not invite you to Yemen' and stated that the Czechoslovaks were not responsible for the work of Egyptian service members. Nevertheless, he expressed his readiness to properly train the Egyptian technicians in the operation and maintenance of Z-126 aircraft. The offer was accepted and the training lasting one week duly took place. After that, Egyptian and Yemeni officials were informed by Lieutenant Colonel Mad'arka that Czechoslovak technicians would not work on C-11 and Z-126 trainers anymore.

Yemeni Colonel al-Sallal continually insisted that Lieutenant Colonel Mad'arka cooperate with the Egyptians closely. These requests were motivated by doubts about the competence of Egyptian military advisors. However, for Czechoslovak technicians it would mean menial works for them in repairing what the Egyptians broke down and cleaning up their mess. Yemeni officials started to realise that the technical expertise of the instructors was not on the level they originally expected. Mistrust arose after the

Egyptians damaged two Il-14 transport aircraft in a short period of time which was coupled with frequent unserviceability of aircraft and the ground support equipment they maintained. Therefore, the Yemenis wanted the Czechoslovak personnel to discreetly check the work of the Egyptians. In August, the Czechoslovak team carried out new conservation of all the automobiles at Sana'a airfield, all B-33 ground attack airplanes, and the Z-126s which were not operated by the Egyptians.

On 13 June 1959, shortly after the arrival of Egyptian instructors in Yemen, Lieutenant Colonel Maďarka sent a report to Prague with a request for withdrawal of the Czechoslovak technical team back to Czechoslovakia as the presence of its members was not needed anymore. Colonel Foršt was subsequently sent to Yemen in order to discuss this matter with Yemeni officials who agreed with the premature return of the Czechoslovak technicians. Thus, the group of Lieutenant Colonel Maďarka ended its activities at Sana'a airfield on 28 August 1959 and was flown back to Czechoslovakia from Taiz on 7 September.[26]

CZECHOSLOVAK FACT-FINDING MISSION

The assistance provided by Czechoslovakia for the Yemeni armed forces had bordered on fiasco so far. However, there was a more pressing issue in Prague – the almost complete failure of Yemenis to pay for weapons and military advisors properly. Despite repeated urgings that included negotiations with crown prince Muhammad al-Badr, Yemen paid only one instalment to the value of 5.040 million CSK with great delay, the Soviet share of which was 3.629 million CSK. Upon such unsatisfactory development, the Politburo ÚV KSČ decided in the resolution of 24 March 1959 that any future deliveries of armament and provision of military assistance for Yemen would be possible only on the condition of advance payment in freely convertible currency.[27]

In December 1959, the Czechoslovak government informed Moscow in an aide-mémoire that it was ready to cooperate with the Soviet Union on providing additional military assistance for Yemen and on finding a solution regarding the payment conditions of the agreement from 11 July 1956. The Soviets responded on 1 February 1960. According to their opinion, it would be 'useful' to postpone this matter and solve it later, with respect to the situation in Yemen. The Yemenis made themselves known in late September 1960. The Czechoslovak Ministry of Foreign Affairs received a diplomatic note in which the Yemenis requested the provision of four instructors for flying training on aircraft delivered from Czechoslovakia three years earlier. Contrary to the previous resolution of the Politburo ÚV KSČ from 24 March 1959, political aspects prevailed, and Prague decided to send a military team to Yemen with the task of ascertaining the actual technical condition of the aircraft.[28]

The Czechoslovak group was led by Colonel Jaroslav Foršt and its further members were Colonel Mikuláš Šinglovič,

Lieutenant Colonel Jan Maďarka and the interpreter Josef Muzikář. They flew from Prague on 27 March 1961. Just one day earlier, two young Yemeni officers made an attempt upon Imam Ahmad bin Yahya's life during his visit to Hudaydah hospital. Although he survived, he was left gravely crippled. Some 40 military servicemen were immediately taken into custody. Thus, the Czechoslovak officials appeared in the Mutawakkilite Kingdom right in the middle of very tumultuous circumstances. However, they were able to find out swiftly why the Yemenis needed Czechoslovak instructor pilots again. When the Imam returned home from recent medical treatment in Italy, he decided to expel almost all Egyptian military specialists during late 1959. Therefore, only one advisor remained at Sana'a airfield – the physical training instructor.

In the meantime, most of the armament delivered to Yemen to date was concentrated at Sana'a and Soviet military experts had trained Yemeni soldiers in the use of tanks, infantry, and artillery weapons. The basics of tactics and maintenance of the armament were taught as well. Moreover, Moscow delivered new PAR-3B non-directional radio beacons. At that time, some 20 Soviet military advisors were present at Sana'a. They were complemented by two crews of Il-14s (Moscow delivered two aircraft of this type that had been manufactured in Czechoslovakia), one crew for an Mi-4

Imam Ahmed Yahya, seen in the late 1950s. (Author's collection)

Imam's palace in Ta'iz during the 1950s. (Author's collection)

Army trucks underway on the streets of Ta'iz during a parade in 1952. (Author's collection)

The building of the Ministry of Foreign Affairs in Ta'iz in 1952. (Author's collection)

Although three C-11 trainers (manufactured in 1954) were in comparatively better condition, they were in need of an overhaul. On the other hand, although four Z-126 Trenérs (airframes of all Zlins were produced in 1957 with engines manufactured in 1955), previously used by the Egyptians, had been standing in the open air for almost two years, their engines were started up without problems. Nevertheless, their technical condition was not optimal, and the aircraft required overhaul too. The remaining six Zlins were stored in a partially disassembled state in the former farm. Therefore, they were generally in a good state and, after a maintenance check, could be used for the potential training of Yemeni pilots without problems. Moreover, it was found that a large part of the ground support equipment (fuel trucks, tractors, power generating set) had been almost unused from the moment the last Czechoslovak advisor left Yemen in August 1959.

Czechoslovak officers wanted to discuss their findings, including possible Czechoslovak involvement in the basic training of some 10–15 Yemeni pilots on overhauled Z-126s and 16–20 aircraft technicians, directly with al-Badr. However, the crown prince was very busy during these days and thus a summarising aide-mémoire was sent to him on 19 April

helicopter, and 14 sailors who were deployed at Hudaydah. The commander of the Soviet advisor group was Colonel Radionov.

Yemeni state institutions were paralysed after the plot to assassinate the Imam. Thus, the Czechoslovak military team could work at Sana'a airfield only after two urgings from crown prince al-Badr. Czechoslovak officers began their work on 10 April with the inspection of 24 B-33 and CB-33 aircraft manufactured in 1954. All 'Kombajns' were unairworthy and in need of an engine- and airframe overhaul in Czechoslovakia because no facilities for such a task were available locally. Czechoslovak aircraft repair plants ceased to carry out higher levels of maintenance on this type in 1956: moreover, stocks of spare parts were depleted and the transport of the aircraft back to Czechoslovakia would be uneconomical. Not surprisingly, it was proposed to scrap all B-33s and CB-33s.

instead. In the meantime, Yemeni pilot cadets, whose training was started by the Egyptians, were relegated to paratrooper training after the Egyptian advisors were expelled from Yemen. They conducted their first parachute jumps from an Il-14 at the time of the Czechoslovak officers' stay in the Mutawakkilite Kingdom. Thereafter, they were sent back to Sana'a airfield to anticipate the renewal of the pilot training. The members of the Czechoslovak fact-finding mission departed Yemen on 27 April 1961.[29]

YEMENI CIVIL WAR
Although the Ministry of National Defence approved the sending of Czechoslovak instructors to train Yemeni pilots and maintenance personnel using Z-126s in June 1961, the Ministry of Foreign Trade stopped the whole affair because of the continuing Yemeni inability

Muhammad al-Badr seen in September 1962, only days before the coup that resulted in his deposing and exile in Saudi Arabia. (Author's collection)

The Dar al-Bashair royal palace in Sana'a, seen after being shelled during the coup of 26 September 1962. (Author's collection)

President Sallal, together with supporting troops (armed with PPSh-41 sub machine guns) and tribesmen, in Sana'a in October 1962. (Author's collection)

to pay for armament delivered within the frame of the agreement from 11 July 1956.[30]

However, the Yemeni ruling dynasty had more pressing issues to solve than to check Prague's payment schedule. Imam Ahmad bin Yahya died in his sleep on 19 September 1962 and his son, crown prince Muhammad al-Badr, was proclaimed Imam the next day. In the meantime, the unpopularity of the Yemeni government reached such proportions that Colonel Abdullah al-Sallal, whom al-Badr had appointed the commander of the Royal Guard, staged a successful coup, and declared himself president of the Yemen Arab Republic on 26 September. During the next day, Radio Sana'a announced that the new Imam had been killed and the revolution won in the country. In fact, al-Badr managed to escape to the Saudi Arabian border where he rallied popular support from northern Shia tribes to retake power. Therefore, the events escalated very swiftly into a full-scale civil war. With covert support from Great Britain, financed by the Kingdom of Saudi Arabia, Royalist forces obtained military aid: simultaneously, Republicans were supported by an Egyptian military intervention, including dozens of thousands of troops, supported by aircraft and heavy weapons of Soviet and Czechoslovak origin. Moscow threw its former friend al-Badr overboard and Prague followed the suit.

On 17 November 1962, during the returning flight from the Soviet Union, the government delegation of the Yemen Arab Republic arrived in Prague. Yemeni officials requested the delivery of 20 Yak-11 training aircraft, five Mi-4 helicopters, infantry weapons, motorcycles, trucks, radio stations, additional military equipment, and foodstuffs. The issue of payment was not discussed: due to their own critical economic situation the Yemenis expected the delivery to be free of charge. At the same time, they rejected taking over the financial obligations of the former Mutawakkilite Kingdom. As in the past, political aspects precluded the adoption of a 'negative attitude' towards Yemeni requests. Hence, the Presidium ÚV KSČ authorised the dispatch of a military mission to the Yemen Arab Republic in order to ascertain the condition of the Czechoslovak

armaments delivered previously and to discuss potential new supplies of weapons.[31]

As of early 1963, Egyptian forces operating in Yemen numbered some 44,000 soldiers, supported by one tank battalion of T-34/85 tanks and 14 T-54 tanks of the United Arab Republic Army. Moreover, Moscow delivered an additional 56 T-34/85 tanks for the Yemeni military. The contingent of the United Arab Republic Air Force operated from airfields at the newly constructed Sana'a airfield 12km (seven miles) outside the city and the old Sana'a. Its complement included 10 Il-14 transports, 28 Yak-11 trainers used for ground attack duties, seven Mi-4 helicopters, and nine Il-28 bombers.

In an operation completely under Soviet control, an air bridge between Sana'a and Cairo was established using An-12 transport aircraft, more than 30 of these were deployed at Almazza air base near the Egyptian capital: three to six An-12s flew between Egypt and Yemen every day. The main effort was supplemented by transport flights undertaken by Egyptian-crewed Il-14 aircraft. According to the opinions of Soviet advisors deployed in Yemen, the

An SU-100 self-propelled anti-tank gun that fired at the Dir al-Bashir palace during the coup of 26 September 1962. (Author's collection)

morale of Egyptian ground troops and the standard of their combat operations control was low.

The Soviet military experts, reportedly numbering around 400 personnel, worked at Sana'a, Hudaydah, and Taiz. They were tasked with maintenance and repair of damaged armament and training of Yemeni technicians in these activities. All newly delivered maintenance equipment and spare parts were concentrated in Soviet advisory teams in order to prevent their destruction, damage, or loss in Yemeni hands. The Soviet military group was commanded by Colonel Kuzovatkin.[32]

MILITARY ASSISTANCE FOR THE YEMEN ARAB REPUBLIC

The new Czechoslovak mission, led again by Colonel Foršt, arrived in the Yemen Arab Republic on 26 January 1963. Czechoslovak officers could observe that weapons delivered from Czechoslovakia are 'fully employed and serve in the fight against foreign intervention forces'. This was, however, not true for the B-33 ground attack aircraft that were in totally unusable condition. Superficial inspection of B-33 and Z-126 airplanes at Sana'a airfield was undertaken, together with the visit of military warehouses at Sana'a. The issue of spare parts for tanks and artillery armament was discussed with resident Soviet experts. It was confirmed that it was no longer possible to bring the 'Kombajns' into airworthy condition while Z-126s could be used for the pilot training, providing that spare parts for them could be delivered and thorough inspection performed. Most of the spare parts for T-34/85 tanks had already been used up. Some important spare parts were depleted in the case of M1942 and vz. 43 guns as well. Czechoslovak officials returned to Prague on 14 February 1963.

One of the most important outcomes for Prague was the fact that Abdullah al-Sallal decided to take over old debts from the times of the former Mutawakkilite Kingdom. On 4 June 1963, the Presidium ÚV KSČ decided to forgive 2.9 million CSK for delivered but unusable B-33 airplanes and to reschedule the payment of instalments into the years 1968 to 1972. At the same time, it was approved to deliver spare parts for all Yemeni Zlins and to carry out their repair so they would be airworthy again, providing that the activities of Czechoslovak technicians would be paid in cash. The reason for this was that Yemeni officials planned to use these airplanes for basic flying training of their pilots with the assistance of Egyptian instructors

from September 1963. However, this undertaking failed too because Yemeni officials did not respond to the proposals of the HTS.[33]

Therefore, another round of discussions related to military assistance for Yemen took place during the visit of the delegation led by Abdullah al-Sallal in Czechoslovakia from 31 March to 4 April 1964. The Yemeni president presented a large set of requirements in the economic, medical, and military sphere which, amongst other points, included 'the delivery of any kind of weapons'. During the negotiations with the Czechoslovak Minister of National Defence Army General Bohumír Lomský on 31 March, his Yemeni counterpart Hasan el Dafei informed him that the delivery of spare parts for Z-126 trainers was no longer necessary because the airplanes were in dilapidated condition without the possibility of making them airworthy again. Prague decided to comply at least partially with Yemeni wishes and gifted mostly unsaleable armament consisting of 3,000 vz. 41 S sub machine guns, 18 vz. 52 anti-tank guns, 12 vz. 43 mortars with related ammunition, several hundreds of aircraft bombs, and 20 tents. The donated arms to the overall value of 7.224 million CSK (listed in Table 14) were handed over to the Soviets, who organised their further transport, at Čierná nad Tisou on 20 and 21 July. The cargo was delivered to Hudaydah harbour on the board of the Soviet merchant ship *Daryal* on 10 September 1964.[34]

ARTILLERY INSTRUCTORS

Together with guns and mortars, two Czechoslovak instructors and one interpreter (Milan Fiedler) were dispatched to Yemen. While Major Josef Hofman (the school battalion commander at the Higher Artillery Training School [*Vyšší dělostřelecké učiliště*]) was tasked to train Yemeni artillery crews, Major Ladislav Košík (the production chief at the Military Repair Plant Moldava nad Bodvou [*Vojenský opravárenský závod Moldava nad Bodvou*]) was to instruct local personnel in the maintenance and repairs of delivered artillery weapons.

The arms and ammunition were unloaded from the Soviet ship under the supervision of Czechoslovak instructors. Despite repeated warnings, local porters broke all possible safety measures related to ammunition handling and storage. Fortunately, no accident happened. Four days after the unloading, Egyptian troops showed up at the port and, upon permission from the Yemeni ministry of defence, seized all aircraft bombs that were subsequently transported to Hudaydah airfield as the Yemeni military still did not have a functional air arm.[36]

The remaining materiel was moved to Sana'a using trucks of the Yemeni Army. Although Yemeni officials wanted to present the newly delivered arms at the military parade commemorating the second anniversary of the revolution on 26 September 1964 in the capital, they were not able to provide suitable vehicles for the task at hand. After numerous urgings, just seven trucks were given for Czechoslovak disposal but only five of them could tow the guns.

Table 14: Czechoslovak arms export to Yemen, 1960–1974[35]

Type	Number of examples	Year of delivery	Note
vz. 41 S, 7.62mm sub machine gun	3,000	1964	Czechoslovak designation of Soviet PPSh-41, from the stocks of the Czechoslovak People's Army
vz. 52, 7.62mm rifle	6	1960	from the stocks of the Czechoslovak People's Army
7.62mm round	2,159,160	1964	for vz. 41 S, from the stocks of the Czechoslovak People's Army
vz. 52, 7.62mm round	1,800	1960	from the stocks of the Czechoslovak People's Army
vz. 52, 85mm anti-tank gun	18	1964	from the stocks of the Czechoslovak People's Army
vz. 43, 160mm mortar	12	1964	the Czechoslovak licence of Soviet M1943 (MT-13), from the stocks of the Czechoslovak People's Army
85-JO-TK 44, K 52, PLK 39, 85mm fragmentation round	3,600	1964	from the stocks of the Czechoslovak People's Army
85-JPSv-TK 44, K 52, PLK 39, 85mm armour-piercing round	2,160	1964	from the stocks of the Czechoslovak People's Army
160-EOF-M 43, 160mm high explosive round	720	1964	from the stocks of the Czechoslovak People's Army
artillery optical and measuring equipment	-	1964	from the stocks of the Czechoslovak People's Army
PTAB-2,5, anti-tank shaped charge bomblet	1,008	1964	from the stocks of the Czechoslovak People's Army
ZAB-2,5, incendiary bomblet	1,000	1964	from the stocks of the Czechoslovak People's Army
AO-2,5, fragmentation bomblet	800	1964	from the stocks of the Czechoslovak People's Army
RBK-250, submunition container	100	1964	from the stocks of the Czechoslovak People's Army
FAB-70, general purpose bomb	500	1964	from the stocks of the Czechoslovak People's Army
OFAB-100M, high explosive bomb	300	1964	from the stocks of the Czechoslovak People's Army
FAB-250, general purpose bomb	400	1964	from the stocks of the Czechoslovak People's Army
tent for 10 men	20	1964	from the stocks of the Czechoslovak People's Army
various pistols	10	1968	from the stocks of the HTS
vz. 52/57, 7.62mm rifle	5	1968	
vz. 98 N, 7.92mm rifle	1,000	1968	Czechoslovak designation of German Karabiner 98k, from the stocks of the HTS
vz. 58, 7.62mm assault rifle	5	1968	
vz. 47, 7.92mm round	2,776,900	1968	
winter combat clothing and personal equipment	7,000	1968	from the stocks of the Czechoslovak People's Army

Yemeni government officials. The vz. 43 mortars, despite their obsolescence, became one of the highlights of the show.

Czechoslovak instructors met the chief of Yemeni artillery troops on 27 September and discussed with him their future activities in the Yemen Arab Republic. Yemeni officers informed them that there would be basically no work for Major Košík because all artillery technicians were currently trained by the group of 20 Soviet advisors in the repair workshop established by the Soviets. Thus, Major Košík handed over to the Soviet experts the spare parts, accessories, tools, and jigs for maintenance of vz. 52 and vz. 43. Moreover, he carried out short training of Soviet technicians related to the maintenance and design differences of the newly delivered weapons. This knowledge was to be later passed on to the Yemeni trainees. With no other work to do, the Czechoslovak officer left Yemen on 8 October and after the stopovers at Asmara and Cairo, he returned to Prague on 14 October 1964 shortly after midnight.

Meanwhile, beginning on 29 September, Major Hofman led the training of 18 Yemeni lieutenants, mostly graduates of the Egyptian military school. The knowledge of artillery expertise on the part of the trainees was absolutely minimal or completely non-existent. Major Josef Hofman started the undertaking with the teaching of general topics so the young officers could serve as firing platoon commanders. The instruction on the operation of the vz. 52 anti-tank gun was provided during October and was followed by analogous training related to the vz. 43 mortar in

The actual movement of three vz. 52 guns, two vz. 43 mortars, a portion of the ammunition, and all optical equipment took place only on 25 September. Due to the arduous terrain, the convoy arrived in Sana'a at night. During the next day, the guns and mortars were presented at the parade and caught the attention of attending November. In the beginning, Major Hofman was assisted by Major Košík who carried out basic instruction in design, maintenance, and technical inspection of delivered guns and mortars. All lectures were prepared in written form and translated into Arabic. The training course culminated with a short tactical exercise coupled with live

Combatants of one of local militias that supported the coup against the Imam in September 1962. (Author's collection)

Army vehicles – including two BTR-40s (centre), a single BTR-152 armoured personnel carrier (left) and two SU-100 self-propelled assault guns (right rear) – operated by Republicans in Ma'rib, during the coup of September 1962. (Author's collection)

from 26 May 1964, nothing materialised due to the Yemeni inability to select suitable candidates and to find the money for their travel to and from Czechoslovakia.[38]

AL-SALLAL'S DEMISE

In the meantime, the Yemeni Civil War raged on. Despite the large-scale deployment of Egyptian troops, the conflict developed into a stalemate by the mid-1960s. The new situation had been created after the June 1967 Arab-Israeli War in which Egypt suffered a major defeat. Hence, the further stay of Egyptian military units in the Yemen Arab Republic became financially unendurable for Cairo. During the Arab League summit, lasting from 29 August to 1 September at Khartoum, Egyptian leader Gamal Abdel Nasser and King Faisal of Saudi Arabia reached an agreement that assumed the withdrawal of Egyptian troops from Yemen and the cessation of Saudi Arabia's military assistance to the Yemeni monarchist forces.

Nor did the agreement between Nasser and Faisal lead to a solution to the Yemeni problem, which was further complicated by the fact that Yemeni President al-Sallal was critical of the deal. Against this background, al-Sallal was ousted in a bloodless coup led by Abdul Rahman al-Iryani on 5 November 1967 and exiled to Egypt. Cairo honoured the commitment from Khartoum and withdrew its troops by the end of November. After their withdrawal, however, the monarchist forces resumed fighting and, with the continued support of Saudi Arabia, attempted to encircle and

firing from vz. 52 guns. The successful exercise was attended by Vice President Hassan al-Amri, top-ranking officials from the Yemeni ministry of defence and general staff, and Egypt's senior officers commanding Egyptian military forces deployed to the Yemen Arab Republic. Moreover, the public was informed about the event by Sana'a Radio during the same day.[37]

Even though the Presidium ÚV KSČ granted its approval for the follow-on one-year training of up to 20 Yemenis in an artillery-technical course for vz. 52 guns and vz. 43 mortars in the resolution

conquer the capital city of Sana'a. Meanwhile, the Republican forces managed to defend the city mainly thanks to supplies of military hardware from the Soviet Union. In this critical situation, the government of the Yemeni Arab Republic turned to Czechoslovakia (and other communist and Arab countries) with a request for urgent assistance.

On 28 December 1967, the Yemeni *chargé d'affaires* presented a request for donations in the form of 30,000 sub machine guns with 100,000 magazines, 30,000 complete winter uniforms, blankets for

A Soviet-supplied T-34/85 medium tank of the Republicans, outside the walls of Sana'a in September 1962. (Author's collection)

SU-100s, T-34/85 (centre background) and a jeep of the Yemeni Army seen after the coup of 26 September 1962. (Author's collection)

(1969) of postponed credits for the weapons delivered in the frame of the agreement from 11 July 1956. Moreover, the training of foreign aircrews was always undertaken under very lucrative conditions for Czechoslovakia, thus the instruction of Yemeni transport pilots was rejected as well. Finally, the Yemenis requested the delivery of MiG-17 fighter aircraft together with anti-aircraft machine guns and cannons. Instead, Czechoslovakia offered battle dress uniforms and obsolete small arms such as vz. 52 rifles, Sa 23 and Sa 25 sub machine guns, vz. 26 light machine guns, vz. 37 heavy machine guns, vz. 27 pistols or P-27 bazookas. However, no deal materialised.[40]

The fighting for the Yemeni capital became the turning point of the war. The Republican units succeeded in retaining the control of the city and by February 1968, lifted the siege. Clashes continued in parallel with peace talks until December 1970, when a ceasefire came into effect. Meanwhile, in May 1970, the Prime Minister of Yemen asked his Czechoslovak counterpart for the provision of military-economic assistance. Prague indicated that it could not comply with Yemeni wishes.[41]

30,000 soldiers, food, and canned goods. However, the Czechoslovak Ministry of National Defence had no surplus machine guns. Hence, in the resolution from 25 January 1968, the Presidium ÚV KSČ approved the donation of 7,000 pieces of complete winter combat clothing to the value of 5,250,000 CSK. The uniforms, together with other kinds of military materiel, were sent to the Yemen Arab Republic during 1968 (see Table 14).[39]

LAST STAGES OF THE INTERNAL CONFLICT

The civil war in the Yemen Arab Republic was still on and Sana'a was in constant need of military assistance. Therefore, in 1969, Yemeni representatives requested Czechoslovakia for the training of transport and fighter pilots. The training on MiG-17s was denied immediately because of the low number of these aircraft in the Czechoslovak Air Force inventory. Besides, Czechoslovak officials were very well aware of continuous Yemeni financial difficulties: Sana'a failed to pay both the first (1968) and the second instalment

PERIOD OF STAGNATION

In the meantime, independent South Yemen, which was established on 30 November 1967, became Moscow's favourite in the south of the Arabian Peninsula. In 1970, the country was transformed into the Marxist socialist republic and renamed as the People's Democratic Republic of Yemen. Prague followed in the Soviet steps and political relations between Czechoslovakia and the Yemen Arab Republic (North Yemen) stagnated. This development was further fuelled by the neutral or slightly pro-Western political orientation of the then North Yemeni leadership. Hence, the official talks between the representatives of both countries were often limited only to the issue of old debts for the arms delivered at the times of the Mutawakkilite Kingdom.[42]

In 1979, North Yemeni officials requested the delivery of 50 T-55 tanks from Czechoslovak licence production. However, since Sana'a still did nothing to pay the old debts, the request was flatly rejected. North Yemeni representatives were greatly dissatisfied with Prague's stance and, instead, bought an identical number of T-55 tanks

A column of T-34/85s on the streets of Sana'a during the siege of late 1967. (Author's collection)

during the same year in Poland which also produced these vehicles under licence.[43]

The matter of financial claims related to the arms agreement from 11 July 1956, was seemingly solved on 6 November 1980 when representatives of the HTS and North Yemeni government signed The Protocol on the Method of Settlement of the Claim. As of 31 October 1980, the North Yemeni debt was 4,581,512 GBP. Prague accepted North Yemeni wishes and waived the amount of interest to the value of 944,573 GBP. Simultaneously, the amount of the debt was reduced by 500,000 GBP. The remaining value was frozen for the next five years, and the debt was to be repaid in the subsequent years. The adoption of the Yemeni proposal meant that Czechoslovakia would receive 3,136,939 GBP in 15 annual instalments, of which 24 percent (752,865 GBP) would be retained and the remaining 76 percent would be remitted to Moscow, which accepted this scheme. Czechoslovak officials had no other choice than to comment bitterly that 'achieving a more favourable solution

in the current political and economic situation of the Yemen Arab Republic is not realistic'.[44]

Another opportunity for Prague to supply military hardware to North Yemen came in April 1985, when Minister of Foreign Affairs Bohuslav Chňoupek made an official visit to the Yemen Arab Republic. During negotiations, President Ali Abdullah Saleh showed extraordinary interest in importing the Czechoslovak armament. Due to the continued difficult financial situation, North Yemeni officials requested a government loan of 4 to 5 million USD, with a maturity of six to seven years. The leadership of the Yemen Arab Republic anticipated that the country's solvency would improve within two to three years when it was expected that the oil from recently discovered deposits could be exported.[45]

THE CONTRACT THAT NEVER MATERIALISED

Correspondingly, North Yemenis presented an extensive list of demanded armament which included, among other items, 200 T-55 and 32 T-72 tanks, three squadrons of L-39 Albatros jet trainers, 300 BTR-60 armoured personnel carriers, 20 S-125 Pechora (ASCC/ NATO reporting name 'SA-3 Goa') batteries, 200 BMP-1 or BMP-2 infantry fighting vehicles, 50 D-30 howitzers or 100 BM-21 multiple rocket launchers. After a swift examination, the HTS officials found out that the actual value of requested weapons was not the 4 or 5 million USD anticipated by Yemenis, but almost 500 million USD! In any event, Czechoslovakia was able to deliver only 36 L-39 aircraft, infantry fighting vehicles, ammunition, and pistols. While the production of T-55 tanks had already ceased, T-72s could not be delivered either since Moscow did not grant its approval for supplies of these tanks to North Yemen. The remaining weapons were not produced in Czechoslovakia at all. Anyway, the HTS had the opportunity to deliver armament to a value of 120 to 150 million USD.

In order to be sure that no diplomatic collision would occur, Prague asked the Soviet Union and the People's Democratic Republic of Yemen for an opinion on the possible arms trade. Both states expressed their agreement with Prague's business. At the same time, the Soviets alerted Czechoslovak representatives that they provided armament for the North Yemeni military on a credit basis too, but due to the economic difficulties of the Yemen Arab Republic, the instalments were then usually forgiven. Being aware of constant North Yemeni financial problems, the HTS representative provided an offer for credit worth 50 to 60 million USD to the officials of the General Staff during negotiations at Sana'a in July 1985.[46]

The North Yemenis responded to the Czechoslovak offer almost a year later, during a meeting of representatives of both Foreign Ministries on 30 July 1986. Deputy Minister of Foreign Affairs A M al-Iryani complained that prices were very high and the conditions of payment completely unacceptable (credit payable

An SPK-5 crane (background) with an armoured recovery vehicle on chassis of the T-34 medium tank, underway in Sana'a in the early 1970s. (Author's collection)

in 5 years, 10 percent down payment, and 8 percent interest rate). Simultaneously, he confirmed interest in discussing these matters further. However, al-Iryani was to learn very early, to his own displeasure, the specifics of the communist command economy. Deputy Minister of Foreign Trade František Langer informed him in a letter that credit and materiel funds of the Czechoslovak 8th five-year plan (1986–1990) were completely exhausted in the meantime. Nevertheless, if North Yemen was still interested, Czechoslovakia could provide some types of infantry weapons, ammunition, vehicles, and even BVP-1 infantry fighting vehicles (after the consent from the Soviet Union) but on condition of payment in cash. Otherwise, new credit on the acquisition of arms could be provided only in the next five-year plan beginning 1991.[47]

Apparently, no deliveries of military hardware of any kind materialised. However, Prague still considered Sana'a as one of its prospective clients and wanted to get Soviet approval for the export of licenced T-72 tanks to the Yemen Arab Republic. During negotiations with the Deputy Chairman of the Council of Ministers of the Union of Soviet Socialist Republics Igor Belousov in early April 1989, Czechoslovak officials were delighted to hear that VT-72 armoured recovery vehicles and MT-72 armoured bridge layers could be exported to Egypt and North Yemen from 1989. But Belousov added that 'the supply of T-72 battle tanks to Egypt, [and] the Yemen Arab Republic is currently not recommended'. In any case, the then Czechoslovak leadership had more pressing issues to solve. Communist rule crumbled just a couple of months later under the weight of its own economic mismanagement and the new government in Prague had more useful things to do than to deliver the armour to the insolvent totalitarian states in the Middle East.[48]

4

SOUTH YEMEN (OPERATION 625, COUNTRY 633)

On 30 November 1967, two British protectorates located at the southern end of the Arabian Peninsula – the Federation of South Arabia and the Protectorate of South Arabia – merged to become independent as the People's Republic of Southern Yemen with the Marxist-oriented National Liberation Front (NLF) consolidating its control of the country. Prague and Aden had established official diplomatic relations on 30 May 1968. Despite the political orientation of the NLF, the Czechoslovak communist leadership was initially ready to provide military assistance to its rival – the Front for the Liberation of Occupied South Yemen (FLOSY).

SUPPORTING FLOSY

On 10 December 1963, a state of emergency was declared in the newly created State of Aden (a member of the Federation of South Arabia) when two local insurgent organisations – the NLF and FLOSY – rebelled against British rule. The insurgency in Aden escalated and hastened the end of the British presence in the south of the Arabian Peninsula. However, the two movements were at odds and when not fighting the British, they were busy battling with each other. Furthermore, after some time, unofficial secret talks started between the British and the NLF with the intention to defeat Egypt-supported FLOSY. Optimistic prospects of FLOSY further diminished after the Six-Day War. In August 1967, in order to make up for the losses suffered during the fighting with the Israel Defence Forces, the Egyptian President Nasser recalled his troops deployed to fight insurgents in the civil war raging in the neighbouring Yemen Arab Republic (YAR).

It was against this backdrop that, on 26 October 1967, Mohammed Salim Basindawa, who was responsible for the combat activity of the FLOSY units, arrived in Prague. Informed beforehand by the embassy in Cairo, the Czechoslovak communist leadership was already aware that his task was to obtain 200 pistols and 100 sub machine guns with related ammunition for further fighting because the Egyptians, facing considerable economic problems after the Six-Day War, sharply limited their military assistance to FLOSY. Left with only little option, FLOSY's only hope for survival was the Soviet Bloc. Thus, after visiting Prague, Basindawa's mission then continued to East Germany and the Soviet Union with the same purpose. He was successful at least in Czechoslovakia as the Presidium ÚV KSČ approved the delivery of an increased quantity of arms worth 244,000 CSK on 14 November 1967 (as detailed in Table 15).

On 5 December 1967, the Presidium ÚV KSČ confirmed the independence of the People's Republic of Southern Yemen led by the NLF. Therefore, preferring to act with caution, the Czechoslovak Ministry of Foreign Affairs recommended suspending temporarily the delivery of infantry weapons for FLOSY. Eventually, Czechoslovakia delivered no weapons to the insurgents. On 7 November 1967, when attacking a federal army base, FLOSY suffered such heavy losses that its military forces basically ceased to exist.[1]

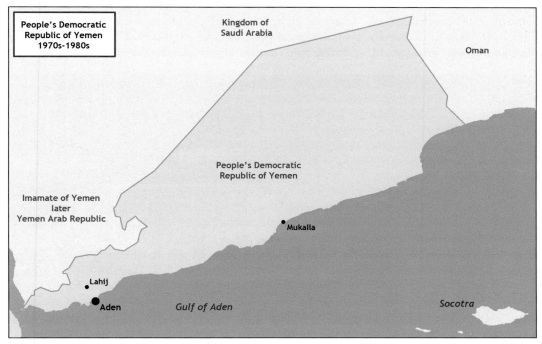

(Map by Tom Cooper)

Table 15: Czechoslovak arms to be delivered to FLOSY (unrealised)[2]

Type	Number of examples	Note
vz. 52, 7.62mm pistol	300	from the stocks of the Czechoslovak People's Army
Sa 23 and Sa 25, 9mm sub machine gun	200	from the stocks of the Czechoslovak People's Army
7.62mm round	60,000	from the stocks of the Czechoslovak People's Army
9mm round	240,000	from the stocks of the Czechoslovak People's Army

ARMAMENT FOR THE PDRY

In June 1969, a hardline Marxist wing of the NLF gained power, and on 1 December 1970 reorganised the country into the People's Democratic Republic of Yemen (PDRY). Under the leadership of Abdul Fattah Ismail, Marxist-Leninist scientific socialism became the official state ideology. The new government introduced a program of nationalisation, central planning, put limits on housing ownership, and implemented collectivisation. The NLF's harsh policies led even the Czechoslovak *chargé d'affaires* in the country to describe the newly emerged situation in the PDRY as 'military communism of minimal food rations'.

Due to its political agenda, it was no surprise that the newly emerged political elite preferred cooperation with the Union of Soviet Socialist Republics and its satellites. While East Germany gifted armament worth 3 million East German marks in 1969 and East German advisors subsequently trained South Yemeni security and intelligence forces, Czechoslovak military assistance had to wait several years longer. During his official visit to Czechoslovakia between 6 and 9 February 1972, South Yemeni Foreign Minister Muhammad Saleh Aulaki discussed, among other matters, potential deliveries of arms and provision of training for South Yemeni troops with the Czechoslovak Minister of National Defence Army General Martin Dzúr. Although no specific agreement was concluded in this matter, Aulaki returned home with a long-term credit worth 5 million USD provided in the frame of signed protocol related to mutual economic cooperation. Czechoslovak officials initially intended to use 40 percent of this sum for deliveries of armament. However, this proposal was not accepted by Aden. In June 1972, a Czechoslovak military delegation led by Deputy Chief of the General Staff of the Czechoslovak People's Army visited the People's Democratic Republic of Yemen.[3]

In the meantime, the governments of the PDRY and the YAR gave refuge and support to opponents of the other. Increasing tension culminated in September 1972 when fighting erupted in the area of Qa'tabah. The conflict was short-lived and led to the Cairo Agreement from 28 October 1972, which set forth a

Prime Minister Ali Nasir Muhammad (standing in the vehicle, in civilian clothes), and his Minister of Defence, Saleh Muslih Qassem, seen while inspecting units participating in a military parade in Aden in the mid-1970s. (Author's collection)

plan to unify the two countries. The PDRY accepted the agreement only in order to immediately stop enemy military actions and to buy a time for political, economic, and military reinforcement that could enable Aden to reach the upper hand in the planned union of the two Yemeni states. Therefore, a South Yemeni delegation of top-level officials hurried to the Soviet Union only a couple of weeks later. Moscow promised to construct a thermal powerplant, hospital and to provide assistance in geological survey, and reconstruction of various facilities. At the same time, the Soviets decided to increase their military assistance to the PDRY armed forces.[4]

Aden was seeking help in Prague as well. On 12 December 1972, the PDRY embassy in Moscow provided a list of topics for negotiations to be held during the planned visit of Ali Nasir Muhammad, South Yemen's prime minister and minister of defence, in Czechoslovakia. Included was a requirement for extensive deliveries of arms and related ammunition such as infantry weapons (7.62mm pistols, SKS carbines, AK-47 assault rifles, RPK machine guns, RG-42 and F-1 hand grenades, RPG-7 anti-tank rocket-propelled grenades), 120mm and 160mm mortars, B-10 recoilless guns, 122mm field guns, 85mm and 100mm anti-tank guns, 37mm and 57mm anti-aircraft guns, 12.7mm and 14.5mm anti-aircraft machine guns (DShK and ZPU-4), mines, T-54/55 tanks, BTR-152 armoured personnel carriers, BRDM-2 armoured scout cars, trucks, buses, medical supplies, clothes for 50,000 troops, L-29 or

Prime Minister Ali Nasir Muhammed attending another military parade in Aden, this time in 1981. He is seen shaking hands with Minister of Defence Saleh Muslih Qassem. (Author's collection)

L-39 training aircraft, spare parts for MiG-17, MiG-17F, and An-24B aircraft, as well as various aircraft bombs, gun ammunition, and S-5M unguided rockets for MiG-17s.[5]

After urging from Aden, a delegation led by Ali Nasir Muhammad and composed of, among others, Ali Ahmed Nasser Antar (the first deputy minister of defence and the commander-in-chief of PDRY armed forces), Major Ahmad Saleh Hagib (military consultant of the prime minister), Major Abdallah Musibili (military attaché) arrived in Czechoslovakia on 1 March and stayed here until 3 March 1973. For discussions related to military deliveries, the Federal Ministry of National Defence (*Federální ministerstvo národní obrany*) established a special committee led by Deputy Chief of the General Staff Major General Vojtěch Srovnal. During negotiations with Antar, Czechoslovak representatives agreed with free of charge delivery of arms worth 54.5 million CSK as listed in Table 16 (the actual cost of the arms was 41,905,000 CSK, further 12,750,000 CSK were transportation costs). At the same time, the South Yemeni request for delivery of L-29 Delfins and training of the People's Democratic Republic of Yemen Air Force (PDRYAF) personnel in the PDRY was refused. In turn, an offer for the training of up to

Table 16: Czechoslovak arms delivered to the People's Democratic Republic of Yemen in 1973[7]

Type	Number of examples	Note
vz. 44/67, 26.5mm signal pistol	200	from the stocks of the Federal Ministry of Interior
26.5mm signal round	10,000	from the stocks of the Federal Ministry of National Defence
vz. 27, 7.65mm pistol	100	from the stocks of the Federal Ministry of National Defence
vz. 52, 7.62mm rifle	3,200	from the stocks of the Federal Ministry of National Defence
vz. 26, 7.92mm light machine gun	200	from the stocks of the HTS
vz. 37, 7.92mm heavy machine gun	100	from the stocks of the Federal Ministry of National Defence
7.65mm pistol round	12,000	from the stocks of the Federal Ministry of National Defence
vz. 52, 7.62mm round	2,500,000	from the stocks of the Federal Ministry of National Defence
vz. 47, 7.92mm round	1,000,000	from the stocks of the Federal Ministry of National Defence
RG-4, hand grenade	5,000	from the stocks of the Federal Ministry of Interior
P-27, light anti-tank weapon	50	from the stocks of the Federal Ministry of National Defence
round for P-27	1,000	from the stocks of the Ministry of National Defence
82mm mortar	34	vz. 52?, from the stocks of the Federal Ministry of Interior
vz. 38, 122mm howitzer	12	the Czechoslovak licence of M1938 (M-30), from the stocks of the Federal Ministry of National Defence
82mm fragmentation mortar round	1,100	from the stocks of the Federal Ministry of Interior
122mm fragmentation round	2,000	from the stocks of the Federal Ministry of National Defence
85-JOF-TK 44, K 52, PLK 39, 85mm high explosive round	13,000	for T-34/85 tank, from the stocks of the Federal Ministry of National Defence
85-JPSv-TK 44, K 52, PLK 39, 85mm armour-piercing round	7,000	for T-34/85 tank, from the stocks of the Federal Ministry of National Defence
OZT, 23mm high explosive incendiary round with tracer	200,000	for NR-23 aircraft cannon (MiG-17), from the stocks of the Federal Ministry of National Defence
OZT, 37mm high explosive incendiary round with tracer	100,000	for N-37 aircraft cannon (MiG-17), from the stocks of the Federal Ministry of National Defence
BZT, 37mm armour-piercing incendiary round with tracer	100,000	for N-37 aircraft cannon (MiG-17), from the stocks of the Federal Ministry of National Defence
ZAB-2,5, incendiary bomblet	2,000	from the stocks of the Federal Ministry of National Defence
OFAB-100M, high explosive bomb	500	from the stocks of the Federal Ministry of National Defence
PP-Mi Šr, anti-personnel shrapnel mine	20,000	from the stocks of the Federal Ministry of National Defence
PT-Mi K, metal anti-tank mine	1,000	from the stocks of the Federal Ministry of National Defence
PP-Mi Ba II, Bakelite anti-tank mine	1,000	from the stocks of the Federal Ministry of National Defence
fuel rubber bag 3,000l	50	from the stocks of the Federal Ministry of National Defence
fuel rubber bag 5,000l	30	from the stocks of the Federal Ministry of National Defence
vacuum bottle 12l	300	from the stocks of the Federal Ministry of National Defence
military blanket	5,000	from the stocks of the Federal Ministry of National Defence
eating utensils	4,000 sets	from the stocks of the Federal Ministry of National Defence
dehydrated potatoes	4,000kg	from the stocks of the Federal Ministry of National Defence

36 PDRYAF specialists in Czechoslovakia was offered. Apparently, this offer was not used due to the lack of South Yemeni personnel suitable for the training in the establishments of the Czechoslovak People's Army.

The provided weapons, generally considered by Prague as obsolete and without possibility to be sold, were taken from long-term storage. The arms were delivered by 17 railway transports to the port of Ploče in southern Yugoslavia and, between 13 and 21 September, loaded on the Czechoslovak cargo ship *Mír* that shipped them to Aden on 16 October 1973. The freight was unloaded here for two days. Despite the obsolescence of the delivered armament, the supply was greatly appreciated personally by Prime Minister Ali Nasir Muhammad.[6]

SOVIET INVOLVEMENT

As of November 1973, the Soviet advisory group deployed to the PDRY was commanded by an officer of the rank of Major General. Soviet military advisors were present at every level of command of the South Yemeni armed forces. More than 100 Soviet military advisors assisted in the training of the PDRY Navy. At the same time, some 200 South Yemeni soldiers were trained in Soviet military schools, their number was increased to 600 in early 1974. Generous military assistance from Moscow (until February 1974, weapons worth 37 million rubles were provided free of charge) resulted in Soviet naval forces gaining access to naval facilities in the People's Democratic Republic of Yemen under an agreement in which the Soviet Navy could deploy up to seven ships in Aden harbour. Soviet vessels were used for the transport of local troops along the coast and to Socotra Island. One of them was BDK-66 (pennant number 344) large landing ship of the Project 1171 class that served for the redeployment of South Yemeni soldiers to the border with Oman in the time of mutual tensions during spring 1974. After landing of small unit organised by Iran on Socotra, Soviet military vessels guarded access to this island as well. Furthermore, the Soviets undertook reconnaissance of the island's coastline and prepared plans for its defence. According to the Soviet naval officers deployed to South Yemen, local troops were very poorly equipped and many times during redeployments did not even have their own food.[8]

The sorry state of the South Yemeni economy meant that in early 1974 payment of civilian credits worth 34 million rubles provided by Moscow to Aden had to be postponed and interest amounts were forgiven completely. When discussing this matter in July 1974, South Yemeni Finance Minister Fadhle Mohsina was literally offering his own shirt to Soviet commercial attaché Kazantsev because, according to Mohsina's words, the 'National Treasury has nothing more'. Despite economic hardship, South Yemeni top-ranking political delegations were warmly welcomed in Moscow and other Warsaw Pact capitals as the political establishment in the PDRY was considered as the sole genuine communist regime in the Arab world.

Thus, another delegation led by the Chairman of the Presidium of the Supreme People's Council Abdul Fattah Ismail was staying in the Soviet Union between 18 and 24 July 1974. When using the usually available passenger aircraft, the South Yemeni delegation would have to make a technical stopover in Cairo. Afraid that the Egyptians could learn about the travel to Moscow, the Soviet Union, upon South Yemeni insistence, provided specially modified Il-18 passenger aircraft with reduced seating capacity but with extended range. Thus, the South Yemeni delegation arrived in Moscow after a nonstop flight from Aden lasting 10 hours. Present was First Deputy Minister of Defence Antar (currently on studies in the Union of Soviet Socialist Republics) and commander of Aden military

Table 17: Czechoslovak arms delivered to the People's Democratic Republic of Yemen within the frame of Contract No. 21-6-27 in 1977[12]

Type	Number of examples	Note
vz. 27, 7.65mm pistol	2,000	from the stocks of the Federal Ministry of National Defence
vz. 52/57, 7.62mm rifle	3,000	including spare parts (30 sets 1:100) from the stocks of the Federal Ministry of National Defence
RPG-7, anti-tank rocket-propelled grenade launcher	200	including spare parts (22 sets 1:9) from the stocks of the Federal Ministry of National Defence
PG-7V, anti-tank rocket-propelled grenade	2,502	from the stocks of the Federal Ministry of National Defence
vz. 43, 160mm mortar	50	including spare parts (10 sets 1:6), from the stocks of the Federal Ministry of National Defence
160-EOF-M 43, 160mm high explosive round	50,000	from the stocks of the Federal Ministry of National Defence
85-JOF-TK 44, K 52, PLK 39, 85mm high explosive round	30,000	for T-34/85 tank, from the stocks of the Federal Ministry of National Defence
85-JPSv-TK 44, K 52, PLK 39, 85mm armour-piercing round	17,502	for T-34/85 tank, from the stocks of the Federal Ministry of National Defence
OTČSv, 23mm high explosive round with tracer	20,016	for NR-23 aircraft cannon (MiG-17), from the stocks of the Federal Ministry of National Defence
OZT, 23mm high explosive incendiary round with tracer	20,016	for NR-23 aircraft cannon (MiG-17), from the stocks of the Federal Ministry of National Defence
BZ, 23mm armour-piercing incendiary round	20,016	for NR-23 aircraft cannon (MiG-17), from the stocks of the Federal Ministry of National Defence
ammunition belt link	60,250	from the stocks of the Federal Ministry of National Defence

school Major Ahmed Salem Obaid as well. However, South Yemeni military officials were not completely satisfied with the outcomes of the negotiations. Moscow agreed with the delivery of infantry armament for the People's Militia but, at the same time, refused to provide the latest weapon systems to the PDRY armed forces so they would not be able to stage offensive operations against South Yemen's neighbours. Soviet instructors were to continue in practical control of the PDRY Air Force and Air Defence Forces while the Soviet Navy was to provide training for personnel of its South Yemeni counterpart. As in the past, in case of need, Soviet military vessels were to protect the coast of the PDRY, including Socotra Island.[9]

WEAPONS FOR FREE AND ON CREDIT

South Yemeni military delegation led by First Deputy Minister of Defence Ali Ahmed Nasser Antar visited Czechoslovakia between 11 and 16 November 1974. During negotiations with the Federal Ministry of National Defence, Antar forwarded a letter for the Czechoslovak Prime Minister Lubomír Štrougal with a request for the delivery of infantry, aviation, artillery, and logistics materiel including tank spare parts. In the next month, Prime Minister Ali Nasir Muhammad sent a further letter to Lubomír Štrougal with a request for granting credit for the acquisition of six L-29 Delfin training aircraft and related training of pilots and ground support personnel. Production of this type had already halted, however, therefore the South Yemeni requirement in this matter was not accepted. After considering the miserable state of the South Yemeni economy and its own delivery possibilities, the Presidium ÚV KSČ approved the provision of credit for the supply of military materiel up to the value of 5.1 million USD (104.6 million CSK) on 31 October 1975.[10]

A corresponding credit agreement with the interest rate of 3 percent per annum between the Czechoslovak and South Yemeni governments was signed in Aden on 30 June 1976. South Yemen was to pay five equal annual instalments, each representing the amount of 1,020,000 USD, within the years 1981 to 1985. Respective deliveries were defined in Contract No. 21-6-27 and were composed of items listed in Table 17. All weapons, ammunition, and spare parts were transported in several large trains totalling some 325 railway cars to the Yugoslav port of Ploče. Two shipments by the Czechoslovak cargo ship *Sitno* were needed to haul the materiel to Aden. The loading on board *Sitno* took place at Ploče in March and April 1977.[11]

Further negotiations related to the deliveries of armament took place in 1977. The party and government delegation led by the Chairman of the Presidium of the Supreme People's Council Abdul Fattah Ismail arrived in Czechoslovakia on 14 April and stayed there for a further four days. As expected by Czechoslovak officials, the South Yemenis placed emphasis on 'one-sided material help from the Czechoslovak side', or in other words – on obtaining the largest amount of civilian and military goods under the best financial conditions possible, ideally free of charge. The military part of negotiations was managed by the deputy director of the HTS of the Federal Ministry of Foreign Trade R Jiřík and Captain Salah Al Eisi. The Yemenis requested credit worth 10 million USD and handed over the extensive list of armaments including 130mm guns, 23mm anti-aircraft guns, 14.5mm anti-aircraft machine guns, 82mm recoilless guns, L-29 Delfin training aircraft, and 9K32 Strela-2 (ASCC/NATO reporting name 'SA-7 Grail') man-portable air-defence systems.

At the same time, they asked for free of charge delivery of weapons and equipment for the People's Militia led by Hussain Qumatah. These paramilitary units were trained by Cuban advisors (as of July 1974, some 100 Cuban troops provided training for South Yemeni militiamen and insurgents from different Marxist paramilitary organisations based in the PDRY) and in addition to their role as one of the pillars of the South Yemeni communist regime served as a means for reducing local unemployment. While employed members of the People's Militia were to receive no pay for their service, their unemployed fellow members were to obtain food and clothes worth minimum salary. During the negotiations, Czechoslovak representatives promised to deliver materiel worth 2 million CSK. However, upon South Yemeni insistence, this assistance was further increased to an overall value of 4 million CSK (delivered arms and equipment are listed in Table 18). On the other hand, credit provided for the purchase of arms was reduced to one-half.[13]

This credit worth 5 million USD (ca. 76 million CSK) was approved by the Czechoslovak government under similar conditions to the first one (interest rate of 3 percent per annum, five years long postponement of payment) in June 1977. This time, the provided funds were spent on the acquisition of armament and military equipment for the PDRY army. The corresponding credit agreement was concluded on 29 January 1978 and related Contract No. 21-8-19 for the shipment of assault rifles, signal pistols, RPG-7s, and ammunition for T-55 tanks (for details see Table 19) was signed in the South Yemeni capital in April 1978. Both armament for the People's Militia and materiel for the South Yemeni army were loaded on board the Czechoslovak merchant ship *Sitno* in the port of Ploče on 5 October 1978. The vessel delivered the cargo to Aden on 15 October 1978.[14]

Table 18: Czechoslovak arms and equipment delivered for People's Militia according to the resolution of the Presidium ÚV KSČ from 27 May 1977[15]

Type	Number of examples	Note
vz. 44, 26.5mm signal pistol	100	from the stocks of the Federal Ministry of National Defence
26.5mm signal round	10,020	from the stocks of the Federal Ministry of National Defence
vz. 26, 7.92mm light machine gun	850	including spare parts (43 sets 1:20), from the stocks of the Federal Ministry of National Defence
vz. 37, 7.92mm heavy machine gun	150	including spare parts (15 sets 1:10, 6 sets 1:30), from the stocks of the Federal Ministry of National Defence
vz. 47, 7.92mm round	1,504,000	from the stocks of the Federal Ministry of National Defence
binocular 6x30	75	from the stocks of the Federal Ministry of National Defence
Adrianova, compass	2,175	from the stocks of the Federal Ministry of National Defence

Table 19: Czechoslovak arms delivered to the People's Democratic Republic of Yemen within the frame of Contract No. 21-8-19[16]

Type	Number of examples	Note
vz. 44, 26.5mm signal pistol	150	from the stocks of the Federal Ministry of National Defence
26.5mm signal round	15,360	from the stocks of the Federal Ministry of National Defence
vz. 58 P, 7.62mm assault rifle	5,000	including spare parts (100 sets 1:100)
vz. 58 V, 7.62mm assault rifle	5,000	including spare parts (100 sets 1:100)
vz. 43, 7.62mm training round	1,001,000	from the stocks of the Federal Ministry of National Defence
RPG-7, anti-tank rocket-propelled grenade launcher	300	from the stocks of the Federal Ministry of National Defence
PG-7V, anti-tank rocket-propelled grenade	3,000	from the stocks of the Federal Ministry of National Defence
100-JOF-ShK 44, K 53, TK, 100mm high explosive round	2,500	from the stocks of the Federal Ministry of National Defence
100-JPSv-ShK 44, K 53, TK, 100mm armour-piercing round	2,500	from the stocks of the Federal Ministry of National Defence
M-10, gas mask	5,000	from the stocks of the Federal Ministry of National Defence
VOP 63/69, chemical protection suit	5,000	from the stocks of the Federal Ministry of National Defence
DK-70, dosimeter	5,000	from the stocks of the Federal Ministry of National Defence
VDK-70, analyser for DK-70	20	from the stocks of the Federal Ministry of National Defence
eating utensils	30,000	from the stocks of the Federal Ministry of National Defence
military flask	15,000	from the stocks of the Federal Ministry of National Defence

Another conflict between North and South Yemen prompted Aden to beg for further military assistance from Prague. Tensions between the YAR and the PDRY escalated after the president of North Yemen, Ahmad al-Ghashmi, was killed on 24 June 1978 and his counterpart in South Yemen, Salim Rubai Ali, was executed after a short battle in Almodowar Palace with forces loyal to Prime Minister Ali Nasir Muhammad just two days later. In the meantime, the PDRY supported the North Yemeni opposition concentrated in the National Democratic Front (NDF). South Yemeni top-ranking officials started to publicly present the alleged capability of the NDF, with the backing of the PDRY, to overthrow the regime in Sana'a. Despite the warnings from Moscow that caution was needed, NDF insurgents supported by South Yemeni special forces were dispatched into action against the YAR. This led to small-scale fighting along the border which degenerated into a full-blown war in February 1979. Following the invasion by three brigades of the PDRY army, North Yemen appeared on the brink of a decisive defeat. However, this was prevented when Aden's forces halted further advance and politicians of both sides signed the Kuwait Agreement on 20 March 1979 that ended the hostilities.

During the time of the fighting, in the second half of February 1979, a Hungarian military delegation led by the Minister of Defence Lajos Czinege visited South Yemen and promised to provide medical equipment for Aden military hospital and another military materiel worth 20 to 25 million USD. Prague was not so generous – a donation of military clothing, personal equipment, and medicaments to the value of 3.296 million CSK was approved by the Czechoslovak government on 8 March 1979. The material was embarked on the East German cargo ship *Fläming* in the port of Rostock on 28 July 1979.

The South Yemeni top political leadership was apparently still not satisfied. Therefore, Prime Minister Ali Nasir Muhammad requested further deliveries of arms during his next visit to Czechoslovakia between 17 and 19 April 1979. The Czechoslovak government complied with Aden's wishes and approved the donation of arms and ammunition to the value of 10 million CSK as listed in Table 20. One of the members of Muhammad's delegation was Chief of the General Staff Colonel Husainoon who asked for further military assistance because of the newly emerged problems of the South Yemeni ammunition plant. The factory, with an annual output of 10 million rounds for infantry

Table 20: Czechoslovak arms and military equipment delivered to the People's Democratic Republic of Yemen according to the resolution of the Czechoslovak government from 15 May 1979[18]

Type	Number of examples	Note
vz. 44/67, 26.5mm signal pistol	50	
26.5mm signal round	16,500	
vz. 58, 7.62mm assault rifle	2,000	
RG-4, hand grenade	5,000	
PT-Mi K, metal anti-tank mine	5,000	with RO-3 and RO-5 fuse
85mm tank round	2,100	for T-34/85 tanks
100mm tank round	4,000	for T-55 tanks
vz. 53, tent (5x5 metres)	10	

weapons, was built with the help of the People's Republic of China. However, Beijing stopped the supplies of basic materials without which the production was not possible. Therefore, Husainoon requested the sending of the Czechoslovak expert group that could review the possibility of substitute deliveries from Czechoslovakia and the feasibility of the ammunition plant's extension with Czechoslovak participation. This request was approved by the Czechoslovak government as well.[17]

DONATIONS FROM PRAGUE

Following another round of power struggles in Aden, Abdul Fattah Ismail was removed from his office of the Chairman of the Presidium

of the Supreme People's Council in March 1980. This position was subsequently taken over by Ali Nasir Muhammad. South Yemeni military delegation under a new political arrangement led by Minister of Defence Ali Ahmed Nasser Antar showed up in Prague in May 1980 and, as usual, demanded donations of armament and other material that could be used by South Yemeni armed forces. Antar's requirement was composed of infantry weapons (pistols, AKM and AKMS assault rifles, RPK light machine guns, SG-43 medium machine guns, RPG-7 anti-tank rocket-propelled grenades), DShK anti-aircraft machine guns, and B-10 recoilless guns with respective ammunition, medicaments, and medical equipment, construction materials (cement, prefabricated wood, steel profiles), sports

Table 21: Czechoslovak arms and military equipment delivered to the People's Democratic Republic of Yemen according to the resolution of the Presidium ÚV KSČ from 12 September 1980[20]

Type	Number of examples/price	Note
vz. 52, 7.62mm pistol	500	from the stocks of the Federal Ministry of National Defence
vz. 58 P, 7.62mm assault rifle	1,500	including spare parts (30 sets 1:100), from the stocks of the Federal Ministry of National Defence
vz. 58 V, 7.62mm assault rifle	1,500	
vz. 43, 7.62mm machine gun	300	the Czechoslovak licence of SG-43, including spare parts (30 sets II), from the stocks of the Federal Ministry of National Defence
7.62mm pistol round	60,000	from the stocks of the Federal Ministry of National Defence
vz. 43, 7.62mm round	4,500,000	from the stocks of the Federal Ministry of National Defence
vz. 59, 7.62mm round	1,000,000	from the stocks of the Federal Ministry of National Defence
RPG-7, anti-tank rocket-propelled grenade launcher	100	from the stocks of the Federal Ministry of National Defence
PG-7V, anti-tank rocket-propelled grenade	3,600	from the stocks of the Federal Ministry of National Defence
vz. 59A, 82mm recoilless gun	12	including spare parts (23 sets 1:1, 2 sets 1:6), from the stocks of the Federal Ministry of National Defence
82-JOF-BzK 59, 82mm high explosive round	2,400	ammunition for vz. 59A recoilless gun, from the stocks of the Federal Ministry of National Defence
82-JPrSv-BzK 59, 82mm high explosive anti-tank round	2,400	ammunition for vz. 59A recoilless gun, from the stocks of the Federal Ministry of National Defence
PT-Mi K, metal anti-tank mine	5,000	with RO-5 fuse, from the stocks of the Federal Ministry of National Defence
PP-Mi Šr, anti-personnel shrapnel mine	20,000	from the stocks of the Federal Ministry of National Defence
RO-8, fuse	15,000	for PP-Mi Šr anti-personnel shrapnel mines, from the stocks of the Federal Ministry of National Defence
RO-1, fuse	5,000	for PP-Mi Šr anti-personnel shrapnel mines, from the stocks of the Federal Ministry of National Defence
two-way connector for PP-Mi Šr	2,500	from the stocks of the Federal Ministry of National Defence
Náložka 100g, explosive block	5,000	from the stocks of the Federal Ministry of National Defence
Náložka 200g, explosive block	5,000	from the stocks of the Federal Ministry of National Defence
Náložka 400g, explosive block	2,500	from the stocks of the Federal Ministry of National Defence
Náložka 1kg, explosive block in metal casing	1,000	from the stocks of the Federal Ministry of National Defence
Rozbuška Ž-1, detonator	2,000	from the stocks of the Federal Ministry of National Defence
Rozbuška Ž, detonator	25,000	from the stocks of the Federal Ministry of National Defence
detonating cord	2,000	from the stocks of the Federal Ministry of National Defence
safety fuse	100	from the stocks of the Federal Ministry of National Defence
cultural and educational material (radio receivers, tape recorders, projectors, billiards, cameras, movie cameras, musical instruments, etc.)	268,300 CSK	from the stocks of the Federal Ministry of National Defence

Table 22: Czechoslovak arms and equipment delivered to the People's Democratic Republic of Yemen according to the resolution of the Presidium ÚV KSČ from 25 June 1982[22]

Type	Number of examples	Note
Sa 24, 7.62mm sub machine gun	5,000	including spare parts (70 sets 1:100), from the stocks of the Czechoslovak People's Army
Sa 26, 7.62mm sub machine gun	2,000	
vz. 43, 7.62mm machine gun	50	the Czechoslovak licence of SG-43, including spare parts (5 sets II), from the stocks of the Czechoslovak People's Army
7.62mm pistol round	3,200,000	from the stocks of the Czechoslovak People's Army
vz. 59, 7.62mm round	1,926,000	from the stocks of the HTS
F-1, hand grenade	30,000	from the stocks of the Czechoslovak People's Army
PT-Mi K, metal anti-tank mine	5,000	with RO-5 fuse, from the stocks of the Czechoslovak People's Army
PP-Mi Šr, anti-personnel shrapnel mine	10,000	from the stocks of the Czechoslovak People's Army
RO-8, fuse	7,000	for PP-Mi Šr anti-personnel shrapnel mines, from the stocks of the Czechoslovak People's Army
RO-1, fuse	3,000	for PP-Mi Šr anti-personnel shrapnel mines, from the stocks of the Czechoslovak People's Army
Náložka 200g, explosive block	5,084	from the stocks of the Czechoslovak People's Army
Náložka 1kg, explosive block in metal casing	1,000	from the stocks of the Czechoslovak People's Army
Rozbuška Ž, detonator	21,000	from the stocks of the Czechoslovak People's Army
W3P, mine detector	30	from the stocks of the Czechoslovak People's Army

equipment, and assistance for children of nomads and Bedouins (clothes, school supplies, canned food). The Federal Ministry of National Defence obliged South Yemeni pleas and provided a large part of requested weapons or their Czechoslovak equivalents worth 24,810,493 CSK (including costs for their overhaul) from its stocks as detailed in Table 21. The request for delivery of goods of civilian nature was forwarded to the Federal Ministry of Foreign Trade.[19]

The Czechoslovak top-level political delegation visited South Yemen on 13 and 14 September 1981. Like many times before, one of the discussed topics was free of charge provision of military assistance for the PDRY armed

Sa 26 sub machine gun, together with Sa 24 equipped with fixed butt, was manufactured in Závody přesného strojírenství Uherský Brod between 1951 and 1953. (Author's collection)

Vz. 52/57 rifle was produced in Czechoslovakia in the 1950s at Závody přesného strojírenství Uherský Brod and Považské strojárne in Považská Bystrica. (Author's collection)

forces. Chief of the General Staff Col A A Alejwa requested not only deliveries of armoured vehicles, infantry weapons, and other equipment (BVP-1 infantry fighting vehicles, Sa 24 and Sa 26 sub machine guns, vz. 43 machine guns, mines or mine detectors) but the training of 12 pilots on L-39 and MiG-21 aircraft in Czechoslovakia as well. While it was not possible to provide some of the requested items such as infantry fighting vehicles, optical, and logistic material, the Czechoslovak authorities generally accepted

South Yemeni requirements (as listed in Table 22) including the training of the PDRYAF personnel. The Presidium ÚV KSČ granted this permission despite the overstretched capacity of the Military Aviation University at Košice that could be used for prospective training of Iraqi or Libyan personnel based on a commercial basis. Upon permission from Moscow, the master's education and military training of 12 South Yemeni students started in 1982. The first to graduate were three command post operators on 17 July 1987. Five

Table 23: Czechoslovak arms and equipment provided for People's Militia according to the resolution of the Czechoslovak government from 25 October 1984[24]

Type	Number of examples	Note
vz. 44/67, 26.5mm signal pistol	250	from the stocks of the Czechoslovak People's Army
26.5mm signal round	10,000	from the stocks of the Czechoslovak People's Army
Sa 24, 7.62mm sub machine gun	1,000	including spare parts (30 sets), from the stocks of the Czechoslovak People's Army
Sa 26, 7.62mm sub machine gun	2,000	
vz. 52/57, 7.62mm light machine gun	100	including spare parts (5 sets), from the stocks of the Czechoslovak People's Army
7.62mm pistol round	3,000,000	from the stocks of the Czechoslovak People's Army
7.62mm sub machine gun round	1,000,000	from the stocks of the Czechoslovak People's Militia
7.62mm sub machine gun round	500,000	from the stocks of the Czechoslovak People's Militia
hand grenade	5,000	from the stocks of the Czechoslovak People's Militia
RPG-75, single-shot anti-tank weapon	200	from the stocks of the Czechoslovak People's Army
vz. 54, compass	250	from the stocks of the Czechoslovak People's Army
commander ruler	500	from the stocks of the Czechoslovak People's Army
pocket bandages	10,000	from the stocks of the Czechoslovak People's Army
poncho	6,300	from the stocks of the Czechoslovak People's Army
raincoat	4,000	from the stocks of the Czechoslovak People's Army
plastic water bottle 25l	250	from the stocks of the Federal Ministry of Foreign Trade
eating utensils	7,100	from the stocks of the Federal Ministry of Foreign Trade
eating bowl	7,100	from the stocks of the Federal Ministry of Foreign Trade

MiG-21 and four Mi-2 pilots completed their training on 31 October of the same year. South Yemeni chief of the general staff requested the transfer of four helicopter pilots to Mi-8 helicopters in his letter from 23 December 1986. However, this demand was rejected and the student pilots continued in their training amounting to a total of 45 flight hours on the Mi-2 helicopter.[21]

Another round of military assistance took place in 1984 when a South Yemeni delegation of the People's Militia forwarded the requirement for the supply of materiel for complete equipping of three People's Militia brigades. With constant South Yemeni financial problems, communist officials became more alert because Czechoslovakia already had its own share of economic difficulties. Up to this time, Prague provided four civilian and two military credits to the overall value of 43 million USD (military share 10.1 million USD). While the payment of 40 million USD had to be postponed in 1982, the maturity of two military credits was extended for a further five years. Under these circumstances, the Czechoslovak government decided to donate armament, ammunition, and further equipment worth only some

A vz. 59 82mm recoilless gun in service with the Czechoslovak People's Army. (Author's collection)

ZiL-131 trucks towing M1943 mortars and MT-12 anti-tank guns of the People's Democratic Republic of Yemen Army, during a parade in Aden in the 1980s. Note, the troops seated on the flat bed of the trucks are armed with Czechoslovak-made vz. 58 assault rifles. (Author's collection)

13 million CSK (including transportation cost of 4.5 million CSK) listed in Table 23. During 20 and 30 May 1985, the material was loaded up on Czechoslovak cargo ship *Blaník* that transported it to Aden harbour. The handover protocol was signed on 24 July 1985.[23]

MEDICAL ASSISTANCE AND INTERNECINE WARFARE

In 1981, Czechoslovak and South Yemeni ministries of defence signed an agreement related to military medical cooperation. However, this 'cooperation' was a one-sided affair only. According to the terms of the agreement, the Czechoslovak side was obliged to provide annually specialised medical treatment in the Central Military Hospital Prague (*Ústřední vojenská nemocnice Praha*) for up to 20 wounded or ill South Yemeni soldiers until the year 1991. Furthermore, selected soldiers from the PDRY could make use of Czechoslovak military recreational facilities and the South Yemeni ministry of defence obtained several shipments of medicaments (provided in the frame of different arms donations) as listed in Tables 24, 25, and 26. The medical assistance was provided at the Czechoslovak expense only.[25]

Table 24: Medical treatment of South Yemeni soldiers in the Central Military Hospital Prague 1981–1988[26]

Year	Number of treated soldiers
1982	8
1983	21
1984	16
1985	24
1986	33 (including 28 treated after 'The Events of '86')
1987	16
1988	4

Table 25: Recreational stay of South Yemeni soldiers in Czechoslovakia 1981–1987[27]

Year	Number of soldiers	Facility
1981	information not available	information not available
1982	information not available	information not available
1983	6	Military Sanatorium Tatranské Matliare
1984	6	Military Spa Institute Karlovy Vary
1985	6	Military Spa Institute Karlovy Vary
1986	0	-
1987	5	Military Sanatorium Tatranské Matliare

Table 26: Deliveries of medicaments for South Yemeni Ministry of Defence from Czechoslovakia 1981–1987[28]

Year	Delivered material
1984	medicaments (55,000 CSK), bandages (420,000 CSK)
1985	10,000 pocket bandages (62,000 CSK)
1987	medicaments (70,000 CSK)

Czechoslovak military medical assistance came as a blessing for some South Yemeni soldiers as another round of internecine fighting broke out in the People's Democratic Republic of Yemen. Ideological and tribal tensions between two factions of the ruling Yemeni Socialist Party (YSP), led by Abdul Fattah Ismail and Ali Nasir Muhammad respectively, served as a cause for a new wave of infighting. Their struggle for the leadership of the YSP resulted in a

T-34/85 medium tanks during another parade in Aden. During the short war with the Yemen Arab Republic of 1979, the better-trained and maintained People's Democratic Republic of Yemen soundly defeated its opponent. (Author's collection)

BMP-1s of the People's Democratic Republic of Yemen Army on a military parade in Aden during the early 1980s. (Author's collection)

costly conflict that lasted 11 days. On 13 January 1986, bodyguards of Ali Nasir Muhammad opened fire on members of the Yemeni Socialist Party politburo that held a meeting in the presidential palace. While Muhammad's supporters were not present in the room, Vice President Ali Ahmad Nasir Antar, Minister of Defence Saleh Muslih Qassem, and the YSP disciplinary chief Ali Shayi Hadi were killed in the shootout. Furthermore, Abdul Fattah Ismail died later during the day. The conflict quickly escalated into a civil war

that resulted in thousands of casualties, including almost 2,500 members of the YSP. Power in Aden was subsequently assumed by Haidar Abu Bakr al-Attas who became the new Chairman of the Presidium of the Supreme People's Council.

Moscow came immediately to the rescue and, by the end of 1989, provided 300 million rubles for the restoration of the ruined economy and a further 500 million rubles for the reconstruction of South Yemeni armed forces. After initial confusion in Prague, the Czechoslovak communist leadership accepted the new regime in Aden and decided to provide medical treatment for up to 50 wounded South Yemeni troops at Czechoslovak expense. Soldiers from the PDRY wounded during 'The Events of '86' were treated in the Union of Soviet Socialist Republics, East Germany, and Bulgaria as well. South Yemeni authorities selected 28 men who underwent treatment in several Czechoslovak military medical facilities listed in Table 27.[29]

Table 27: Treatment of South Yemeni troops in Czechoslovak military hospitals related to 'The Events of '86'[30]

Military medical facility	Number of soldiers
Central Military Hospital Prague	16
Military Hospital Plzeň	6
Military Hospital České Budějovice	6
Follow-up treatment was carried out in the Military Rehabilitation Institute Slapy	

ECONOMIC FAILURE

In October 1987, the South Yemeni delegation requested credit for the purchase of 31 BVP-1 or BVP-2 infantry fighting vehicles and four L-39 Albatros training aircraft. This request was promptly turned down by Prague that had started to feel the consequences of its own economic mismanagement. Apparently, the last shipment of armament from communist Czechoslovakia to South Yemen was realised in the frame of the agreement from 27 February 1987. The hand over of this materiel (listed in Table 28), which was provided free of charge again, took place in Aden on 15 November 1987 (in total, eight free of charge military deliveries took place between 1977 and 1987).[31]

Up to late 1988, Czechoslovakia had provided to South Yemen free of charge military assistance worth approximately 260 million CSK. Hardline Marxist policies of the Aden regime meant that it was positively described as 'progressive' or even 'avant-garde' by the communist officials in Prague. However, the same ill-conceived policies led to the situation that the PDRY constantly balanced on the edge of economic collapse. The administration of the Yemeni Socialist Party could manage to survive day-to-day only thanks to donations or loans from other communist countries and its massive security and military apparatus. Thus, it was no surprise that the General Secretary of the YSP Ali Salem al-Beidh asked for financial concessions during his visit to Prague in January 1989. From all provided credits, the PDRY did not pay 16.08 million USD (including 8.8 million USD of military assistance) and owed interest of a further 4.36 million USD. The Czechoslovak leadership accepted his pleas and decided to postpone the payment of instalments from civilian credits until the end of 1995, and, at the same time, started to consider the write-off of debts for military deliveries. Despite the inability to pay properly for provided loans, al-Beidh was swift to request further civilian credit to the value of 10 million USD for the reconstruction of the refinery in Aden. Already disgusted by South Yemeni incompetence and never-ending requests for donations and credits, the General Secretary of the Communist Party of Czechoslovakia Miloš Jakeš reminded him that 'our cooperation must be mutually beneficial'. However, its own problems caused the collapse of the communist regime in Prague just 10 months later.[33]

Simultaneously, the rule of the Communist Party of the Soviet Union, Aden's principal sponsor, started to crumble as well. As of November 1989, the Soviet Union provided one-half of all loans that the PDRY had obtained since the beginning of its existence. At that time, several hundreds of Soviet military advisors were still present at South Yemeni military installations: Soviet warships operating in the Persian Gulf and the Indian Ocean continued in their routine and used naval facilities at Socotra Island as their replenishment base. Furthermore, information related to the military-strategic

The Aero L-39 Albatros remained one of the 'export hits' of Czechoslovakia throughout the 1980s. however, Aden's plan for acquiring enough to equip three squadrons with them never materialised. (Author's collection)

Table 28: Czechoslovak arms delivered to the People's Democratic Republic of Yemen in 1987[32]		
Type	Number of examples	Note
vz. 44, 26.5mm signal pistol	50	from the stocks of the Czechoslovak People's Army
26.5mm signal round	75,000	from the stocks of the Czechoslovak People's Army
vz. 52, 7.62mm pistol	500	from the stocks of the Czechoslovak People's Army
Sa 26, 7.62mm sub machine gun	2.000	from the stocks of the Czechoslovak People's Army, including spare parts (20 sets), additional 281 sub machine guns of unknown type delivered from the stocks of the HTS
vz. 52/57, 7.62mm rifle	500	from the stocks of the Czechoslovak People's Army, including spare parts (5 sets)
vz. 52/57, 7.62mm machine gun	50	from the stocks of the Czechoslovak People's Army
vz. 42 N, 7.92mm machine gun	78	from the stocks of the HTS
7.62mm pistol round	2,000,000	from the stocks of the Czechoslovak People's Army
vz. 43, 7.62mm round	120,000	from the stocks of the Czechoslovak People's Army
vz. 47, 7.92mm round	400,000	in total 5,840,000 round of 7.62mm and 7.92mm rifle and machine gun ammunition delivered from the stocks of the Czechoslovak People's Army and the HTS
RG-4M, hand grenade	20,000	from the stocks of the Czechoslovak People's Army
F-1, hand grenade	20,000	from the stocks of the Czechoslovak People's Army
vz. 56, 5.6mm rifle	100	from the stocks of the Czechoslovak People's Army
5.6mm round	50,000	from the stocks of the Czechoslovak People's Army
TP-25, field telephone	200	from the stocks of the Czechoslovak People's Army
Adrianova, compass	100	from the stocks of the Czechoslovak People's Army
commander ruler	100	from the stocks of the Czechoslovak People's Army
Blůza vz. 60, field jacket	5,000	from the stocks of the Czechoslovak People's Army
Kalhoty vz. 60, trousers	5,000	from the stocks of the Czechoslovak People's Army
poncho	2,500	from the stocks of the Czechoslovak People's Army
Várnice 14, vacuum bottle	25	from the stocks of the Czechoslovak People's Army
field bandages	500	
vz. 54, field bed	500	from the stocks of the Czechoslovak People's Army
vz. 61, metallic box for documents	500	from the stocks of the Czechoslovak People's Army
sugar	80 tonnes	
meat cans	15 tonnes	
medical material	1 box	from the stocks of the Czechoslovak People's Army

situation on the Arabian Peninsula obtained by Soviet spy satellites was provided to the South Yemeni armed forces as well.[34]

The decline and following breakdown of European communist donors forced the YSP leadership to consider the unification of South and North Yemen seriously. Left with little option, the regime in Aden embarked on the unification process and the Republic of Yemen came into existence on 22 May 1990 when North and South merged to form one state. While Yemen was ravaged by civil war in 1994, successor states of Czechoslovakia, the Czech and the Slovak Republic, could only count financial losses from the times of cooperation between former communist regimes in Prague and Aden. In the end, Yemeni debts were restructured and sold to the International Development Association, the part of the World Bank that helps the world's poorest countries, for 10 percent of their original value.[35]

POST SCRIPTUM: CZECHOSLOVAK ARMS FOR UNITED YEMEN

In 1989–1990, North and South Yemen entered negotiations that led to the union of the country. Unsurprising political differences, and the failure of integration of their armed forces resulted in the Yemeni Civil War of 1994, in which the South was soundly defeated and conquered. In the course of their reforms of the 1990s and 2000s, and with help of income from oil sources discovered in the centre of the country, the reformed armed forces of the Yemen Arab Republic returned to the practice of purchasing Czechoslovak-made weapons. In 1998, an agreement was signed with the manufacturer - Aero Vodochody, in Prague, for delivery of 12 Aero L-39C Albatros training jets – left-overs from a series originally intended for the Soviet Union, but never delivered. The aircraft were shipped to Aden in 2000, and entered service with the Flight School at Anad AB. During the same year, Sana'a followed with an order for a batch of T-55AM1 and T-55AM2 main battle tanks from surplus stocks of the Czech Republic: these were delivered by the end of 2000.

Finally, in 2004, the Yemeni government placed several orders from Ukraine for deliveries of overhauled aircraft and equipment. Amongst these were 14 L-39Cs from surplus stocks of the local air force: these were refurbished at the Odessa Aviarem and delivered in 2005 and 2006. As far as is known, in 2014, the Yemen Air Force still operated 22 out of these 26 L-39s, and some were transferred to its No. 12 Squadron, which deployed them for ground attacks on both the Houthi insurgency in the north, and al-Qaida of the Arabian Peninsula in the south. However, by the time the central government was overrun by the Houthis, in September 2014, fewer than 10 were still operational. In turn, most of these were destroyed during the subsequent, Saudi-led military intervention in the country.

Table 29: T-55AM1 and T-55AM2 delivered to Yemen from the Czech Republic

Type	Number of examples	Year of delivery
T-55AM1 (and T-55AM2?)	97	2000
T-55AM2	35	2002

Note: VT-55A armoured recovery vehicles were delivered together with the tanks. The shipment in 2002 included also 30 D10-T2S 100 mm main guns.

Photo caption: One of the T-55AM2 medium tanks delivered to Yemen from the Czech Republic at the turn of the millennium (Author's collection)

BIBLIOGRAPHY

ARCHIVE SOURCES

Archiv Ministerstva zahraničních věcí (AMZV), Praha (Archive of the Ministry of Foreign Affairs, Prague)
Fond Teritoriální odbory – tajné (TO-T), 1955-1959 (Fund Territorial Departments – Secret, 1955–1959)
Fond Teritoriální odbory – tajné (TO-T), 1970-1974 (Fund Territorial Departments – Secret, 1970–1974)
Fond Teritoriální odbory – tajné (TO-T), 1975-1979 (Fund Territorial Departments – Secret, 1975–1979)
Fond Teritoriální odbory – tajné (TO-T), 1980-1989 (Fund Territorial Departments – Secret, 1980–1989)

Národní archiv (NA), Praha (National Archive, Prague)
Fond Politické byro ÚV KSČ 1954-1962, 1261/0/11 (Fund Political Bureau ÚV KSČ 1954-1962, 1261/0/11)
Fond Předsednictvo ÚV KSČ 1962-1966, 1261/0/4 (Fund Presidium ÚV KSČ 1962-1966, 1261/0/4)
Fond Předsednictvo ÚV KSČ 1966-1971, 1261/0/5 (Fund Presidium ÚV KSČ 1966-1971, 1261/0/5)
Fond Předsednictvo ÚV KSČ 1971-1976, 1261/0/6 (Fund Presidium ÚV KSČ 1971-1976, 1261/0/6)
Fond Předsednictvo ÚV KSČ 1976-1981, 1261/0/7 (Fund Presidium ÚV KSČ 1976-1981, 1261/0/7)
Fond Předsednictvo ÚV KSČ 1981-1986, 1261/0/8 (Fund Presidium ÚV KSČ 1981-1986, 1261/0/8)
Fond Předsednictvo ÚV KSČ 1986-1989, 1261/0/9 (Fund Presidium ÚV KSČ 1986-1989, 1261/0/9)
Fond Kancelář 1. tajemníka ÚV KSČ Antonína Novotného – II. část, 1261/0/44 (Fund Office of First Secretary ÚV KSČ Antonín Novotný – II part, 1261/0/44)

Vojenský ústřední archiv – Vojenský historický archiv (VÚA-VHA), Praha (Military Central Archive – Military Historical Archive, Prague)
Fond Ministerstvo národní obrany (MNO), 1951-1980, 1989 (Fund Ministry of National Defence, 1951-1980, 1989)

Internal Documents
CIA/Directorate of Intelligence, *Recent Trends in Iranian Arms Procurement*, May 1972

Diploma theses
Vyhlídal, Milan, *Československá pomoc při výstavbě vojenského školství v arabském světě v letech 1948 – 1989* (Brno: Filozofická fakulta, Masarykova univerzita, 2010)

Literature
Fojtík, Jakub, *Albatros. AERO L-39, L-59, L-139* (Bratislava: Magnet Press Slovakia, 2016)
Fojtík, Jakub, *Delfín. AERO L-29* (Bratislava: Magnet Press Slovakia, 2018)
Francev, Vladimír, *Československé zbraně ve světě* (Praha: Grada Publishing, 2015)
Francev, Vladimír, *Československé tankové síly* (Praha: Grada Publishing, 2012)
Irra, Miroslav, *L-39 Albatros, 2. díl* (Nevojice: Jakab, 2017)

Stojanov, Robert, *Finanční pohledávky České republiky u rozvojových zemí* (Praha: Ekumenická akademie, 2019)

Zídek, Petr & Sieber, Karel, *Československo a Blízký východ v letech 1948-1989* (Praha: Ústav mezinárodních vztahů, 2009)

Periodicals

Jančár, Milan, Irácké Zliny, *Letectví+kosmonautika*, 6/2004

Štaigl, Jan & Turza, Peter, Zbrojná výroba na Slovensku v rokoch 1969-1992 (1. časť), *Vojenská história*, 2/2013

Štaigl, Jan & Turza, Peter, Zbrojná výroba na Slovensku v rokoch 1969-1992 (2. časť), *Vojenská história*, 3/2013

Internet

www.aktualne.cz

www.senat.cz

www.valka.cz

www.vojenstvi.cz

NOTES

CHAPTER 1

1 Zídek & Sieber, *Československo a Blízký východ v letech 1948-1989*, pp. 111–112. Francev, *Československé zbraně ve světě*, pp. 70–72.

2 Francev, *Československé zbraně ve světě*, pp. 70–72.

3 AMZV, TO-T 1975-1979, Írán, karton 1, obal 6, č.j. 014/782/75-7, ÍRÁN _ příprava návštěvy předsedy vlády Íránu A. A. Hoveydy v ČSSR, předložení návrhu materiálu do PÚV KSČ, 1975.

4 VÚA-VHA, MNO, 1968, karton 62, sl. 30-3/3, Výkazy jmenovitých položek za I. – IV. čtvrtletí 1964, 19. února 1965. VÚA-VHA, MNO, 1968, karton 62, sl. 30-3/3, Výkazy jmenovitých položek za I. – IV. čtvrtletí 1965, 29. ledna 1966. VÚA-VHA, MNO, 1968, karton 80, sl. 22-1, č.j. 012297/68, Komplexní rozbor zahraničních styků ministerstva národní obrany, uskutečněných v roce 1967, 11. března 1968. VÚA-VHA, MNO, 1969, karton 27, sl. 7/1-1, č.j. 020659, Komplexní rozbor zahraničních styků ministerstva národní obrany, uskutečněných v roce 1968, 28. března 1969. VÚA-VHA, MNO, 1969, karton 175, Evidence GŠ/SMP-5 – vývozní skupina.

5 Within the frame of the federalisation of Czechoslovakia, the Czech Socialist Republic and the Slovak Socialist Republic were established on 1 January 1969. This was associated with renaming of ministries with statewide authority that added the word Federal into their official titles.

6 VÚA-VHA, MNO, 1969, karton 211, sl. 31D-31, č.j.020788/1969, Odpověď na dopis č. 022.905/69-7 z 6. června 1969, 13. srpna 1969. CIA/Directorate of Intelligence, *Recent Trends in Iranian Arms Procurement*, May 1972.

7 AMZV, TO-T 1975-1979, Írán, karton 2, obal 12, č.j. 012314, Záznam o jednání s generálem Toufanianem, 14. března 1978. AMZV, TO-T 1980-1989, Írán, karton 2, obal 6, č.j. 017128/83, Informace o vztazích ve speciální oblasti s Íránem, 8. prosince 1983.

8 AMZV, TO-T 1975-1979, Írán, karton 1, obal 8, č.j. 014293, Podkladové materiály ZÚ Teherán k přípravě návštěvy šáha v ČSSR, 8. června 1977. AMZV, TO-T 1975-1979, Írán, karton 2, obal 16, č.j. 01061/76, Íránský vojenský průmysl, 30. června 1976. AMZV, TO-T 1975-1979, Írán, karton 2, obal 16, č.j. 01072, ČSSR-Irán: Problematika vývozu investičních celků do Íránu, 12. července 1976. CIA/Directorate of Intelligence, *Recent*

Trends in Iranian Arms Procurement, May 1972. Zídek & Sieber, *Československo a Blízký východ v letech 1948-1989*, pp. 111–112.

9 AMZV, TO-T 1970-1974, Írán, karton 2, obal 4, č.j. 021.518/72-7, Politická zpráva ZÚ Teherán č. 5/72-: Vývoj hospodářských vztahů a současná obchodně-politická situace, 28. února 1972. AMZV, TO-T 1975-1979, Írán, karton 2, obal 12, č.j. 13920, Zaslání záznamu a zprávy k problematice spolupráce ČSSR s MSK Tabriz, 29. května 1977. AMZV, TO-T 1975-1979, Írán, karton 2, obal 16, č.j. 01061/76, Íránský vojenský průmysl, 30. června 1976. AMZV, TO-T 1975-1979, Írán, karton 4, obal 17, č.j. 01031/78, Írán – zpráva o technické pomoci za rok 1977, 22. března 1978. AMZV, TO-T 1975-1979, Írán, karton 4, obal 22, č.j. 01042/77, ČSSR-Írán – zajišťování výstavby vojenských investičních celků dodávaných OZO Omnipol do Íránu a některé nové skutečnosti ve vztahu k ČSSR v oblasti speciální techniky, 6. dubna 1977. AMZV, TO-T 1980-1989, Írán, karton 2, obal 6, č.j. 017128/83, Informace o vztazích ve speciální oblasti s Íránem, 8. prosince 1983.

10 AMZV, TO-T 1975-1979, Írán, karton 2, obal 16, č.j. 01061/76, Íránský vojenský průmysl, 30. června 1976.

11 CIA/Directorate of Intelligence, *Recent Trends in Iranian Arms Procurement*, May 1972.

12 AMZV, TO-T 1975-1979, Írán, karton 2, obal 15, č.j. 012.644/75-7, dopis místopředsedy vlády ČSSR s. Gregora předsedovi íránské vlády A.A. Hovejdovi z r. 1972, 1. dubna 1975. AMZV, TO-T 1975-1979, Írán, karton 3, obal 26, č.j. 01005/78, Záznam z porady diplomatických pracovníků, 22. ledna 1979. AMZV, TO-T 1975-1979, Írán, karton 4, obal 17, č.j. 01031/78, Írán – zpráva o technické pomoci za rok 1977, 22. března 1978. AMZV, TO-T 1975-1979, Írán, karton 4, obal 22, č.j. 01042/77, ČSSR-Írán – zajišťování výstavby vojenských investičních celků dodávaných OZO Omnipol do Íránu a některé nové skutečnosti ve vztahu k ČSSR v oblasti speciální techniky, 6. dubna 1977. AMZV, TO-T 1980-1989, Írán, karton 2, obal 6, č.j. 017128/83, Informace o vztazích ve speciální oblasti s Íránem, 8. prosince 1983.

13 AMZV, TO-T 1975-1979, Írán, karton 2, obal 12, č.j. 013066, Správa o návšteve stavby A-23 v Isfahane, 21. dubna 1979.

14 AMZV, TO-T 1980-1989, Írán, karton 1, obal 4, č.j. 01021/84, K obchodně politickým a ekonomickým vztahům ČSSR-ÍIR, 25. prosince 1983. AMZV, TO-T 1980-1989, Írán, karton 2, obal 6, č.j. 017128/83, Informace o vztazích ve speciální oblasti s Íránem, 8. prosince 1983. AMZV, TO-T 1980-1989, Írán, karton 2, obal 10, Záznamy o rozhovorech, 16.6.1983, 3.10.1983. AMZV, TO-T 1980-1989, Írán, karton 3, obal 11, Záznamy o rozhovorech 15.2.1984, 27.2.1984, 15.3.1984, 16.5.1984, 25.3.1985. NA, A ÚV KSČ, fond 1261/0/8 (Předsednictvo ÚV KSČ 1981-1986), P 13/86, k informaci bod 10, Informace o průběhu a výsledcích návštěvy ministra zahraničních věcí Íránské islámské republiky Ali Akbar Velajátího v Československé socialistické republice, 21. července 1986.

15 VÚA-VHA, MNO, 1989, karton 60, č.j. 001777, Rozpis prováděcího plánu na rok 1989 a příprava prováděcího plánu na rok 1990, Dodatek k návrhu státního plánu na rok 1989 a zaměření přípravy na rok 1990 (po projednání návrhu státního plánu ve vládě ČSSR dne 19. července 1988), červenec 1988.

16 AMZV, TO-T 1980-1989, Irák, karton 5, obal 19, Záznamy o rozhovorech, 3.7.1984, 16.9.1984, 22.10.1984, 13.12.1984. AMZV, TO-T 1980-1989, Irák, karton 5, obal 20, Záznamy o rozhovorech, 23.1.1985.

17 AMZV, TO-T 1980-1989, Írán, karton 2, obal 6, č.j. 017128/83, Informace o vztazích ve speciální oblasti s Íránem, 8. prosince

1983. AMZV, TO-T 1980-1989, Írán, karton 2, obal 8, č.j. 01048/81, Záznamy z rozhovorů se členy islámské vlády Íránu, 13. září 1981. AMZV, TO-T 1980-1989, Írán, karton 3, obal 15, č.j. 013.444/83-7, Možnost dodávky lehké munice, příp. ručních granátů do Íránu, 23. května 1983.

18 NA, A ÚV KSČ, fond 1261/0/9 (Předsednictvo ÚV KSČ 1986-1989), P 103/89, bod 2, Zpráva o oficiální návštěvě předsedy vlády ČSSR s. L. ADAMCE v Íránské islámské republice, 2. února. NA, A ÚV KSČ, fond 1261/0/9 (Předsednictvo ÚV KSČ 1986-1989), P 112/89, bod 5, Informace o jednání s místopředsedou ray ministrů SSSR s I. S. BĚLOUSOVEM o dodávkách speciální techniky do SSSR v období 1991 – 1995, 13. dubna 1989.

CHAPTER 2

1 Zídek & Sieber, *Československo a Blízký východ v letech 1948-1989*, p. 91.

2 Francev, *Československé zbraně ve světě*, p. 133.

3 AMZV, TO-O 1945-1959, Izrael, karton 4, obal 3, č. 3472/8/48, Protest irácké vlády proti dodávkám zbraní z ČSR do Izraele. Zájem o nákup lehčích zbraní v ČSR, 14. září 1948.

4 VÚA-VHA, MNO, 1955, karton 663, sign. 54/2/11/7, č.j. 050232, Vývoz zbraní do Iraku, 27. ledna 1955.

5 Zídek & Sieber, *Československo a Blízký východ v letech 1948-1989*, pp. 92–93.

6 VÚA-VHA, MNO, 1960, karton 42, sign. 38/6-6, č.j. 13144/NM-SVŠ, Povolení studia iráckému studentu na VA AZ, směr vojenskoprůmyslový – 1960, 17. září 1960. VÚA-VHA, MNO, 1965, karton 254, sign. 38/6-6, č.j. 09006/10, rozbor zahraničních akcí – předložení, 20. únor 1965.

7 VÚA-VHA, MNO, 1960, karton 386, sign. 40/1/1, č.j. 012584-NGŠ, Účast MNO na nabídce mapovacích prací pro Irák, 18. říjen 1960. VÚA-VHA, MNO, 1960, karton 461, sign. 30/2/4/46, č.j. 0017237, Zmapování území Iráku, 14. září 1960.

8 NA, A ÚV KSČ, fond 1261/0/44 (Kancelář 1. tajemníka ÚV KSČ Antonína Novotného – II. část), karton 105 (Irák), inv. č. 193, obal 21, Telegramy, šifry, depeše ZÚ (1959) 1961-1964 (1967). VÚA-VHA, MNO, 1963, karton 296, sign. 24/3/10 (31/2/14), č.j. 010840-OZS/1963, Poskytnutí asylu dvěma iráckým důstojníkům, 30. září 1963. VÚA-VHA, MNO, 1963, karton 297, sign. 31/9/36, č.j. 0122/1963, Žádost o udělení asylu iráckým státním příslušníkům, 17. června 1963. Zídek & Sieber, *Československo a Blízký východ v letech 1948-1989*, p. 95.

9 Zídek & Sieber, *Československo a Blízký východ v letech 1948-1989*, pp. 94–95.

10 NA, A ÚV KSČ, fond 1261/0/44 (Kancelář 1. tajemníka ÚV KSČ Antonína Novotného – II. část), karton 105 (Irák), inv. č. 195, obal 39, Rozhovory s mluvčím Demokratické strany Kurdistánu Džabalem Talabanym na MZV, 1963.

11 NA, A ÚV KSČ, fond 1261/0/4 (Předsednictvo ÚV KSČ 1962-1966), sv. 78, ar.j. 82, bod 26, Situace v Demokratické straně Kurdistánu, 14. září 1964.

12 VÚA-VHA, MNO, 1964, karton 326, sign. L/104, č.j. 003556/OTP, Situace v Demokratické straně Kurdistánu, 25. října 1964. VÚA-VHA, MNO, 1964, karton 326, sign. L/119, č.j. 003611/OTP, Materiál pro Kurdistán, 31. říjen 1964.

13 NA, A ÚV KSČ, fond 1261/0/44 (Kancelář 1. tajemníka ÚV KSČ Antonína Novotného – II. část), karton 105 (Irák), inv. č. 195, obal 43, Zrušení vojenských dodávek pro Demokratickou stranu Kurdistánu, 1966. VÚA-VHA, MNO, 1966, karton 35, sl. 24/5/2, Dodávka ručních zbraní a munice Dem. straně Kurdistánu, 14. března 1966.

14 VÚA-VHA, MNO, 1964, karton 326, sign. L/104, č.j. 003556/OTP, Situace v Demokratické straně Kurdistánu, 25. října 1964. VÚA-VHA, MNO, 1966, karton 35, sign. 24/5/2, Dodávka ručních zbraní a munice Dem. straně Kurdistánu, 14. března 1966.

15 NA, A ÚV KSČ, fond 1261/0/44 (Kancelář 1. tajemníka ÚV KSČ Antonína Novotného – II. část), karton 105 (Irák), inv. č. 195, obal 44, Dopis předsedy DSK M.Barzáního prezidentu A.Novotnému (žádost o materiální pomoc), 1966. VÚA-VHA, MNO, 1966, karton 35, sl. 24/5/2, Dodávka ručních zbraní a munice Dem. straně Kurdistánu, 14. března 1966.

16 VÚA-VHA, MNO, 1964, karton 22, sign. 24/5/1-30, č.j. 0050928/HTS-05, Zpráva o výsledcích průzkumu možností odbytu speciálního materiálu, 30. června 1964. VÚA-VHA, MNO, 1965, karton 233, sign. K/17, č.j. 004178, Stručná zpráva o poskytování technické pomoci rozvojovým zemím za rok 1964.

17 VÚA-VHA, MNO, 1968, karton 62, sl. 30-3/3, Výkazy jmenovitých položek za I. – IV. čtvrtletí 1965, 29. ledna 1966.

18 NA, A ÚV KSČ, fond 1261/0/4 (Předsednictvo ÚV KSČ 1962-1966), sv. 98-99, ar.j. 104, bod 5, Dohoda mezi Československou socialistickou republikou a Iráckou republikou o dodávkách vojenské techniky, 24. března 1965. NA, A ÚV KSČ, fond 1261/0/44 (Kancelář 1. tajemníka ÚV KSČ Antonína Novotného – II. část), karton 105 (Irák), inv. č. 193, obal 18, Dohoda mezi ČSSR a Irákem o dodávkách vojenské techniky Iráku, 1965. VÚA-VHA, MNO, 1966, karton 187, sl. 1/-, č.j. 04137/OTP, Uvolnění 50 ks velitelských tanků T-54 A/K pro Irák, březen 1965.

19 NA, A ÚV KSČ, fond 1261/0/44 (Kancelář 1. tajemníka ÚV KSČ Antonína Novotného – II. část), karton 105 (Irák), inv. č. 193, obal 18, Dohoda mezi ČSSR a Irákem o dodávkách vojenské techniky Iráku, 1965.

20 NA, A ÚV KSČ, fond 1261/0/44 (Kancelář 1. tajemníka ÚV KSČ Antonína Novotného – II. část), karton 105 (Irák), inv. č. 193, obal 18, Dohoda mezi ČSSR a Irákem o dodávkách vojenské techniky Iráku, 1965. NA, A ÚV KSČ, fond 1261/0/4 (Předsednictvo ÚV KSČ 1962-1966), sv. 108, ar.j. 111, bod 16, Jednání o dodávkách vojenské techniky Irácké republice, 22. května 1965. NA, A ÚV KSČ, fond 1261/0/4 (Předsednictvo ÚV KSČ 1962-1966), sv. 113-114, ar.j. 117, bod 8, Zpráva o řešení požadavku Irácké republiky o zvýšení dodávek letecké speciální techniky, 17. července 1965. NA, A ÚV KSČ, fond 1261/0/4 (Předsednictvo ÚV KSČ 1962-1966), sv. 117, ar.j. 122, bod 4, Zajištění potřeb Čs. lidové armády v případě zvýšených dodávek letecké speciální techniky do Irácké republiky, 30. srpna 1965. NA, A ÚV KSČ, fond 1261/0/44 (Kancelář 1. tajemníka ÚV KSČ Antonína Novotného – II. část), karton 105 (Irák), inv. č. 193, obal 19, Jednání o dodávkách vojenské techniky a zvýšení dodávek letecké vojenské techniky, 1965. VÚA-VHA, MNO, 1966, karton 187, sl. 1/-, č.j. 002532, Řešení požadavku Irácké republiky, srpen 1965.

21 NA, A ÚV KSČ, fond 1261/0/44 (Kancelář 1. tajemníka ÚV KSČ Antonína Novotného – II. část), karton 105 (Irák), inv. č. 193, obal 20, Zpráva o vývoji styků mezi ČSSR a Irákem v oblasti speciálních materiálů, 1967. VÚA-VHA, MNO, 1967, karton 35, sign. 24/5/1-20, č.j. 0020800/sekr.min., Poskytnutí další technické pomoci Iráku, 4. května 1967. VÚA-VHA, MNO, 1969, karton 27, sl. 7/1-1, č.j. 020659, Komplexní rozbor zahraničních styků ministerstva národní obrany, uskutečněných v roce 1968, 28. března 1969.

22 NA, A ÚV KSČ, fond 1261/0/44 (Kancelář 1. tajemníka ÚV KSČ Antonína Novotného – II. část), karton 105 (Irák), inv. č. 193, obal 20, Zpráva o vývoji styků mezi ČSSR a Irákem v oblasti

speciálních materiálů, 1967. VÚA-VHA, MNO, 1967, karton 158, sl. 27/1/2, č.j. 00750/10-67, Komplexní rozbor zahraničních styků MNO v r. 1966, 10. dubna 1967.

23 VÚA-VHA, MNO, 1968, karton 83, sl. 31D-41, Dílčí zpráva o práci pracovní skupiny pro výstavbu letiště a letecké školy v IRAKU. Fojtík, *Delfin*, p. 117.

24 VÚA-VHA, MNO, 1966, karton 245, sl. D/59, Vyhodnocení 1. čtvrtletí 1968. Fojtík, *Delfin*, p. 118.

25 Jančár, *Irácké Zliny*, pp. 93–94.

26 VÚA-VHA, MNO, 1969, karton 383, sl. 38/3-9, č.j. 080991, Jednání s velitelem iráckého letectva dne 14.2.1969 na SZS, 19. února 1969. VÚA-VHA, MNO, 1969, karton 207, sl. 50, č.j. 129/860, Přelet letounů MiG-15UTI do Iráku, 3. září 1969. VÚA-VHA, MNO, 1971, karton 143, sl. 30/3/17, Dodávkové příkazy ročník 1971. VÚA-VHA, MNO, 1977, karton 112, č.j. 006141, Vývoz a technická pomoc Iráku.

27 VÚA-VHA, MNO, 1967, karton 162, sl. 31D-69, č.j. 05269/SZS, Přecvičení iráckých pilotů a techniků na L-29 – kurs čís. 262. VÚA-VHA, MNO, 1967, karton 159, sl. 31D-46, č.j. 02867/17, Přecvičení iráckých pilotů a techniků na L-29 – ukončení, listopad 1967. VÚA-VHA, MNO, 1967, karton 159, sl. 31D-46, č.j. 066169, Ukončení přeškolovacího kursu iráckých specialistů na L-29, 18. listopadu 1967.

28 VÚA-VHA, MNO, 1969, karton 27, sl. 7/1-1, č.j. 020659, Komplexní rozbor zahraničních styků ministerstva národní obrany, uskutečněných v roce 1968, 28. března 1969. VÚA-VHA, MNO, 1969, karton 211, sl. 31D-37, č.j. 021152/SZS-1969, Návštěva iráckého viceprezidenta a pozvání ministra obrany irácké armády, 9. září 1969.

29 VÚA-VHA, MNO, 1967, karton 159, sl. 31D-46, č.j. 066169, Ukončení přeškolovacího kursu iráckých specialistů na L-29, 18. listopadu 1967.

30 VÚA-VHA, MNO, 1966, karton 245, sl. D/59, Vyhodnocení 1. čtvrtletí 1968. VÚA-VHA, MNO, 1968, karton 83, sl. 31D-41, Dílčí zpráva o práci pracovní skupiny pro výstavbu letiště a letecké školy v IRAKU. VÚA-VHA, MNO, 1968, karton 83, sl. 31D-43, Zpráva projekční skupiny Vojenského projektového ústavu a MNO z pobytu v Iráku.

31 VÚA-VHA, MNO, 1966, karton 245, sl. D/59, Vyhodnocení 1. čtvrtletí 1968.

32 VÚA-VHA, MNO, 1969, karton 27, sl. 7/1-1, č.j. 020659, Komplexní rozbor zahraničních styků ministerstva národní obrany, uskutečněných v roce 1968, 28. března 1969. VÚA-VHA, MNO, 1969, karton 211, sl. 31D-45, č.j. 02558/SZS, Technická pomoc Iráku, říjen 1967. VÚA-VHA, MNO, 1970, karton 139, sl. 22-4/1, č.j. 0152708/67, Zpráva ze služební cesty do Iráku ve dnech 22.10.-13.11.1967, 17. listopadu 1967.

33 VÚA-VHA, MNO, 1969, karton 27, sl. 7/1-1, č.j. 020659, Komplexní rozbor zahraničních styků ministerstva národní obrany, uskutečněných v roce 1968, 28. března 1969. VÚA-VHA, MNO, 1969, karton 211, sl. 31D-45, č.j. 02558/SZS, Technická pomoc Iráku, říjen 1967. VÚA-VHA, MNO, 1970, karton 139, sl. 22-4/1, č.j. 0152708/67, Zpráva ze služební cesty do Iráku ve dnech 22.10.-13.11.1967, 17. listopadu 1967. VÚA-VHA, MNO, 1966, karton 245, sl. D/59, Vyhodnocení 1. čtvrtletí 1968.

34 VÚA-VHA, MNO, 1970, karton 139, 22-4/2, č.j. 01622063, Výcvik iráckých pilotů, prosinec 1969.

35 VÚA-VHA, MNO, 1969, karton 383, sl. 38/3-26, č.j. 020665, Změny a další požadavky ve výcviku iráckých pilotů, 15. května 1969. VÚA-VHA, MNO, 1970, karton 139, 22-4/2, č.j. 020937/SZS, Zpráva ze služební cesty do Iráku ve dnech 22.6.-4.7.1969.

36 VÚA-VHA, MNO, 1969, karton 27, sl. 7/1-1, č.j. 020659, Komplexní rozbor zahraničních styků ministerstva národní obrany, uskutečněných v roce 1968, 28. března 1969.

37 VÚA-VHA, MNO, 1969, karton 170, sl. 15/15, č.j. L086072, Zpráva o vyšetřování letecké nehody, 7. listopadu 1969.

38 VÚA-VHA, MNO, 1970, karton 153, sl. 38/14, č.j. 15489/40-1970, Propuštění z dalšího výcviku na Su-7BM por. Abdul Muniam Al HASSANA, 16. září 1970. VÚA-VHA, MNO, 1971, karton 138, sl. 12/17, Výcvik iráckých pilotů, 2. dubna 1971. VÚA-VHA, MNO, 1977, karton 112, č.j. 006141, Přehled o čs. vojenské technické pomoci poskytované Irácké republice v letech 1967 – 1972. Dúbravčík, *Osmadvacítka*, p. 161.

39 NA, A ÚV KSČ, fond 1261/0/44 (Kancelář 1. tajemníka ÚV KSČ Antonína Novotného – II. část), karton 105 (Irák), inv. č. 193, obal 20, Zpráva o vývoji styků mezi ČSSR a Irákem v oblasti speciálních materiálů, 1967.

40 VÚA-VHA, MNO, 1969, karton 211, sl. 31D-3, č.j. 020028/SZS-1969, Návštěva irácké vládní delegace, 14. ledna 1969. VÚA-VHA, MNO, 1969, karton 211, sl. 31D-37, č.j. 021152/SZS-1969, Návštěva iráckého viceprezidenta a pozvání ministra obrany irácké armády, 9. září 1969. VÚA-VHA, MNO, 1970, karton 3, sign. 1/12/2/9, č.j. 0164954/70-05, Návrh na uzavření dohody s Iráckou republikou o dodávkách speciálního materiálu a platbách za ně, 24. února 1970.

41 VÚA-VHA, MNO, 1970, karton 143, sl. 30/3-17, Cestovní zpráva ze služební cesty do Iráku ze dne 18.11.-9.12.

42 VÚA-VHA, MNO, 1969, karton 201, sl. 30/3, č.j. 6842 14/1969, Uvolnění 4 ks 30mm PLDvK vz. 43 pro IRAK.

43 VÚA-VHA, MNO, 1970, karton 3, sign. 1/12/2/9, č.j. 0164954/70-05, Návrh na uzavření dohody s Iráckou republikou o dodávkách speciálního materiálu a platbách za ně, 24. února 1970.

44 VÚA-VHA, MNO, 1970, karton 24, sign. 2/7/1, č.j. 02474/SÚP-1970, Informační podklad pro s. ministra národní obrany související s pobytem irácké voj. delegace v ČSSR.

45 VÚA-VHA, MNO, 1969, karton 201, sl. 30/3, dopis generálního ředitele MZO/HTS, 6. srpna 1969.

46 VÚA-VHA, MNO, 1969, karton 201, sl. 30/3, Podklady pro jednání ministra zahraničního obchodu s Ing. Tabačka s ministrem národní obrany generálplukovníkem s. Ing. Dzúrem, 2. dubna 1969. VÚA-VHA, MNO, 1969, karton 201, sl. 30/3, č.j. 004020-14, Vývoz vojenské techniky do zahraničí. VÚA-VHA, MNO, 1969, karton 211, sl. 31D-37, č.j. 021152/SZS-1969, Návštěva iráckého viceprezidenta a pozvání ministra obrany irácké armády, 9. září 1969. VÚA-VHA, MNO, 1970, karton 24, sign. 2/7/1, č.j. 02474/SÚP-1970, Informační podklad pro s. ministra národní obrany související s pobytem irácké voj. delegace v ČSSR. VÚA-VHA, MNO, 1970, karton 144, sl. 30/3-17, č.j. 09337/SÚP-1970, Vyslání nakládací skupiny do PLR, 26. srpna 1970. VÚA-VHA, MNO, 1970, karton 144, sl. 30/3-17, VÚA-VHA, MNO, 1970, karton 144, sl. 30/3-17, č.j. 27/3/Pa/33, dopis HTS, 27. března 1970. VÚA-VHA, MNO, 1970, karton 144, sl. 30/3-17, č.j. 6559, Jednání k zabezpečení výuky a dodávek, 31. března 1970. VÚA-VHA, MNO, 1977, karton 112, č.j. 006141, Podkladový materiál k návštěvě irácké delegace o čs. technické pomoci Iraku.

47 Within the frame of the federalisation of Czechoslovakia, the Czech Socialist Republic and the Slovak Socialist Republic were established on 1 January 1969. This was associated with renaming of ministries with statewide authority that added the word Federal into their official titles.

48 VÚA-VHA, MNO, 1969, karton 211, sl. 31D-37, č.j. 021152/
    SZS-1969, Návštěva iráckého viceprezidenta a pozvání ministra
    obrany irácké armády, 9. září 1969. VÚA-VHA, MNO, 1970,
    karton 24, sign. 2/7/1, č.j. 02474/SÚP-1970, Informační podklad
    pro s. ministra národní obrany související s pobytem irácké voj.
    delegace v ČSSR.

49 VÚA-VHA, MNO, 1969, karton 27, sl. 7/1-1, č.j. 020659,
    Komplexní rozbor zahraničních styků ministerstva národní
    obrany, uskutečněných v roce 1968, 28. března 1969. VÚA-VHA,
    MNO, 1969, karton 207, sl. 50/17, č.j. 12549, Hodnocení kursu
    302 B, 19. prosince 1969. VÚA-VHA, MNO, 1969, karton 211, sl.
    31D-37, č.j. 021152/SZS-1969, Návštěva iráckého viceprezidenta a
    pozvání ministra obrany irácké armády, 9. září 1969. VÚA-VHA,
    MNO, 1970, karton 137, sl. 12/21, č.j. 012152, Zaslání Výroční
    zprávy ZF za rok 1969, 5. ledna 1970.

50 VÚA-VHA, MNO, 1977, karton 112, č.j. 006141, Přehled o čs.
    vojenské technické pomoci poskytované Irácké republice v letech
    1967 – 1972.

51 VÚA-VHA, MNO, 1970, karton 142, sl. 30/5, č.j. 01025/23 – 1970,
    Zpráva o služební cestě do Iráku, 3. leden 1970. VÚA-VHA,
    MNO, 1970, karton 153, sl. 31-4/57, č.j. 40503-34/29, Akce 760 a
    762 – podklady, 26. březen 1970.

52 VÚA-VHA, MNO, 1970, karton 3, sl. 1/12/2/9, č.j. 0164954/70-
    05, Návrh na uzavření dohody s Iráckou republikou o dodávkách
    speciálního materiálu a platbách za ně, 24. února 1970. VÚA-
    VHA, MNO, 1970, karton 24, sign. 2/7/1, č.j. 02474/SÚP-1970,
    Dodatek k informaci o problematice československo-iráckých
    vztahů ve speciální oblasti. VÚA-VHA, MNO, 1970, karton
    144, sl. 30/3-17, č.j. 04960/70-101, Záznam z jednání PV dne
    12.3.1970. VÚA-VHA, MNO, 1972, karton 93, sl. 86/1, Návštěva
    irácké vojenské delegace v ČSSR 30.5.-8.6.1972.

53 VÚA-VHA, MNO, 1971, karton 143, sl. 30/14, č. 021.054/71-8,
    Bagdád – záznam o návštěvě velvyslance u ministra obrany, 24.
    února 1971.

54 VÚA-VHA, MNO, 1972, karton 93, sl. 86/1, Návštěva irácké
    vojenské delegace v ČSSR 30.5.-8.6.1972.

55 NA, A ÚV KSČ, fond 1261/0/6 (Předsednictvo ÚV KSČ 1971-
    1976), sv. 77, ar.j. 73, k informaci bod 6, Zpráva o podepsání nové
    dohody s Iráckou republikou o dodávkách speciálního materiálu,
    10. dubna 1973.

56 NA, A ÚV KSČ, fond 1261/0/6 (Předsednictvo ÚV KSČ 1971-
    1976), sv. 77, ar.j. 73, k informaci bod 6, Zpráva o podepsání nové
    dohody s Iráckou republikou o dodávkách speciálního materiálu,
    10. dubna 1973.

57 NA, A ÚV KSČ, fond 1261/0/6 (Předsednictvo ÚV KSČ 1971-
    1976), sv. 108, ar.j. 109, bod 5, Rozšíření úvěrového rámce na
    dodávky speciálního materiálu do Iráku, 30. ledna 1974. VÚA-
    VHA, MNO, 1973, karton 100, sl. 53/3, č.j. 007230, Akce 99 –
    přehled písemností, Telegram z Bagdádu, 14. října 1973.

58 VÚA-VHA, MNO, 1974, karton 120, sl. 85/12, výměnný dopis, 3.
    dubna 1974.

59 VÚA-VHA, MNO, 1974, karton 120, sl. 85/12, výměnný dopis, 3.
    dubna 1974.

60 VÚA-VHA, MNO, 1968, karton 62, sl. 30-3/3, Výkazy
    jmenovitých položek za I. – IV. čtvrtletí 1964, 19. února 1965.
    VÚA-VHA, MNO, 1967, karton 158, sl. 27/1/2, č.j. 00750/10-67,
    Komplexní rozbor zahraničních styků MNO v r. 1966, 10. dubna
    1967. VÚA-VHA, MNO, 1968, karton 80, sl. 22/1, č.j. 012297/68,
    Komplexní rozbor zahraničních styků ministerstva národní
    obrany, uskutečněných v roce 1967, 11. března 1968. VÚA-VHA,
    MNO, 1969, karton 27, sl. 7/1-1, č.j. 020659, Komplexní rozbor

    zahraničních styků ministerstva národní obrany, uskutečněných
    v roce 1968, 28. března 1969. VÚA-VHA, MNO, 1969, karton
    201, sl. 30/3, Vývoz 1969. VÚA-VHA, MNO, 1969, karton 211, sl.
    31D-37, č.j. 021152/SZS-1969, Návštěva iráckého viceprezidenta a
    pozvání ministra obrany irácké armády, 9. září 1969. VÚA-VHA,
    MNO, 1974, karton 120, sl. 84/13, č.j. 08006/21-19-74, návštěva
    vojenské obchodní delegace Iráku, 26. srpna 1974. VÚA-VHA,
    MNO, 1974, karton 120, sl. 84/14, č.j. 008069/12-FMNO/14-1974,
    Přehled zahraničních odběratelů speciálního materiálu z ČSSR v
    letech 1970-1974. Fojtík, *Delfín*, p. 162.

61 VÚA-VHA, MNO, 1976, karton 100, sl. 86/2, č.j. 04332, Vyslání
    2 pracovníků FMNO – OZ 026, leden 1976. VÚA-VHA, MNO,
    1977, karton 112, k č.j. 061866-84, Návrh na doplnění
    zprávy. VÚA-VHA, MNO, 1977, karton 112, č.j. 006141,
    Podkladový materiál, Přijetí ministra obrany Iráku.

62 VÚA-VHA, MNO, 1977, karton 112, č.j. 006141, č.j. 037087/HT,
    Zranění pplk. Ing. Karla Matějíčka, listopad 1974.

63 VÚA-VHA, MNO, 1977, karton 112, č.j. 006141, č.j. 09392/SÚP,
    Příprava školení iráckých specialistů pro JVBT-55, leden 1975.

64 VÚA-VHA, MNO, 1976, karton 102, č.j. 006123, Výcvik iráckých
    specialistů pro 30 mm PLDvK vz. 53/70.

65 VÚA-VHA, MNO, 1977, karton 112, č.j. 006141, k č.j. 06141/19-
    72/SÚP-77, Stanovisko GŠ/SÚP ke zprávám čs. velvyslance v
    Bagdádu č. 0160 a 0186.

66 VÚA-VHA, MNO, 1977, karton 112, č.j. 006141, č.j. 071982-84,
    Výcvik iráckých letovodů, 18. září 1973. VÚA-VHA, MNO, 1977,
    karton 112, č.j. 006141, k č.j. 001101, Stanovisko NGŠ ČSLA-1.
    ZMNO k č.j. 082897-84, VÚA-VHA, MNO, 1977, karton 112, č.j.
    006141, č.j. 7527-14/76, Účast iráckých vojenských představitelů
    při ukončení výcviku letovodů, 23. dubna 1976.

67 NA, A ÚV KSČ, fond 1261/0/6 (Předsednictvo ÚV KSČ 1971-
    1976), sv. 108, ar.j. 109, bod 5, Rozšíření úvěrového rámce na
    dodávky speciálního materiálu do Iráku, 30. ledna 1974. VÚA-
    VHA, MNO, 1974, karton 120, sl. 85/12, č.j. 08648/SÚP, Úvěrová
    dohoda s Irákem, 31. května 1974. VÚA-VHA, MNO, 1977,
    karton 112, č.j. 006141, č.j. 04351/SÚP, Výstavba radioopravny v
    Iráku, srpen 1972.

68 VÚA-VHA, MNO, 1977, karton 112, č.j. 006141, č.j. 06094-6,
    Zpráva o výsledku jednání v Iráku o výstavbě opravny vozidel, 20.
    července 1973.

69 VÚA-VHA, MNO, 1974, karton 120, sl. 85/12, č.j. 08648/SÚP,
    Úvěrová dohoda s Irákem, 31. května 1974. VÚA-VHA, MNO,
    1977, karton 112, č.j. 006141, č.j. 4064/SÚP, Výstavba opravny
    vojenské techniky v Iráku v sovětsko-čs. spolupráci, září 1974.
    VÚA-VHA, MNO, 1977, karton 112, č.j. 006141, č.j. 09218/
    SÚP, Výstavba opravny vojenské techniky v Iráku v sovětsko-čs.
    spolupráci, 28. listopadu 1974.

70 VÚA-VHA, MNO, 1977, karton 112, č.j. 006141, č.j. 001101/19,
    Technická pomoc Iráku.

71 VÚA-VHA, MNO, 1977, karton 112, č.j. 006141, č.j. 08371/SÚP,
    Výstavba letecké opravny v Iráku, 22. července 1974. VÚA-VHA,
    MNO, 1977, karton 112, č.j. 006141, č.j. 09105/SÚP-74, Výstavba
    letecké opravny v Iráku, prosinec 1974.

72 VÚA-VHA, MNO, 1977, karton 112, č.j. 006141, č.j. 090969-
    84, Zavedení generálních oprav letounů L-29 v Iráku, 12.
    května 1975.

73 VÚA-VHA, MNO, 1979, karton 183, č.j. 04121, k č.j. 004121-
    16/14-1979, Zpráva o realizaci vývozu a technické pomoci za IV.
    čtvrtletí 1979.

74 VÚA-VHA, MNO, 1977, karton 112, č.j. 006141, č.j. 062284-84, 13. listopadu 1972, Uzavření dohody na dodávky speciálního materiálu – Irák. Fojtík, *Albatros*, pp. 123–124.

75 Irra, *L-39 Albatros, 2. díl*, pp. 29–32.

76 Fojtík, *Albatros*, p. 124.

77 NA, A ÚV KSČ, fond 1261/0/7 (Předsednictvo ÚV KSČ 1976-1979), sv. 32, ar.j. 37, bod 3, Zpráva o požadavcích irácké strany na spolupráci ve vojenském vysokém technickém školství, 15. března 1977. VÚA-VHA, MNO, 1969, karton 211, sl. 31D-21, č.j. 020674/SZS, Příprava k návštěvě irácké vojenské delegace, květen 1969. VÚA-VHA, MNO, 1972, karton 69, č.j. 05383, Zpráva o pobytu delegace vojenského školství v Iráku, 31. března 1972. Podkladový materiál, Přijetí ministra obrany Iráku. VÚA-VHA, MNO, 1977, karton 112, č.j. 006141, č.j. 08409/SÚP, Návštěva irácké vojenské delegace na VAAZ v Brně, 28. března 1974.

78 NA, A ÚV KSČ, fond 1261/0/7 (Předsednictvo ÚV KSČ 1976-1979), sv. 32, ar.j. 37, bod 3, Zpráva o požadavcích irácké strany na spolupráci ve vojenském vysokém technickém školství, 15. března 1977. Vyhlídal, *Československá pomoc při výstavbě vojenského školství*, pp. 19–20.

79 NA, A ÚV KSČ, fond 1261/0/7 (Předsednictvo ÚV KSČ 1976-1981), P 144/80, bod 9, Zpráva o speciální technické pomoci poskytované iráckým ozbrojeným silám ve vojenském vysokém technickém školství podle usnesení PV ČSSR č. 68 ze dne 10. března 1977 a o nových požadavcích irácké strany v uvedené oblasti, 10. července 1980. VÚA-VHA, MNO, 1977, karton 112, č.j. 006141, č.j. 001101/19, Technická pomoc Iráku.

80 Vyhlídal, *Československá pomoc při výstavbě vojenského školství*, pp. 21–23.

81 NA, A ÚV KSČ, fond 1261/0/7 (Předsednictvo ÚV KSČ 1976-1981), P 144/80, bod 9, Zpráva o speciální technické pomoci poskytované iráckým ozbrojeným silám ve vojenském vysokém technickém školství podle usnesení PV ČSSR č. 68 ze dne 10. března 1977 a o nových požadavcích irácké strany v uvedené oblasti, 10. července 1980. VÚA-VHA, MNO, 1979, karton 183, č.j. 04121, příloha k č.j. 004121/14-1979, Finanční vyhodnocení technické pomoci poskytované Čs. lidovou armádou ve 4. čtvrtletí 1979.

82 AMZV, TO-T 1980-1989, Irák, karton 8, obal 38, č.j. 01122/82, Zpráva o iráckém zbrojním průmyslu a jeho dalším rozvoji, 28. dubna 1982.

83 AMZV, TO-T 1980-1989, Irák, karton 8, obal 38, č.j. 01122/82, Zpráva o iráckém zbrojním průmyslu a jeho dalším rozvoji, 28. dubna 1982. AMZV, TO-T 1980-1989, Irák, karton 6, obal 27, č.j. 0133/80, Súčasná ekonomická situácia v Iraku, 15. prosince 1980. AMZV, TO-T 1980-1989, Irák, karton 6, obal 27, č.j. 013.766/81, Odpověď s. ministra na dopis s. ministra Barčáka, 15. června 1981.

84 NA, A ÚV KSČ, fond 1261/0/7 (Předsednictvo ÚV KSČ 1976-1981), sv. 53, ar.j. 59, bod 2, Zpráva o jednání s Irákem o výstavbě na klíč závodu na výrobu pěchotní munice /akce Beta/, 14. listopadu 1977.

85 NA, A ÚV KSČ, fond 1261/0/7 (Předsednictvo ÚV KSČ 1976-1981), sv. 53, ar.j. 59, bod 2, Zpráva o jednání s Irákem o výstavbě na klíč závodu na výrobu pěchotní munice /akce Beta/, 14. listopadu 1977. AMZV, TO-T 1975-1979, Irák, karton 1, obal 4, č.j. 02912/78-11, Podklady k ekonomické části jednání předsedy vlády ČSSR s. L. Štrougala v Irácké republice, 15. listopadu 1978. AMZV, TO-T 1980-1989, Irák, karton 6, obal 27, č.j. 0133/80, Súčasná ekonomická situácia v Iraku, 15. prosince 1980. AMZV, TO-T 1980-1989, Irák, karton 8, obal 38, č.j. 01122/82,

Zpráva o iráckém zbrojním průmyslu a jeho dalším rozvoji, 28. dubna 1982.

86 AMZV, TO-T 1980-1989, Irák, karton 6, obal 27, č.j. 012033/81, Informace o stavu čs. závazků na dodávky speciálního materiálu do Iráku.

87 AMZV, TO-T 1980-1989, Irák, karton 8, obal 38, č.j. 089/81, Zpráva o činnosti a perspektivách v oblasti FMZO-HTS v Iráku, 11. srpna 1981.

88 AMZV, TO-T 1980-1989, Irák, karton 8, obal 38, č.j. 089/81, Zpráva o činnosti a perspektivách v oblasti FMZO-HTS v Iráku, 11. srpna 1981. VÚA-VHA, MNO, 1977, karton 112, č.j. 006141, Telegram z Bagdádu, 16. května 1977.

89 Zídek & Sieber, *Československo a Blízký východ v letech 1948-1989*, p. 106.

90 AMZV, TO-T 1980-1989, Irák, karton 6, obal 27, č.j. 012033/81, Informace o stavu čs. závazků na dodávky speciálního materiálu do Iráku.

91 AMZV, TO-T 1980-1989, Irák, karton 6, obal 27, č.j. 012033/81, Informace o stavu čs. závazků na dodávky speciálního materiálu do Iráku.

92 Zídek & Sieber, *Československo a Blízký východ v letech 1948-1989*, p. 107.

93 AMZV, TO-T 1980-1989, Irák, karton 6, obal 27, č.j. 013.766/81, Odpověď s. ministra na dopis s. ministra Barčáka, 15. června 1981.

94 AMZV, TO-T 1980-1989, Irák, karton 6, obal 27, č.j. 013.766/81, Odpověď s. ministra na dopis s. ministra Barčáka, 15. června 1981. AMZV, TO-T 1980-1989, Irák, karton 6, obal 27, č.j. 0133/80, Súčasná ekonomická situácia v Iraku, 15. prosince 1980. AMZV, TO-T 1980-1989, Irák, karton 8, obal 38, č.j. 089/81, Zpráva o činnosti a perspektivách v oblasti FMZO-HTS v Iráku, 11. srpna 1981.

95 Zídek & Sieber, *Československo a Blízký východ v letech 1948-1989*, p. 108.

96 AMZV, TO-T 1980-1989, Irák, karton 6, obal 27, č.j. 013.766/81, Odpověď s. ministra na dopis s. ministra Barčáka, 15. června 1981. AMZV, TO-T 1980-1989, Irák, karton 7, obal 30, č.j. 063/82, Správa o vzájemných vzťahoch v období 1979-1981 medzi ČSSR a Irakom, 9. března 1982. AMZV, TO-T 1980-1989, Irák, karton 8, obal 38, č.j. 089/81, Zpráva o činnosti a perspektivách v oblasti FMZO-HTS v Iráku, 11. srpna 1981.

97 Vyhlídal, *Československá pomoc při výstavbě vojenského školství*, pp. 34–36.

98 Vyhlídal, *Československá pomoc při výstavbě vojenského školství*, pp. 37–39.

99 Vyhlídal, *Československá pomoc při výstavbě vojenského školství*, pp. 41–45.

100 AMZV, TO-T 1980-1989, Irák, karton 8, obal 39, č.j. 01345/83, Zpráva o technické pomoci a vědeckotechnické spolupráci mezi ČSSR a Iráckou republikou za rok 1983, 15. listopadu 1983.

101 Vyhlídal, *Československá pomoc při výstavbě vojenského školství*, p. 47.

102 Vyhlídal, *Československá pomoc při výstavbě vojenského školství*, p. 27.

103 Francev, *Československé tankové síly*, p. 162. Štaigl & Turza, *Zbrojná výroba na Slovensku v rokoch 1969-1992 (1. časť)*, p. 93. Štaigl & Turza, *Zbrojná výroba na Slovensku v rokoch 1969-1992 (2. časť)*, p. 91.

104 AMZV, TO-T 1980-1989, Irák, karton 7, obal 30, č.j. 063/82, Správa o vzájemných vzťahoch v období 1979-1981 medzi ČSSR a Irakom, 9. března 1982.

105 Zídek & Sieber, *Československo a Blízký východ v letech 1948-1989*, p. 110.

106 AMZV, TO-T 1980-1989, Irák, karton 6, obal 26, č.j. 046 965, Informace o jednání v oblasti speciálu s iráckou delegací 24. až 30.11.1986, 1. prosince 1986.

107 AMZV, TO-T 1980-1989, Irák, karton 6, obal 27, č.j. 01028/89, Roční zpráva 1988 – OBO, 25. března 1989. AMZV, TO-T 1980-1989, Irák, karton 8, obal 36, č.j. 01005/88, Zpráva o plnění záměrů čs. zahraniční politiky vůči Irácké republice v roce 1987, 18. ledna 1988.

108 NA, A ÚV KSČ, fond 1261/0/9 (Předsednictvo ÚV KSČ 1986-1989), P 131/89, bod 13, Uskutečnění oficiální návštěvy předsedy vlády ČSSR s. L. ADAMCE v Irácké republice a Egyptské arabské republice ve dnech 14. – 19. října 1989, 19. září 1989. NA, A ÚV KSČ, fond 1261/0/9 (Předsednictvo ÚV KSČ 1986-1989), P 136/89, bod 5, Oficiální návštěva předsedy vlády ČSSR s. L. ADAMCE v Irácké republice a Egyptské arabské republice, 24. října 1989.

109 Stojanov, *Finanční pohledávky České republiky u rozvojových zemí*, p. 12. ČTK, Země loni dlužily Česku 12 miliard korun. Dluh klesl, peníze uhradilo Srbsko i Irák, *Aktuálně.cz*, https://zpravy. aktualne.cz/ekonomika/dluhy-statu-vuci-cesku-se-loni-snizily-na-12-miliard-korun/r~8034f978ae2a11eab115ac1f6b220ee8/ (accessed 11 October 2020).

CHAPTER 3

1 Zídek & Sieber, *Československo a Blízký východ v letech 1948-1989*, pp. 148–149.

2 AMZV, TO-T 1955-1959, Jemen, karton 1, obal 124/211, č.j. 7938/dův.hl.št.prům/49, Jemen – dodávka 10.000 pušek K 98, 250 kul. vz.26, 150 kul. vz. 37 s municí, 29. říjen 1949.

3 NA, A ÚV KSČ, Politické byro ÚV KSČ 1954-1962 (1261/0/11), sv. 103, ar.j. 120, bod 23, Jednání o dodávkách vojenské techniky do Finska, Švédska a Jemenu, 24. května 1956.

4 NA, A ÚV KSČ, Politické byro ÚV KSČ 1954-1962 (1261/0/11), sv. 108, ar.j. 126, bod 22, Dodávky speciálního materiálu z ČSR do Jemenu, 9. července 1956.

5 NA, A ÚV KSČ, Politické byro ÚV KSČ 1954-1962 (1261/0/11), sv. 211, ar.j. 287, bod 6, Československo-jemenské styky, 12. března 1959.

6 VÚA-VHA, MNO, 1962, karton 367, sign. 30-2/4, Souhrnné dokumenty o vývozu, Přehled o vývozu vojenské techniky do kapitalistických států, 6. února 1959.

7 VÚA-VHA, MNO, 1956, karton 522, sign. 26/7/7-329, č.j. 023293, seznam leteckého, tankového a dělostřeleckého materiálu, 30. července 1956. VÚA-VHA, MNO, 1956, karton 522, sign. 26/7/7-330, Seznam materiálů které ministerstvo národní obrany uvolňuje ze svých zásob pro vývoz do Jemenu podle usnesení politického byra ÚV KSČ z 9.7.56, srpen 1956. VÚA-VHA, MNO, 1956, karton 523, sign. 26/7/7-490, č.j. 05068/NGŠ 1956, Vyslání čs. specialistů do Jemenu, 5. říjen 1956. VÚA-VHA, MNO, 1957, karton 399, sign. 30-4/168, k č.j. 002949-1/SMP-5, Informační zpráva pro ZNGŠ jako přednes k jednání kolegia min. NO 10.9.1957. VÚA-VHA, MNO, 1962, karton 367, sign. 30/2/4, Souhrnné dokumenty o vývozu, Přehled o vývozu voj. techniky do kapitalistických států, 6. února 1959. VÚA-VHA, MNO, 1963 karton 360, sign. D/20, č.j. 02092/OTP, Návrh na tech. pomoc Jemenské arabské republice, únor 1963. VÚA-VHA, MNO, 1969, karton 172, Evidence GŠ/SMP-5 – vývozní skupina. VÚA-VHA, MNO, 1969, karton 173, Evidence GŠ/SMP-5 – vývozní skupina. VÚA-VHA, MNO, 1969, karton 174, Evidence GŠ/SMP-5 – vývozní skupina. VÚA-VHA, MNO, 1969, karton 175, Evidence GŠ/SMP-5 – vývozní skupina.

8 NA, A ÚV KSČ, Politické byro ÚV KSČ 1954-1962 (1261/0/11), sv. 150, ar.j. 195, bod 16, Návrh na usnesení politického byra ÚV KSČ o dalších dodávkách vojenské techniky do Mutavakilijského království Jemenu a o poskytnutí technické pomoci, 19. srpna 1957.

9 VÚA-VHA, MNO, 1957, karton 397, sign. 30/2/6-24, č.j. 001265-7, Uvolnění speciálního materiálu pro vývoz do Jemenu, 22. června 1957.

10 NA, A ÚV KSČ, Politické byro ÚV KSČ 1954-1962 (1261/0/11), sv. 150, ar.j. 195, bod 16, Návrh na usnesení politického byra ÚV KSČ o dalších dodávkách vojenské techniky do Mutavakilijského království Jemenu a o poskytnutí technické pomoci, 19. srpna 1957.

11 NA, A ÚV KSČ, fond 1261/0/44 (Kancelář 1. tajemníka ÚV KSČ Antonína Novotného – II. část), karton 111 (Jemen), inv. č. 221, obal 7, Řešení dalších požadavků JAR o dodávky vojenské techniky z ČSSR. 1963. VÚA-VHA, MNO, 1963 karton 360, sign. D/20, č.j. 02092/OTP, Návrh na tech. pomoc Jemenské arabské republice, únor 1963.

12 NA, A ÚV KSČ, Politické byro ÚV KSČ 1954-1962 (1261/0/11), sv. 150, ar.j. 195, bod 16, Návrh na usnesení politického byra ÚV KSČ o dalších dodávkách vojenské techniky do Mutavakilijského království Jemenu a o poskytnutí technické pomoci, 19. srpna 1957.

13 VÚA-VHA, MNO, 1962, karton 367, sign. 30/2/4, Souhrnné dokumenty o vývozu, Přehled o vývozu voj. techniky do kapitalistických států, 6. února 1959. VÚA-VHA, MNO, 1963 karton 360, sign. D/20, č.j. 02092/OTP, Návrh na tech. pomoc Jemenské arabské republice, únor 1963. VÚA-VHA, MNO, 1969, karton 172, Evidence GŠ/SMP-5 – vývozní skupina. VÚA-VHA, MNO, 1969, karton 173, Evidence GŠ/SMP-5 – vývozní skupina. VÚA-VHA, MNO, 1969, karton 174, Evidence GŠ/SMP-5 – vývozní skupina. VÚA-VHA, MNO, 1969, karton 175, Evidence GŠ/SMP-5 – vývozní skupina.

14 NA, A ÚV KSČ, Politické byro ÚV KSČ 1954-1962 (1261/0/11), sv. 151, ar.j. 198, bod 16, Průběh technické pomoci a rozsah dalšího poskytování této pomoci Egyptu, Syrii a Jemenu, 7. září 1957. VÚA-VHA, MNO, 1956, karton 523, sign. 26/7/7-490, č.j. 041229/SMP, Vyslání čs. specialistů do Jemenu, 5. říjen 1956. VÚA-VHA, MNO, 1956, karton 523, sign. 26/7/7-440, č.j. 041270 GŠ/SMP, Vyslání instruktorů do Jemenu, 15. říjen 1956. VÚA-VHA, MNO, 1956, karton 523, sign. 26/7/7-410, č.j. 041107 GŠ/SMP, Výběr instruktorů pro Jemen, 27. srpen 1956.

15 VÚA-VHA, MNO, 1957, karton 395, sign. 30/2, OPIS KONTRAKTU podepsaného mezi Československou republikou a Mutavakilijským královstvím Jemenu o vyslání československých instruktorů do Jemenu a jemenských specialistů do Československa podle dohody ze dne 11. července 1956.

16 NA, A ÚV KSČ, Politické byro ÚV KSČ 1954-1962 (1261/0/11), sv. 151, ar.j. 198, bod 16, Průběh technické pomoci a rozsah dalšího poskytování této pomoci Egyptu, Syrii a Jemenu, 7. září 1957. VÚA-VHA, MNO, 1956, karton 523, sign. 26/7/7-440, č.j. 041270 GŠ/SMP, Vyslání instruktorů do Jemenu, 15. říjen 1956. VÚA-VHA, MNO, 1957, karton 397, sign. 30/2/6-24, Nové požadavky Jemenu, 27. srpna 1957. VÚA-VHA, MNO, 1957, karton 399, sign. 30-4/168, k č.j. 002949-1/SMP-5, Informační zpráva pro ZNGŠ jako přednes k jednání kolegia min. NO 10.9.1957. VÚA-VHA, MNO, 1958, karton 367, sign. 30-3/1,

č.j. 00/5046-8/25-21, Zápis z porady o vyslání čs. specialistů do Jemenu, 9. ledna 1958.

17 VÚA-VHA, MNO, 1957, karton 397, sign. 30/2/6-20, č.j. 01432, Letouny B-33 pro Jemen, 30. května 1957. VÚA-VHA, MNO, 1957, karton 397, sign. 30/2, č.j. 00232/16-SMP-5, Dodávky letounů B-33 do Jemenu, 14. června 1957.

18 VÚA-VHA, MNO, 1956, karton 523, sign. 26/7/7-440, č.j. 041270 GŠ/SMP, Vyslání instruktorů do Jemenu, 15. říjen 1956. VÚA-VHA, MNO, 1957, karton 397, sign. 30/2/6-32, Návrh kontraktu na vyslání specialistů do Jemenu, 19. července 1957. VÚA-VHA, MNO, 1957, karton 397, sign. 30/2/6-37, Vyslání specialistů do země 110, 13. prosince 1957. VÚA-VHA, MNO, 1957, karton 621, sign. 38/10-6, Přehled příslušníků letectva a PVOS, kteří se nacházejí v cizině v rámci akce 105 a 110. VÚA-VHA, MNO, 1958, karton 367, sign. 30-3/1, č.j. 00/5046-8/25-21, Zápis z porady o vyslání čs. specialistů do Jemenu, 9. ledna 1958.

19 VÚA-VHA, MNO, 1958, karton 369, sign. 30/3/3-1, Zabezpečení čs. vojenských instruktorů v Jemenu, 6. dubna 1959. VÚA-VHA, MNO, 1959, karton 354, sign. 30/3/2-5, Vyslání specialistů do země 110, 28. listopadu 1958.

20 VÚA-VHA, MNO, 1958, karton 108, sign. 015042, č.j. 010087/SMP-5, Vyslání čs. odborníků do Jemenu – upřesnění, 24. ledna 1958.

21 VÚA-VHA, MNO, 1958, karton 367, sign. 30-3/22, č.j. 012902, Zpráva o pobytu v Jemenu, 23. listopadu 1958.

22 VÚA-VHA, MNO, 1959, karton 354, sign. 30/3/2-5, Vyslání specialistů do země 110, 28. listopadu 1958. VÚA-VHA, MNO, 1959, karton 351, sign. 30-3/24, Hlášení o situaci v Jemenu, 8. července 1959. VÚA-VHA, MNO, 1959, karton 351, 30-3/24, sign. 30-3/35, č.j. 07446, Situační hlášení Sanaá, 3. květen 1959.

23 VÚA-VHA, MNO, 1958, karton 369, sign. 30/3/3-1, Zabezpečení čs. vojenských instruktorů v Jemenu, 6. dubna 1959.

24 VÚA-VHA, MNO, 1959, karton 351, 30-3/24, sign. 30-3/35, č.j. 07446, Situační hlášení Sanaá, 3. květen 1959.

25 VÚA-VHA, MNO, 1959, karton 351, 30-3/24, sign. 30-3/35, č.j. 046907/OZK-140, Zpráva z kursu č. 534, 6. října 1959.

26 VÚA-VHA, MNO, 1959, karton 351, 30-3/24, sign. 30-3/35, č.j. 046907/OZK-140, Zpráva z kursu č. 534, 6. října 1959.

27 NA, A ÚV KSČ, Politické byro ÚV KSČ 1954-1962 (1261/0/11), sv. 211, ar.j. 287, bod 6, Československo-jemenské styky, 12. března 1959.

28 VÚA-VHA, MNO, 1960, karton 238, sign. 0098, č.j. 0052576 SMP-5, Žádost Jemenu o zahájení leteckého výcviku, 27. říjen 1960. VÚA-VHA, MNO, 1960, karton 463, sign. 30/3/3/20, č.j. 050799/SMP-5, Žádost Jemenu o zahájení výcviku leteckého personálu, listopad 1960.

29 VÚA-VHA, MNO, 1961, karton 453, sign. 30/3/3/11, příloha k č.j. 011636-SMP, Zpráva o služební cestě do Jemenu vykonané ve dnech 27.3.-2.5.1961.

30 VÚA-VHA, MNO, 1961, karton 76, sign. 38/3-79, č.j. 02168, Návrh na možnosti výcviku v Jemenu – zaslání, 15. června 1961. VÚA-VHA, MNO 1962, karton 376, sign. K/106, č.j. 005176/62-OTP, Souhrnná zpráva o poskytování technické pomoci hospodářsky méně vyvinutým zemím za rok 1961, 24. leden 1962.

31 NA, A ÚV KSČ, fond 1261/0/4 (Předsednictvo ÚV KSČ 1962-1966), sv. 1, ar.j. 1, bod 8, Jednání s delegací Jemenské arabské republiky, 27. listopadu 1962. VÚA-VHA, MNO, 1962, karton 24, sign. 32/4-6, č.j. 050799-OTP, Pobyt jemenské vládní delegace v ČSSR. 18. listopadu 1962.

32 VÚA-VHA, MNO, 1963, karton 360, sign. D/20, č.j. 02092/OTP, Návrh na tech. pomoc Jemenské arabské republice, únor 1963.

33 NA, A ÚV KSČ, fond 1261/0/4 (Předsednictvo ÚV KSČ 1962-1966), sv. 22, ar.j. 24, bod 5, Řešení dalších požadavků Jemenské arabské republiky, 28. května 1963. VÚA-VHA, MNO, 1963, karton 360, sign. D/20, č.j. 02092/OTP, Návrh na tech. pomoc Jemenské arabské republice, únor 1963. VÚA-VHA, MNO, 1964, karton 21, inv.č. 32, sign. 24/5/1-9, č.j. 0010861/sekr.min., Návštěva prezidenta Jemenské arabské republiky v ČSSR, 25. března 1964.

34 NA, A ÚV KSČ, fond 1261/0/4 (Předsednictvo ÚV KSČ 1962-1966), sv. 65, ar.j. 69, bod 5, Zpráva o pobytu presidenta Jemenské arabské republiky maršála Abdulláha as-Salláha, 20. května 1964. VÚA-VHA, MNO, 1964, karton 26, sign. 39/1-3, č.j. 010982-22, dopis ministra národní obrany, 1. dubna 1964.

35 VÚA-VHA, MNO, 1964, karton 325, sign. D/66, č.j. 0033690-50/1964, Akce 110 – finanční vyhodnocení, 4. srpna 1964. VÚA-VHA, MNO, 1964, karton 326, sign. D/79, č.j. 003335/OTP, Akce 110, 4. červen 1964. VÚA-VHA, MNO, 1969, karton 27, sl. 7/1-1, č.j. 020659, Komplexní rozbor zahraničních styků ministerstva národní obrany, uskutečněných v roce 1968, 28. března 1969.

36 VÚA-VHA, MNO, 1964, karton 326, sign. D/79, Zpráva o předání vojenského materiálu Jemenské republice, 4. červen 1964.

37 VÚA-VHA, MNO, 1964, karton 326, sign. D/79, Zpráva o činnosti skupiny v Jemenské arabské republice.

38 VÚA-VHA, MNO, 1964, karton 326, sign. D/80, č.j. 03435/OTP, Technická pomoc Jemenské arabské republice, 28. července 1964.

39 NA, A ÚV KSČ, fond 1261/0/5 (Předsednictvo ÚV KSČ 1966-1971), sv. 59, ar.j. 67, bod 3, Poskytnutí československé pomoci Jemenské arabské republice, 20. ledna 1968. VÚA-VHA, MNO, 1970, karton 143, sl. 30 (sběrný arch Vývoz do KS), č.j. 012235/SZS, Akce 110, 18. dubna 1968.

40 VÚA-VHA, MNO, 1969, karton 201, sl. 30/3 (sběrný arch Vývoz do KS), Vyjádření GŠ/Správy ústředního plánování (25).

41 AMZV, TO-T 1970-1974, Jemenská arabská republika, karton 1, obal 2, č.j. 016.045/74-8, Informační zpráva k přijetí velvyslance Jemenské arabské republiky.

42 Zídek & Sieber, *Československo a Blízký východ v letech 1948-1989*, pp. 160–162.

43 AMZV, TO-T 1980-1989, Jemenská arabská republika, karton 1, obal 1, č.j. 011.757/81-8, Informace k současnému vývoji vztahů mezi ČSSR a Jemenskou arabskou republikou, 5. března 1981. AMZV, TO-T 1980-1989, Jemenská arabská republika, karton 1, obal 2, č.j. 014.291/80-8, Materiál pro vládu ČSSR – Návrh na pozvání a uskutečnění návštěvy místopředsedy vlády a ministra zahraničních věcí Jemenské arabské republiky Hasana Makkiho v ČSSR, 18. června 1980.

44 AMZV, TO-T 1980-1989, Jemenská arabská republika, karton 1, obal 4, č.j. 011972/92-81, Zpráva o požadavku Jemenské arabské republiky na změnu úvěrových podmínek, 16. ledna 1981.

45 AMZV, TO-T 1980-1989, Jemenská arabská republika, karton 1, obal 1, č.j. 012.248/85-8, JeAR – List ministra zahr. vecí ČSSR předsedovi vlády ČSSR, 13. června 1985.

46 AMZV, TO-T 1980-1989, Jemenská arabská republika, karton 1, obal 1, č.j. 012.287/85-8, Plnenie záverov z návševy s. ministra v JeAR – list s. ministra Chňoupka ministrovi zahraničného obchodu ČSSR, 18. června 1985. AMZV, TO-T 1980-1989, Jemenská arabská republika, karton 1, obal 4, č.j. 012.944/85-8, Odpoveď na list s. Rohlíčka vo veci dodávok špeciálu do JeAR, 7. června 1985.

47 AMZV, TO-T 1980-1989, Jemenská arabská republika, karton 1, obal 4, č.j. 013.923/86, JeAR – spolupráce ve vojenské oblasti, 20.11.1986.

48 NA, A ÚV KSČ, fond 1261/0/9 (Předsednictvo ÚV KSČ 1986-1989), P 112/89, bod 5, Informace o jednání s místopředsedou rady ministrů SSSR s I. S. BĚLOUSOVEM o dodávkách speciální techniky do SSSR v období 1991 – 1995, 13. dubna 1989.

CHAPTER 4

1 NA, A ÚV KSČ, fond 1261/0/5 (Předsednictvo ÚV KSČ 1966-1971), sv. 48, ar.j. 50, bod 7, Poskytnutí pomoci „Frontě pro osvobození okupovaného jihu Jemenu", 11. listopadu 1967. NA, A ÚV KSČ, fond 1261/0/5 (Předsednictvo ÚV KSČ 1966-1971), sv. 51, ar.j. 52, bod 14, Uznání Lidové republiky Jižního Jemenu jako nezávislého státu, 4. prosince 1967.

2 VÚA-VHA, MNO, 1967, karton 159, sl. 31D-52, č.j. 02386/SZS, Uvolnění pěchotních zbraní a munice pro Jemen/FLOSY, 4. září 1967.

3 AMZV, TO-T 1970-1974, Jemenská lidová demokratická republika, karton 1, obal 6, č.j. 023.430/72-8, Kontrola čs. závazků, vyplývajících z výsledků jednání ministra zahra. věcí ČSSR s partnerem z JLDR M.S.Aulákím, 14. června 1972. AMZV, TO-T 1970-1974, Jemenská lidová demokratická republika, karton 1, obal 6, č.j. 021.100/73-8, Vládní delegace JLDR do ČSSR – podání do předsednictva vlády. AMZV, TO-T 1970-1974, Jemenská lidová demokratická republika, karton 1, obal 6, č.j. 027.102/73-8, JLDR – informace pro presidenta republiky k přijetí nového velvyslance JLDR. AMZV, TO-T 1970-1974, Jemenská lidová demokratická republika, karton 1, obal 8, č.j. 011739, Přehled pomoci socialistických zemí /zastoupených v Adenu/ JLDR – připomínky čs. pomoci, 25. února 1974.

4 AMZV, TO-T 1970-1974, Jemenská lidová demokratická republika, karton 1, obal 6, č.j. 027.029/72-8, Návštěva delegace JLDR v ČSSR, 18. prosince 1972. AMZV, TO-T 1970-1974, Jemenská lidová demokratická republika, karton 1, obal 6, č.j. 021.561/73-8, Zpráva o návštěvě vládní delegace Jemenské lidové demokratické republiky, vedené členem PB Organizace Národní fornty JLDR, předsedou vlády a ministrem obrany Alí Nasir Mohammedem, která se uskutečnila v ČSSR ve dnech 1.-3. března 1973, březen 1973.

5 AMZV, TO-T 1970-1974, Jemenská lidová demokratická republika, karton 1, obal 6, č.j. 026.933/72-8, Příprava návštěvy předsedy vlády JLRD v ČSSR, 15. prosince 1972.

6 AMZV, TO-T 1970-1974, Jemenská lidová demokratická republika, karton 1, obal 7, č.j. 027443, Přijetí a večeře u zástupce náčelníka generálního štábu, 16. listopadu 1973. NA, A ÚV KSČ, fond 1261/0/6 (Předsednictvo ÚV KSČ 1971-1976), sv. 91, ar.j. 86, bod 5, Návrh na poskytnutí bezplatné vojenské pomoci Jemenské lidově demokratické republice v roce 1973, 22. srpna 1973. VÚA-VHA, MNO, 1973, karton 100, sl. 85/6, č.j. 06963/SÚP-73, Jemenská lidově demokratická republika – realizace.

7 NA, A ÚV KSČ, fond 1261/0/6 (Předsednictvo ÚV KSČ 1971-1976), sv. 91, ar.j. 86, bod 5, Návrh na poskytnutí bezplatné vojenské pomoci Jemenské lidově demokratické republice v roce 1973, 22. srpna 1973.

8 AMZV, TO-T 1970-1974, Jemenská lidová demokratická republika, karton 1, obal 7, č.j. 027441, Záznam z konzultace na MZV SSSR, 5.11.1973, 16. listopadu 1973. AMZV, TO-T 1970-1974, Jemenská lidová demokratická republika, karton 1, obal 7, č.j. 013519, Záznam z návštěvy na sovětské vojenské lodi, 20. dubna 1974. AMZV, TO-T 1970-1974, Jemenská lidová demokratická republika, karton 1, obal 8, č.j. 011739, Přehled pomoci socialistických zemí /zastoupených v Adenu/ JLDR – připomínky čs. pomoci, 25. února 1974. AMZV, TO-T 1970-1974,

Jemenská lidová demokratická republika, karton 1, obal 9, č.j. 011738, Politická zpráva č. 1-74, O vnitropolitickém vývoji v JLDR na přelomu let 1973/74, 23. února 1974.

9 AMZV, TO-T 1970-1974, Jemenská lidová demokratická republika, karton 1, obal 5, č.j. 016120, Informace o návštěvě generálního tajemníka strany Národní fronta JLDR v SSSR, 6. srpna 1974. AMZV, TO-T 1970-1974, Jemenská lidová demokratická republika, karton 1, obal 7, č.j. 016118, Záznam z návštěvy u sovětského obchodního přidělence, 13. července 1974.

10 AMZV, TO-T 1980-1989, Jemenská lidová demokratická republika, karton 2, obal 4, č.j. 010.562/80-DP, JEMENSKÁ LIDOVĚ DEMOKRATICKÁ REPUBLIKA – informační materiály k přijetí velvyslance AHMEDA ABDO RAGEHA u čs. představitelů. NA, A ÚV KSČ, fond 1261/0/6 (Předsednictvo ÚV KSČ 1971-1976), sv. 171, ar.j. 177, bod 6, Uzavření dohody na dodávky speciální techniky do Jemenské lidové demokratické republiky, 20. října 1975.

11 VÚA-VHA, MNO, 1977, karton 102, č.j. 006113, Spec. dodávky ze zásob ČSLA do JLDR.

12 VÚA-VHA, MNO, 1977, karton 102, č.j. 006113, Spec. dodávky ze zásob ČSLA do JLDR.

13 AMZV, TO-T 1970-1974, Jemenská lidová demokratická republika, karton 1, obal 7, č.j. 016116, Záznam z návštěvy kubánského velvyslance, 9. července 1974. AMZV, TO-T 1970-1974, Jemenská lidová demokratická republika, karton 1, obal 9, č.j. 011738, Politická zpráva č. 1-74, O vnitropolitickém vývoji v JLDR na přelomu let 1973/74, 23. února 1974. NA, A ÚV KSČ, fond 1261/0/7 (Předsednictvo ÚV KSČ 1976-1981), sv. 39, ar.j. 45, bod 9, Zpráva o návštěvě stranické a vládní delegace Jemenské lidové demokratické republiky v ČSSR ve dnech 14.-18. dubna 1977, 25. května 1977.

14 VÚA-VHA, MNO, 1977, karton 122, č.j. 006189, Jemenská lidově demokratická republika – podklady. Akce „625/A".

15 NA, A ÚV KSČ, fond 1261/0/7 (Předsednictvo ÚV KSČ 1976-1981), sv. 39, ar.j. 45, bod 9, Zpráva o návštěvě stranické a vládní delegace Jemenské lidové demokratické republiky v ČSSR ve dnech 14.-18. dubna 1977, 25. května 1977. VÚA-VHA, MNO, 1977, karton 122, č.j. 006189, Jemenská lidově demokratická republika – podklady. Akce „625/A".

16 VÚA-VHA, MNO, 1977, karton 122, č.j. 006189, Jemenská lidově demokratická republika – podklady. Akce „625/A".

17 AMZV, TO-T 1975-1979, Jemenská lidová demokratická republika, karton 2, obal 13, č.j. 042/79, Vývoj stykov JĽDR s krajinami socialistického společenstva, v oblasti politickej, hospodárskej a kultúrnej, 3. června 1979. AMZV, TO-T 1980-1989, Jemenská lidová demokratická republika, karton 2, obal 4, č.j. 010.562/80-DP, JEMENSKÁ LIDOVĚ DEMOKRATICKÁ REPUBLIKA – informační materiály k přijetí velvyslance AHMEDA ABDO RAGEHA u čs. představitelů. NA, A ÚV KSČ, fond 1261/0/7 (Předsednictvo ÚV KSČ 1976-1981), sv. 103, ar.j. 104, bod 8, Oficiální návštěva člena politického byra ÚV Jemenské socialistické strany, místopředsedy prezídia Nejvyšší lidové rady a předsedy vlády Jemenské lidové demokratické republiky Alí Násira Mohameda v ČSSR, 23. března 1979. NA, A ÚV KSČ, fond 1261/0/7 (Předsednictvo ÚV KSČ 1976-1981), sv. 112, ar.j. 111, k informaci bod 3, Informace o průběhu a výsledcích oficiální návštěvy člena politického byra ÚV Jemenské socialistické strany, místopředsedy prezídia Nejvyšší lidové rady a předsedy vlády Jemenské lidové demokratické republiky Alí Násira Mohameda v ČSSR ve dnech 17. až 19. dubna 1979, 16.

června 1979. VÚA-VHA, MNO, 1978, karton 214, č.j. 08228, Požadavky JLDR na dodávku týlového materiálu (akce „625/B").

18 NA, A ÚV KSČ, fond 1261/0/7 (Předsednictvo ÚV KSČ 1976-1981), sv. 112, ar.j. 111, k informaci bod 3, Informace o průběhu a výsledcích oficiální návštěvy člena politického byra ÚV Jemenské socialistické strany, místopředsedy prezídia Nejvyšší lidové rady a předsedy vlády Jemenské lidové demokratické republiky Alí Násira Mohameda v ČSSR ve dnech 17. až 19. dubna 1979, 16. června 1979.

19 NA, A ÚV KSČ, fond 1261/0/7 (Předsednictvo ÚV KSČ 1976-1981), P 147/80, bod 13, Bezplatná materiální pomoc Jemenské lidové demokratické republice ve vojenské oblasti, 1. září 1980.

20 NA, A ÚV KSČ, fond 1261/0/7 (Předsednictvo ÚV KSČ 1976-1981), P 147/80, bod 13, Bezplatná materiální pomoc Jemenské lidové demokratické republice ve vojenské oblasti, 1. září 1980.

21 AMZV, TO-T 1980-1989, Jemenská lidová demokratická republika, karton 4, obal 11, č.j. 010.961/87-8, Výcvik pilotov JĽDR – list NGŠ ČSLA, 2. února 1987. NA, A ÚV KSČ, fond 1261/0/8 (Předsednictvo ÚV KSČ 1981-1986), P 43/82, bod 5, Zpráva o řešení požadavku JLDR na poskytnutí bezplatné materiální a technické pomoci ve speciální oblasti předloženého během návštěvy čs. stranické a státní delegace v JLDR v září 1981, 22. června 1982.

22 NA, A ÚV KSČ, fond 1261/0/8 (Předsednictvo ÚV KSČ 1981-1986), P 43/82, bod 5, Zpráva o řešení požadavku JLDR na poskytnutí bezplatné materiální a technické pomoci ve speciální oblasti předloženého během návštěvy čs. stranické a státní delegace v JLDR v září 1981, 22. června 1982.

23 AMZV, TO-T 1980-1989, Jemenská lidová demokratická republika, karton 4, obal 12, č.j. 013.832/84-8, List s. min. zahr. vecí ČSSR min. zahr. obchodu ČSSR v rámci pripomienkového konania k návrhu riešenia požadavky LM JĽDR na bezplatnú pomoc, 26. července 1984. AMZV, TO-T 1980-1989, Jemenská lidová demokratická republika, karton 4, obal 12, č.j. 015.567/84-8, Poskytnutie čs. pomoci JĽDR, prosinec 1984. AMZV, TO-T 1980-1989, Jemenská lidová demokratická republika, karton 4, obal 12, č.j. 012.770/85-8, ZÚ Aden – zaslání protokolu o předání pomoci pro LM JLDR, 30. května 1985.

24 AMZV, TO-T 1980-1989, Jemenská lidová demokratická republika, karton 4, obal 12, č.j. 013.832/84-8, List s. min. zahr. vecí ČSSR min. zahr. obchodu ČSSR v rámci pripomienkového konania k návrhu riešenia požadavky LM JĽDR na bezplatnú pomoc, 26. července 1984.

25 AMZV, TO-T 1980-1989, Jemenská lidová demokratická republika, karton 4, obal 11, č.j. 06008/52-19, Odpověď na požadavek č. 111.284/88-8 ze dne 6.6.1988, 28. června 1988.

26 AMZV, TO-T 1980-1989, Jemenská lidová demokratická republika, karton 4, obal 11, č.j. 06008/52-19, Odpověď na požadavek č. 111.284/88-8 ze dne 6.6.1988, 28. června 1988.

27 AMZV, TO-T 1980-1989, Jemenská lidová demokratická republika, karton 4, obal 11, č.j. 06008/52-19, Odpověď na požadavek č. 111.284/88-8 ze dne 6.6.1988, 28. června 1988.

28 AMZV, TO-T 1980-1989, Jemenská lidová demokratická republika, karton 4, obal 11, č.j. 06008/52-19, Odpověď na požadavek č. 111.284/88-8 ze dne 6.6.1988, 28. června 1988.

29 AMZV, TO-T 1980-1989, Jemenská lidová demokratická republika, karton 4, obal 11, č.j. 011397/86-8, Materiál pre vládu ČSSR – návrh na prijatie ranených vojakov JĽDR na liečenie v ČSSR. AMZV, TO-T 1980-1989, Jemenská lidová demokratická republika, karton 4, obal 11, č.j. 06008/52-19, Odpověď na požadavek č. 111.284/88-8 ze dne 6.6.1988, 28. června 1988.

AMZV, TO-T 1980-1989, Jemenská lidová demokratická republika, karton 4, obal 14, č.j. 01.038/89, Zpráva o vztazích JLDR-SSSR, 12. listopadu 1989.

30 AMZV, TO-T 1980-1989, Jemenská lidová demokratická republika, karton 4, obal 11, č.j. 06008/52-19, Odpověď na požadavek č. 111.284/88-8 ze dne 6.6.1988, 28. června 1988.

31 AMZV, TO-T 1980-1989, Jemenská lidová demokratická republika, karton 4, obal 11, č.j. 01057/87, Zaslání předávacího protokolu pro HTS FMZO, 15. listopadu 1987. AMZV, TO-T 1980-1989, Jemenská lidová demokratická republika, karton 4, obal 11, č.j. 06008/52-19, Odpověď na požadavek č. 111.284/88-8 ze dne 6.6.1988, 28. června 1988.

32 AMZV, TO-T 1980-1989, Jemenská lidová demokratická republika, karton 4, obal 11, č.j. 01057/87, Zaslání předávacího protokolu pro HTS FMZO, 15. listopadu 1987.

33 AMZV, TO-T 1980-1989, Jemenská lidová demokratická republika, karton 4, obal 12, č.j. 01029/87, Zpráva o hospodářské situaci JLDR, 27. dubna 1987. NA, A ÚV KSČ, fond 1261/0/9 (Předsednictvo ÚV KSČ 1986-1989), P 102/89, bod 1, Zpráva o průběhu a výsledcích oficiální přátelské návštěvy generálního tajemníka ÚV Jemenské socialistické strany Alí Sálima AL-BEJDA v ČSSR, 26. ledna 1989.

34 AMZV, TO-T 1980-1989, Jemenská lidová demokratická republika, karton 4, obal 14, č.j. 01.038/89, Zpráva o vztazích JLDR-SSSR, 12. listopadu 1989.

35 Zpráva o zahraniční cestě na BAHRAJN a do JEMENU místopředsedy Senátu a Výboru pro hospodářství, zemědělství a dopravu, *Senát Parlamentu České republiky*, https://www.senat.cz/doc2html/136239730/index.html (accessed 18 May 2019).

ABOUT THE AUTHOR

Martin Smisek was born in 1985 and received a master's degree in aerospace engineering at the Czech Technical University in Prague in 2010. In addition to his regular job as a mechanical design engineer, he has written over 70 articles about contemporary armoured vehicles, modern air-launched weapons as well as Czechoslovak military history and local conflicts since 1945. He is the author of the ground-breaking book *Super Sabry nad Československem* (*Super Sabres over Czechoslovakia*) about US spyflights over Czechoslovakia in 1955. Martin Smisek is also a regular contributor of the Czech and Slovak leading military website www.valka.cz.